Money and Banking in Contemporary Japan

Money and Banking in Contemporary Japan

The Theoretical Setting and
Its Application

Yoshio Suzuki

Translated by John G. Greenwood

Foreword by James Tobin and Hugh Patrick

Yale University Press
New Haven and London 1980

Originally published in Japanese by Toyo Keizai Shinposha, Tokyo, under the title *Gendai Nihon Kinyūron*.

Designed by James J. Johnson and set in Monophoto Times Roman type by Asco Trade Typesetting Ltd., Hong Kong. Printed in the United States of America by Vail-Ballou Press, Binghamton, N.Y.

Published in Great Britain, Europe, Africa, and Asia (except Japan) by Yale University Press, Ltd., London. Distributed in Australia and New Zealand by Book & Film Services, Artarmon, N.S.W., Australia; and in Japan by Harper & Row, Publishers, Tokyo Office.

Library of Congress Cataloging in Publication Data

Suzuki, Yoshio, 1931–
    Money and banking in contemporary Japan.

    Translation of Gendai Nihon Kinyūron.
    Bibliography: p.
    Includes index.
    1. Finance—Japan.   2. Banks and banking—Japan.
3. Monetary policy—Japan.   I. Title.
HG188.J3S8413   1980   332.1′0952   79–23627
ISBN 0–300–02255–7

Contents

Tables and Charts

Foreword

Like other branches of our imperfect science, monetary economics seeks theoretical principles and empirical regularities of general relevance. Yet financial institutions and markets differ widely from nation to nation. To understand both their common and their diverse features, it is necessary to combine the detailed information of an insider with international and theoretical perspective. There are conceptual, accounting, and analytical frameworks of broad applicability to monetary and financial systems. By accidents of intellectual history, these frameworks were developed mainly with Anglo-Saxon institutions in mind. To adapt them and apply them to the economy of another culture, while doing justice to both the idiosyncrasy and the commonality of its financial structure, is a difficult and important challenge.

This is especially true for Japan. Like many other features of the Japanese economy, the financial system and the mechanism of monetary policy have mystified Western economists who are not close students of the country. Yet Japan's ever-increasing weight in the world economy and monetary system, and its growing participation in international financial and capital markets, make it pragmatically important, as well as intellectually interesting, to understand Japanese monetary policies and financial institutions.

That is why publication in English of Yoshio Suzuki's prize-winning book is very welcome. Dr. Suzuki is ideally placed to explain the Japanese monetary system to nonspecialists, whether students at Tokyo University (to whom the lectures which formed the basis of this publication were originally addressed) or interested readers throughout the world. He brings to the task the authoritative knowledge of a senior staff economist of the Bank of Japan and the broad perspective of a first-rate economist well-versed in general monetary theory and well acquainted with financial and central banking institutions in other countries.

An American reader of Dr. Suzuki's account will learn a number of interesting features of the Japanese system. He will see that it is difficult to find monetary aggregates whose paths tell most of the story of monetary policies and developments. He will discover that many interest rates are controlled, and that means other than ordinary rate variations are used to bring credit demands into line with supplies. He will appreciate the importance of the reciprocal depositor-borrower relationships of businesses and banks.

But this book is no mere description. It represents a rigorous analytical effort to formulate a general theoretical framework in the light of Japanese institutions and financial circumstances and, equally importantly, to test these hypotheses quantitatively in order to illuminate our understanding of Japanese financial markets, bank behavior, and the actual operation of monetary policy. In the controversy in Japan over the relative importance of Bank of Japan direct controls over commercial bank lending versus indirect controls relying upon restrictions on the terms and cost of Bank of Japan credit and on attendant adjustments in the call market (analogous to the American Federal Funds market), Dr. Suzuki has been at the forefront of those supporting the latter interpretation.

The final section represents an important updating and extension of the study as previously published in Japanese. Dr. Suzuki sees the 1970s as a major historical turning point for the Japanese economy, with fundamental ramifications for the structure of the financial system and for the implementation of monetary policy. He combines projections as to what will occur with a vision of how the system and the goals and techniques of monetary policy should evolve. The new circumstances include less rapid growth, a greater international interdependence in financial as well as commodity markets, and the accumulation of government debt by the financial system as a consequence of increasingly massive deficit-spending programs between 1975 and 1979.

Under these circumstances the pressures to liberalize domestic financial markets—and to let market-determined interest rates allocate funds—have become increasingly strong. Certain of the steps predicted by Dr. Suzuki have occurred, such as the opening of a (still limited) market for bank certificates of deposit (CDs) from spring 1979. His emphasis on the goal of price stability and the use of money-supply targets bear the clear implication that the Bank of Japan will no longer be able to peg the market for the now substantial overhang of government bonds. It is with deep meaning that the author's final words are a call for the "historic need for interest-rate liberalization." Nonetheless, he realizes that the opposing forces are strong, and the problems of adjustment among affected groups substantial. Only time will tell which way Japan will continue—along the previous path so well analyzed by the author, or on to the new path he advocates.

For those of us who have known the author and his work both during his visits to Yale and ours to Japan, it is especially gratifying to have this book published by the Yale University Press. We believe it makes an important contribution both to our general understanding of the nature and operations of financial systems and to the particular case of contemporary Japan.

James Tobin
Hugh Patrick

Translator's Note

In July 1974, the Bank of Japan first announced its intention to pursue a specific monetary growth target. At that time the implications of this decision were not widely understood, and consequently the publicity which the decision received within Japan was limited, while outside Japan the decision passed almost unnoticed. However, as the momentous consequences of the Bank of Japan's switch in policy gradually have become evident in the succeeding years, in a sharply reduced rate of domestic inflation and a strongly rising external exchange rate, foreign interest in the new Japanese monetary policy and its origins has grown.

By good fortune I attended a course of special lectures at the Economics Faculty of the University of Tokyo in 1972–73 given by Yoshio Suzuki, one of the architects of the switch in Japanese monetary policy, and I was flattered to be invited in 1974 to undertake the translation into English of the book that resulted from those lectures. Ironically, the pressures of business life in Hong Kong have been intensified by the change in Bank of Japan policy, making my job as an international investment adviser much more demanding and thereby adding to the delays in translation and in the copy-editing of the manuscript. Nevertheless, it has been my view that the importance of the change in policy far outweighs that of any other single decision in Japanese monetary policy since 1949. It was from this conviction that I felt it worthwhile to make available to the English-speaking world a text which provides the underlying rationale for that decision.

The original Japanese text, *Gendai Nihon Kinyūron*, consisted of over four hundred pages, divided into seventeen chapters. In rendering such a formidable document into acceptable English I faced two major tasks. The first was an editorial problem. My solution has been to concentrate on the core of Suzuki's theoretical framework and the empirical tests directly relating to it, leaving out substantial sections of the book which were either addressed especially to Japanese students or which described monetary developments in the United States or Britain that would already be well known to foreign scholars.

Chapters 1, 2, and 3, which describe the peculiarities of Japan's flow of funds structure and hence provide the institutional framework for the model, have been translated almost in their entirety. Chapter 4, which recapitulates chapters 1–3, has been shortened. Chapters 5, 6, and 7, which are concerned with the behavior of the banks, constitute the core of the book and have been rendered with only minor omissions. Chapter 8, which extends the analysis of banks to corporations and households, is slightly abbreviated. In chapters 9–12, which are concerned with the Bank of Japan's role in the implementation of monetary policy, sections considered too detailed were cut (for example, that on reserve requirements in chapter 12). Chapter 13 contained material of a comparative nature intended to introduce Japanese students to foreign monetary systems, and this has been omitted. The author himself rewrote chapter 15 for the English edition, updating it and including extensive revisions. Chapters 16 and 17 of the original, which discuss some further issues of monetary policy and inflation, have been completely omitted from the English edition. The second problem was to render a series of somewhat discursive Japanese lectures into a form of crisp, written English appropriate to their scientific subject matter. This has not been an easy assignment.

I am grateful to Professor Hugh Patrick and to Yale University Press, as well as to the author himself, for their encouragement and support at different stages of this venture. I have also received helpful comments from other individuals, in particular from my colleague and fellow economist in Hong Kong, Christian Wignall, but the final responsibility for any errors in judgment or understanding and for all remaining faults must be mine.

John G. Greenwood

Hong Kong
June 1979

Preface

This book consists of essays on money and banking in Japan based on a series of special lectures given at the Faculty of Economics of Tokyo University in the winter semester of 1972–73. The lectures provided a good opportunity for me, because although there are many textbooks in Japan on monetary *theory* or on financial *institutions* and financial *history*, there are very few books that analyze Japan's monetary *mechanism* or deal with monetary policy according to the positive, analytical methods of modern economics. Indeed, a systematic treatment is nonexistent. Therefore, having put myself in the predicament of lecturing at my alma mater, I was forcibly confronted with the difficult task of encompassing these subjects within a systematic framework, and this book is the result of that effort.

Today Japan's monetary and financial structure, mechanism, and policy stand at a major turning point. Whereas in the past exports and investment were the leading sectors in the economy, Japan is now moving toward a welfare-oriented economy. Moreover, the world economy is faced with intense inflationary pressures following the collapse of the old Bretton Woods international monetary system and the appearance of constraints on natural resources. Unless the monetary and financial aspects of the export-oriented, investment-led development pattern of the Japanese economy are systematically set down, I am acutely conscious of the danger that it will be difficult to make a balanced appraisal of future changes. Under the daily pressure of work as a member of the Bank of Japan staff I thought it would be extremely difficult to find the time to define this framework, but the commitment of weekly lectures at the university compelled me to find the time.

Economics is traditionally, of course, political economy, and in political economy monetary problems are a particularly practical discipline. When I published *Nihon no tsūka to bukka* [Money and Prices in Japan] (Tōyō Keizai Shimpōsha, 1966), it was my intention to contribute a study of

Japanese monetary policy and Japan's financial institutions that would be useful for the establishment of a *Japanese* monetary economics. Nothing would please me more than if the present study, "Money and Banking in Contemporary Japan," which is a revised version of my lectures at Tokyo University, also contributed in some way to this ambition. I hope that academic economists will be encouraged to further the development of *Japanese* monetary economics, utilizing as a testing ground the statistical or structural facts, together with the economic hypotheses, offered in this book. If by this process the reform of Japan's monetary policy and financial structure is given a firmer theoretical foundation, *Japanese* monetary economics will have advanced decisively into the sphere of political economy. In a period of both internal and external economic upheaval, and at a time when the Japanese people have been subjected to an inflation unprecedented in normal peacetime conditions, surely that is the duty of scholars of *Japanese* monetary economics.

The book is divided into five parts and contains fifteen chapters. Part I, "Japan's Financial Structure," explains the peculiar characteristics of Japan's financial structure by means of international comparisons and examines those characteristics in the context of Japan's institutional arrangements and economic background. For a comprehensive analysis of monetary phenomena a correctly specified and simplified theoretical monetary model is required, but in order to build such a theoretical model for Japan the first prerequisite is an intensive study of the financial structure of the country, its institutional arrangements, and its economic background. In Japan's case, it is particularly necessary to explain the structure of the flow of funds in an export-oriented, investment-led economy and the economic implications of the rigidity of interest rates imposed by the policy of maintaining artificially low interest rates.

Part II, "Japan's Monetary Mechanism," shows how Keynes's $IS = LM$ model as taught in standard economics textbooks can be adapted to incorporate the structural and institutional conditions (e.g. overloan, overborrowing, the imbalance of liquidity between city and local banks, the predominance of indirect financing, and the rigidity of interest rates) examined in part I. Having obtained a general equilibrium model of assets with this revised Keynesian model, I shall present a theoretical and quantitative analysis of the crucial economic units—namely, the behavior of banks and business enterprises.

Part III, "The Instruments of Japanese Monetary Policy," explains the function of each instrument of monetary policy and, using the theoretical and quantitative results of the study of bank behavior in part II, demonstrates the impact of each of these instruments on bank behavior. It is widely believed that in Japan, where controls on bank lending occur in conjunction with a rigid interest-rate structure, the effects of monetary policy cannot be examined by the positive, analytical methods of modern economics. Part III is intended to offer evidence to the contrary.

Part IV, "The Effectiveness of Monetary Policy in Japan," examines the transmission of the effects of policy and the various conditions required for policy to be effective. It also examines the Bank of Japan's policy objectives and its degree of success in achieving them. It is concerned with Japan's monetary policy after 1955 and relies mainly on the theoretical monetary model of part II. The lesson of this section is that one of the major reasons for the effectiveness of monetary policy until the early 1960s was the absence of a mutual trade-off between the policy objectives of internal price stability, equilibrium in the international balance of payments, and an appropriate level of effective demand (or appropriate growth rate) during the period.

Finally, part V, "Prospects for the Future," considers how, in a rapidly changing domestic and foreign environment, Japan's financial structure and monetary mechanism may change and in what ways it is desirable that they *should* change, and it takes a constructive, forward-looking approach to the question of Japanese monetary policy. As Japan moves toward a greater emphasis on social capital and the expansion of social security at home, and as the floating exchange rate system continues domestically and abroad in an environment of varying national inflation rates and constrained supplies of natural resources, the financial environment facing Japan will change dramatically. The dominant belief that price stability strengthened Japan's international competitiveness and was necessary in order to achieve a high growth rate has now been displaced, but there still remains the unanswered problem of how the new objectives of priority for welfare and price stability can be coordinated. Moreover, the artificial low interest rate policy associated with the promotion of exports and investment has now lost its historical validity, and we are left with only the conspicuous distortions it imposed on the efficient distribution of resources and a fair distribution of income. However, progress in liberalizing interest rates was slowed down by the attempt to avoid raising the interest burden of government financing. In one sense it may be said that this confusion over policy intentions lay behind the great inflation that occurred in the fall of 1973. In the trade-off between the three objectives of price stability, equilibrium in the international balance of payments, and growth, my conclusion is that monetary policy should always be assigned to price stability (i.e. a low rate of price increase) and should not be diverted to cope with the balance of payments or the business cycle. I shall also conclude that in the execution of monetary policy the most important operating target should be the level of money supply, and that in the transmission mechanism it is essential to utilize free market interest rates.

In the writing and publication of this book I have received guidance and assistance from many people. In particular, the following read the text at the manuscript stage and provided valuable comments: Motohiko Nishikawa, auditor at the Bank of Japan (part 4); Michio Yoshino, director of the Research Department of the Bank of Japan (part V); Professor Ryūichiro Tachi of the University of Tokyo (parts II and III); Professor Ryutaro Komiya (parts II, III, and V); and Assistant Professor Shōichi Rōyama of Osaka University (part II). The book is based on knowledge I have acquired during research work at the Bank of Japan and in this sense owes much to my superiors, contemporaries, and junior staff at the bank. Throughout the book I have quoted liberally, with the permission of Mr. Yoshino, from the statistical results of quantitative work performed by junior staff there. The original Japanese version of this book was dedicated to Mr. Shigeru Toyama, former executive director of the Bank of Japan, to express my gratitude for the generous support of all my colleagues at the Bank. To all those who have given me instruction and guidance I am deeply grateful.

If there are shortcomings in the book these are my sole responsibility. One thing I wish to make absolutely clear is that the book contains my personal views, which, under the banner of academic freedom, were put forward at my alma mater, and at the present point in time they do not represent the official views of the Bank of Japan. Of course I welcome criticisms of this text, as they will add to the store of knowledge, but they should always be directed to me personally and not to the Bank of Japan.

Finally, I want to express my heartfelt gratitude to the staff of Tōyō Keizai Shinpōsha, especially Mr. Masaaki Ogawa, for their kindness to me during the publication of the book, and to my wife and children for their cooperation in permitting me to write it during their leisure time.

Yoshio Suzuki

Kamitakaidō, Children's Day
May 5, 1974

PART I
Japan's Financial Structure

Part I analyzes the distinctive features of Japan's financial structure from the period of the late 1950s to the early 1970s and the specific conditions in the Japanese economy which helped to create that structure. Conversely, I also consider the impact the financial structure had on the development of the economy.

When I turn to analysis of Japan's financial mechanism in part II, the distinctive features discussed in part I will be explicitly included as the structural and institutional conditions that form the framework for the theoretical model. These distinctive characteristics will also be frequently referred to when, in parts III and IV, I examine the instruments of monetary policy and their effectiveness. Finally, in part V, when I consider the future development of Japan's financial system, I shall examine how the financial structure studied in part I may be expected to change with the new pattern of Japanese economic growth and with any new pattern of developments in Japan's international balance of payments.

1 Four Distinctive Characteristics of Japan's Financial Structure

In comparing Japan's financial structure with those of the United States, Britain, West Germany, or France, there are at least four outstanding and distinctive characteristics to be pointed out. These are the phenomena known as overloan, overborrowing, the imbalance of liquidity between city banks and local banks, and the predominance of indirect financing.

1. *Overloan*

1.1 *Definition and Essential Characteristics*

Overloan is a word frequently used in discussions of the distinctive characteristics of Japan's financial structure and has even gained international currency as "Japanese English." However, its usage is by no means consistent. We start with its meaning and proceed to make a definition.

In general the assets and liabilities of banks may be simplified to the form given in table 1.1. The assets side may be divided into three types: central bank money (or high-powered money), secondary reserve assets (i.e. money-market assets easily convertible into central bank money, such as call loans, short-term government securities, and commercial bills circulating in the bills discount market), and loans and investments (defined to exclude short-term government securities and commercial bills). The liabilities side

Table 1.1 Simplified Bank Balance Sheet

Central bank money Secondary reserve assets	Borrowed funds
Loans and investments	Deposits Capital accounts

may also be divided into three groups: borrowed funds (for example, loans from the central bank and borrowing from the money market such as call money or bills sold), deposits, and capital accounts.

The basic pattern of bank behavior is to utilize deposits and capital from the liabilities side to make loans and investments on the assets side and to make a profit from the interest spread between them. However, since the timing of deposit withdrawals is uncertain, the bank may face a deterioration in its profitability if it is obliged to convert loans or investments into cash at a moment's notice, or if it is obliged to borrow heavily at high cost using those assets as collateral. In an extreme case of loss of confidence, the bank might have to pay an inordinate price to meet its obligations. In order to meet such an emergency the bank must be prepared, to some extent, to hold highly liquid assets as reserves for payment, even at the expense of slightly lower profitability in the short run, so that it can maximize its profit in the long run. It is for this reason that banks hold central bank money (as first-line reserve assets) as well as second-line reserve assets. Also, on the liabilities side, to meet the case where it cannot immediately honor demands for payment of deposits, a bank typically maintains borrowed funds. Thus, borrowed funds on the liabilities side are, in effect, negative reserve assets. Simplifying the principles of bank behavior, one may say that, given a particular interest-rate structure, the objective is to achieve that combination of assets—reserve assets (positive or negative) plus loans and investments—which maximizes profit, using as funding sources equity capital and deposit liabilities whose withdrawal may not be entirely predictable.[1]

1. Attempts to explain the behavior of Japanese banks by the profit-maximization motive have been made by Hiroshi Kawaguchi [19], Hidekazu Eguchi [9], and Shozaburo Fujino [10]. The theory of bank behavior developed in this book is explained in part II, chapter 6 and was suggested by Tobin [59]. It represents a slight modification of Yoshio Suzuki [41] but is basically along the same lines as that analysis.

In the light of uncertainty about future profits, attempts have been made (see, for example, Ishii [14]) to build models of bank behavior based not on profit maximization but on the hypothesis of expected utility maximization. Although interesting from a theoretical point of view, for the purpose of analyzing Japanese bank behavior there do not appear to be any important obstacles to an explanation based on profit maximization as compared with the hypothesis of expected utility maximization.

With respect to the city banks alone, there is the view that they behave, not according to any principles of profit maximization, but are motivated by the attempt to maintain or increase their market share (see, for example, Bunji Kure [24], Kinzō Suzuki [39], EPA Research Institute [20]). However, as explained in chapter 6, section 3, the reason why city banks are very concerned about their rivals' behavior is that, since their point of profit maximization is decisively influenced by the Bank of Japan's credit rationing, they must consider whether in receiving Bank of Japan credit allocations they may not be at a disadvantage in comparison with other banks.

Also, without introducing the general theory of oligopoly, since profit maximization is

Loosely speaking, the phenomenon of overloan is taken to mean the existence of loans and investments funded from sources other than deposits and equity capital, so that reserve assets (taken as the sum of central bank money plus second-line reserve assets minus borrowed funds) are consistently negative. However, in practice the statistical or conceptual distinction between second-line reserve assets and loans and investments (e.g. in the case of bills discounted and other negotiable instruments) is by no means straightforward. Here I shall define overloan rather strictly as the condition when central bank money less borrowed funds is negative.

"The Correction of Overloan," a publication of the Monetary System Research Council [21], in its recommendation of May 9, 1963, defined overloan as "the phenomenon whereby banks' overlending depends primarily on Bank of Japan loans." Since in this case *overlending* is defined as "net bank reserves (equals vault cash plus deposits with the Bank of Japan minus borrowing from the Bank of Japan, or vault cash plus deposits with the Bank of Japan minus external liabilities) being negative," this conforms to the stricter definition given above.

Overloan as used above has two aspects: micro as applied to individual banks and macro when applied to the banking system as a whole. In other words, although one bank may be overlent, another bank may have liquid funds in excess of that margin. Thus, whatever the intrasectoral balance of fund surpluses and deficits between individual banks, for the banking system as a whole there is no net borrowing from the central bank. Where this situation exists in the industrialized countries of North America and Europe, use of the term *overloan* only confuses the issue and is not appropriate.

In referring to overloan as a special characteristic of Japan's financial structure, one is concerned with the banking system as a whole being in debt to the Bank of Japan, not with the condition of individual banks. Since overloan is a macro matter, it is intimately connected with the Bank of

---

achieved through raising market share in a situation where prices (interest rates) are controlled, the vigorous rivalry of city banks is an entirely natural consequence of the profit-maximization principle. In chapter 3, section 2.3, I shall show how, because the interest payable on deposits is restricted to a low level, the marginal cost of raising deposits is low relative to the effective rates paid on loans or to the cost of raising money in the short-term money markets, so that the more deposits they attract, the greater their profit. Also, in chapter 3, section 2.4, and chapter 6, I shall explain how, because the official discount rate is lower than interest rates in the short-term money market, the more the banks borrow from the Bank of Japan, the greater their profit. In this way, the expansion of a bank's operations for the purpose of attracting deposits on the one hand and borrowing from the Bank of Japan on the other, is quite natural from a profit-maximization standpoint, given the controls on interest rates. In a world where a larger market share immediately translates into higher profits, the appearance of the kind of behavior where banks watch their rivals to ensure that they do not lag behind can therefore be rationalized on the basis of profit-maximizing principles.

Japan's method of supplying money and hence the very real importance attached to overloan in monetary theory. If the Bank of Japan meets the cash needs of the city banks and accommodates their overlending not by direct loans but by buying securities from them, their investments decline and the overloan position is eliminated. Thus the two aspects of overloan concern: first, bank behavior and, second, the specific supply channel of central bank credit.

In micro terms, overloan is a problem of behavior for each individual bank. At the same time, however, the individual net overloan position of the city banks is not directly, or at least in the short run, attributable to these institutions but results from certain external conditions. This may be explained by a specific example. For any single financial institution, the net outcome of its lending and borrowing activities is reflected in the net balances of individual accounts resulting from the clearing of checks and bills, domestic settlements, receipts from government relative to tax payments, net purchases or sales of foreign exchange to the Foreign Exchange Special Account, and drawings on the Bank of Japan. If the net balance of these receipts and payments constitutes a negative sum (cash "deficit"), the bank will either borrow in the call market or borrow from the Bank of Japan. Conversely, if there is a net "surplus," the bank will reduce its borrowings from the central bank or otherwise alter its lending and borrowing behavior.

Taking these transactions between financial institutions overall, however, the clearance of checks and bills, domestic settlements, and transactions in the call market constitute internal swaps, and from the standpoint of the banking system as a whole they cancel out. Those that do not cancel out are the receipts of government checks versus tax payments (the net balance of the Treasury with the private sector), transactions with the Foreign Exchange Special Account (the net balance of the Foreign Exchange Special Account with the private sector), net withdrawals of cash from the Bank of Japan (net note issue), and the residual change in borrowings from (or repayments to) the Bank of Japan. Thus, for the banking system as a whole the following equation describes how the counterpart of the net result of the banks' lending and borrowing activities is provided by the Bank of Japan:

Net addition to note issue − (net payments by the Treasury General Account to the private sector + net yen payments by the Foreign Exchange Special Account to the private sector) = Net change in Bank of Japan credit.

(See also table 9.1, Factors for the Supply and Demand for Funds.)[2]

2. Detailed explanations of the relation between an individual bank's fund position and the commercial banking sector's overall fund position or aggregate borrowings from the

In this equation, trends in the note issue on the left-hand side are basically determined by the demand for cash currency by businesses and households, while the net balances with the private sector of the General Account and the Foreign Exchange Special Account are determined by trends in fiscal spending and the international balance of payments. Naturally, these three determinants are neither directly nor in the short run subject to the behavior of commercial banking institutions. (Indirectly, of course, one may say that they are affected by bank-lending activity and hence in turn affect the demand for banknotes, the level of tax payments, and the international payments position, and thus there is a long-term relation between them; on this point see part III, chapter 9, and chapter 10, section 2). In this sense, it is not necessarily appropriate to analyze the overloan position of the banks—that is, the condition when Bank of Japan credit provides the main counterpart of the overall banking system's net lending and borrowing operations—as a direct or short-term aspect of the behavior of the banking system. A better approach is to ask why the Bank of Japan provides credit to the banking system in the form of Bank of Japan loans. The amount must offset the shortage of funds in the money market as determined by the interaction of the demand for banknotes and payments to the private sector by the government (Treasury and Foreign Exchange Special Account); but the crucial question concerns the form or source of the funds.

In the long run, however, because bank lending affects the overall level of economic activity, it also affects the demand for cash, currency, the level of tax payments, and the international balance of payments position. To that extent, the essence of overloan is the persistent failure of city banks to eliminate their Bank of Japan borrowings, that is, the noncorrection of their negative net reserve asset or funds position.[3] Study of the short-run and long-run aspects of the problem will be postponed until chapters 2, 3,

---

Bank of Japan are given in Yoshio Suzuki [40], pp. 31–35, and [41], pp. 78–80. The first clear description of this mechanism in the debate on Japan's monetary policy was given by Motohiko Nishikawa in [28] and [29] (see chap. 9 and chap. 10, sec. 2).

3. "Fund position" is defined as the difference between "surplus funds" and "external liabilities":

Fund position = (Call loans + deposits with other financial institutions + bills bought) − (Call money + borrowings from other financial institutions + bills sold + borrowings from Bank of Japan). If the first expression on the right is greater, the fund position is said to be positive, whereas if external liabilities are greater, the fund position is said to be negative. In terms of table 1.1, the difference between secondary reserve assets and borrowed funds is approximately equivalent to the funds position. As the concept of "fund position" does not include central bank money, the definition does not exactly correspond to reserve assets being positive or negative, or to a looser definition of a bank being a net borrower or overloaned. The basic purpose of the concept of "fund position" is to determine the level of reserve assets or whether the bank is in a net borrowing position or an overloan position. "Central bank money" was customarily omitted only because it was a very small amount.

and 4, and part II, chapter 6, but the conclusion may be stated here. In the Japanese economy certain conditions (e.g. the inevitability of Bank of Japan credit rationing under the artificial low interest-rate policy) necessitate the supply of high-powered money through Bank of Japan loans, and it is this particular method of provision that has induced the city banks to come to rely continuously on Bank of Japan loans, thus perpetuating the overloan situation.

1.2 *Historical Evolution and the Current Situation*
Before proceeding to an analysis of these points in chapter 2, it is worth examining the current overloan position both in an international context and in historical perspective. Taking the accounts of central banks in leading countries at the end of 1972, table 1.2 shows the deposits of commercial banks with the central bank and loans and discounts to the same group of banks. It is immediately apparent that Japan is the only country where the central bank is a net lender: for each of the other four countries, deposits of commercial banks exceed loans from and discounts with the central bank. The omission of vault cash held by financial institutions from liquid assets demonstrates the validity of the strict definition of overloan used above. Omitting vault cash makes the definition one stage stricter, but even against this stricter definition, comparison shows that overloan did not exist in any of these economically advanced countries except Japan. (The historical data, too, show that only France experienced overloan by this definition. This was the case until the end of 1970; but thanks to vigorous central bank purchasing operations, this condition was eliminated during 1971.)

The existence of overloan has characterized Japan's financial structure ever since banks were established in the country. Even the national banks,

Table 1.2   Overloan: An International Comparison (As of December 1972)

	Unit	Deposits of Financial Institutions at the Central Bank *A*	Central Bank Loans to Financial Institutions *B*	(*A − B*)
Japan	¥ billion	374	2,122	−1,748
United States	$ million	28,667	2,088	26,579
United Kingdom	£ million	343	41	302
West Germany	DM million	46,388	20,178	26,210
France	Fr. f. million	48,539	11,352	37,187

Source: Bank of Japan, *Economic Statistics Annual, Foreign Economic Statistics Annual,* [1973].

which began business following the promulgation of the National Banking Act in November 1872, were almost continuously in an overloaned state until they relinquished their note-issuing function and became ordinary banks in 1899. Table 1.3 illustrates this situation, tabulating loans as a percentage of deposits and capital funds employed to test the weaker definition. In addition, to explore the strict definition, borrowings from the Bank of Japan (including, in the case of national banks, their own note issues and bills drawn on themselves)[4] are compared with total funds employed. If vault cash plus deposits with the Bank of Japan are assumed to have been constant at 5 percent of funds employed, then whenever the ratio of Bank of Japan loans to total funds employed exceeded 5 percent, the banks were overloaned according to the strict definition.

Table 1.3 shows how the national banks were almost invariably in an overloan position under the strict definition and how even under the relaxed definition the overloan position persisted, apart from a few exceptional years. For the ordinary banks, between 1893 and the end of the war in 1945 there was no overloan under the weaker definition, but under the stricter definition overloan existed until 1900, although it was quickly eliminated thereafter. Overloan occurred only to a mild degree during the first decade of the Showa era (1925–35); but after 1943 overloan again became a persistent phenomenon.

As table 1.3 shows, the overloan situation of the early Meiji era began to be corrected after 1897 and was dramatically improved after the end of the First World War. The belief that it was shameful for the big banks to be in debt to the Bank of Japan—even temporarily—dates from this period. However, with the enormous increase in loans to the munitions industries by the big banks during the Second World War, this belief vanished along with the huge volume of Bank of Japan loans that supported such activity, and once again the phenomenon of overloan began to predominate among the larger banks.

Overloan in the stricter definition continued to prevail after the end of the war, as evidenced in table 1.4, although it disappeared briefly in 1955 against the background of a balance of payments surplus and a good rice harvest, which resulted in large net disbursements from the Foreign Exchange Special Account and from the government's Foodstuffs Control Special

---

4. Overloan is here based on treatment of national bank notes as a form of borrowing from the central bank. This is because, whenever the central bank replaced national bank notes by central bank currency, loan accounts of the national banks with the Bank of Japan were credited. After these transactions, the Bank of Japan had assumed liability for the notes on issue and had a corresponding asset in the form of a loan to the national bank concerned. In effect, one liability of the national bank's (notes) had been replaced by another (loans from the Bank of Japan). For the detailed historical background to overloan from the Meiji Era until around 1951, see Toshihiko Yoshino [61].

Table 1.3 Two Measures of Overloan, 1873–1951 (In Percent)

	Loans	Bank of Japan Borrowings
Year-end	Deposits + Capital	Total Funds Employed

National Banks

Year-end	Loans / Deposits + Capital	Bank of Japan Borrowings / Total Funds Employed
1873	90	23
74	73	16
75	65	13
76	139	44
77	215	61
78	140	56
79	181	61
80	172	58
81	166	53
82	151	51
83	111	47
84	132	48
85	99	42
86	99	37
87	116	40
88	109	35
89	118	35
90	137	36
91	115	31
92	103	28
93	112	29
94	107	27
95	97	27

All Ordinary Banks

Year-end	Loans / Deposits + Capital	Bank of Japan Borrowings / Total Funds Employed
1893	87	–
94	83	9
95	88	11
96	98	15
97	99	15
98	88	10
99	93	15
1900	93	12
01	86	5
02	83	5
03	83	4
04	81	6
05	79	4
06	82	3
07	85	5
08	76	4
09	77	2
10	78	2
11	82	3
12	83	4
13	85	4
14	84	2
15	79	1

Year-end	Loans / Deposits + Capital	Bank of Japan Borrowings / Total Funds Employed
1920	84	2
21	80	4
22	81	3
23	82	5
24	82	5
25	82	4
26	81	5
27	74	6
28	67	7
29	64	6
30	64	2
31	66	6
32	73	6
33	58	5
34	54	4
35	53	4
36	53	4
37	55	2
38	53	1
39	52	1
40	53	1
41	49	1
42	47	2

All Banks

Year-end	Loans / Deposits + Capital	Bank of Japan Borrowings / Total Funds Employed
1945	73	22
46	74	19
47	71	9
48	80	9
49	92	10
50	102	14
51	108	17

City Banks

Year-end	Loans / Deposits + Capital	Bank of Japan Borrowings / Total Funds Employed
1945	94	29
46	124	28
47	83	14
48	85	13
49	98	13
50	117	19
51	124	25

Local Banks

Year-end	Loans / Deposits + Capital	Bank of Japan Borrowings / Total Funds Employed
1945	31	4
46	42	2
47	47	2
48	67	2
49	79	5

Table 1.4   Borrowings from Bank of Japan as Percentage of Liabilities and Net Worth, 1948–1975

Year-end	City Banks	Local Banks	Long-Term Credit Banks	Trust Banks
1948	9.7	1.4	11.5	–
49	10.1	3.9	11.2	–
50	8.5	5.8	7.2	–
51	11.4	1.7	6.5	–
52	8.9	1.4	5.4	3.9
53	9.6	1.2	4.2	4.5
54	7.7	0.5	2.1	2.2
55	0.9	0	0.1	0
56	2.7	0	1.5	0.6
57	10.2	0.1	1.8	1.3
58	5.9	0.2	0.8	0.6
59	4.5	0.2	0.7	0.3
60	5.5	0.2	0.7	0.3
61	12.3	0.2	1.0	0.1
62	10.5	0.1	0.7	0
63	7.5	0.2	0.5	0
64	5.6	0.2	1.1	0.1
65	6.0	0.3	0.9	0.1
66	6.6	0.3	0.9	0.1
67	5.1	0.3	0.7	0.1
68	5.1	0.3	0.7	0.1
69	5.4	0.2	0.6	0.1
70	5.8	0.3	0.7	0.1
71	1.2	0.2	0.2	0.2
72	3.5	0.4	0.3	0.2
73	3.1	0.2	0.2	0.4
74	2.0	0.2	0.2	0.4
75	1.8	0.2	0.2	0.3

Source: Bank of Japan, *Economic Statistics Annual.*

Account financed by short-term borrowings from the Bank of Japan. However, there was a resurgence of overloan between 1956 and 1970, although during this period it was noticeably a city bank phenomenon.[5] This book deals with the overloan problem as it occurred after 1956 and specifically as it relates to the city banks. In other words, it will be directly linked with the related problems of the imbalance of liquidity between city

5. For the purpose of this book, a detailed explanation of Japan's financial system with a description of the distinctions between commercial banks and the definition of city banks is not included. For these aspects of Japan's financial system, the reader is referred to the publications of the Research Department of the Bank of Japan [1] and [2], and to Toshihiko Yoshino [62].

96	108	24	16	81	2	43	50	15	50	87	7
97	94	29	17	78	2	44	55	11	51	83	2
98	–	62	18	78	2	8.20.45	70	20			
			19	86	5						

Source: Bank of Japan, *Chōsa Geppō*, February 1952.

Notes:
1. National banks' borrowings from the Bank of Japan include banknotes issued and bills issued by each bank.
2. Borrowings from the Bank of Japan by all banks and city banks in 1950 and 1951 include foreign exchange accounts (mainly balances in foreign currency at the Bank of Japan).
3. Deposits of all banks include financial debentures; but checks and bills in process of collection are deducted.
4. Total Funds Employed = Capital + Deposits + Borrowings from the Bank of Japan.

and local banks and the export-oriented, investment-led, high-growth pattern that was the distinguishing feature of the years 1955–70.

During the international monetary crises of May and August 1971, a huge volume of short-term capital flowed into the country, so that the overloan phenomenon disappeared briefly until year-end, but from 1972 on overloan returned (see table 1.4). Looking to the future, although it is possible that there will be a change in the structure of the flow of funds, the overloan situation will not be eliminated unless the artificial low interest-rate policy is abandoned.

2. *Overborrowing*

Because overborrowing is frequently believed to be the counterpart of overloan and because the two sound similar, they are often confused. However, it is not necessarily true to say that overloan and overborrowing are simply the same phenomena viewed from different perspectives.

As pointed out above, the word *overloan* indicates a situation where the banking system is so overlent that it has negative reserve assets and depends upon the Bank of Japan for borrowing. The word *overborrowing*, however, refers to the financing of the corporate sector and indicates a condition of heavy dependence on bank borrowing. In Japan the present situation is that the corporate sector is the main recipient of the banks' overlending, so that overloan and overborrowing are in fact complementary; but this need not always be the case. For example, even if overborrowing were corrected, it would be quite possible for investment in government securities or increased loans to individual consumers to preserve the phenomenon of overloan. Furthermore, if the capital market were to develop so that capital increases by companies or bond issues were to grow while the proportion of loans from banks were to decline, overborrowing would be corrected, but if the banks were to increase greatly their purchases of corporate bonds or equity stock, then banks might continue to be in a position of overloan. Conversely, the Bank of Japan could conduct buying operations to purchase large quantities of long-term bonds and as a result the investments of the banking system as a whole might decline so that borrowings from the Bank of Japan would be zero and overloan would be corrected, but, given only these changes, overborrowing would probably continue to exist.

In this formal scenario the problem of overloan concerns the relation between the Bank of Japan and the city banks (the problem of the provision of high-powered money), while overborrowing concerns the city banks and the companies (the problem of corporate financing), and each is not necessarily the mirror image of the other. However, as will be pointed out below, it was inevitable in the *export-oriented, investment-led rapid growth economy*, and the *low interest dominated, noninternational* financial structure of Japan that overloan and overborrowing should become inextricably entwined.

The extent of the heavy dependence of Japanese companies on bank borrowing, i.e. overborrowing, may be seen in table 1.5. During the five years 1966–70, the average proportion of loan money was 49 percent for Japan but in the range 10–30 percent for the United States, the United Kingdom, West Germany, and France, or about half the level in Japan on the average. This pattern of overborrowing by Japanese companies developed, as will be explained below in table 1.9, during the years 1955–65. The features to notice in table 1.5 are that the Japanese bank loan ratio was high firstly because internal financing was so low, and secondly because the proportion of external financing from the issue of securities (increases in equity capital or bond issues) was also low. As we shall explore in detail below, the first is related to Japan's export-oriented, investment-led rapid growth and the second to the underdevelopment of the capital market (or the preference for indirect financing), which is in turn related to the low interest-rate policy and the policy of noninternationalization.

3. *The Imbalance of Bank Liquidity*

The imbalance of liquidity between city and local banks refers to the phenomenon within the commercial banking system, whereby the city banks continuously have negative reserve assets while other banks have positive reserve assets, so that one group is persistently borrowing and the other persistently lending in the call market, in the interbank lending

Table 1.5   International Comparison of Financing of the Corporate Sector, 1966–1970 (Percentage Composition)

	Internal Finance	*External Finance*			*Total*
			Borrowed Money	*Securities Issued*	
Japan	40.0	60.0	49.0	11.0	100.0
United States	69.4	30.6	12.4	18.2	100.0
United Kingdom	51.4	48.6	10.3	38.3	100.0
West Germany	63.1	36.9	29.6	7.3	100.0
France	65.0	35.0	27.4	7.6	100.0

Source: Bank of Japan Statistics Department, *International Comparative Statistics*, various issues.

market, in the interbank deposit market, and (after 1971) in the bill discount market. (Hereafter these will be collectively referred to as the call market.)

Table 1.6 shows the year-end balance sheets for 1965, 1970, and 1975 of financial institutions, divided into city banks and other financial institutions. The reserve assets of city banks are consistently negative, while those of other institutions are always positive. It will be observed that the difference in behavior which forms the background to this situation is the maintenance of loans and investments by the city banks in excess of their deposits and capital, whereas other banks restrict their loans and investments to the range allowed by their deposits and capital.

Thus the commercial banking system in Japan is comprised of one group of institutions that are regularly net lenders and another group that

Table 1.6   Simplified Balance Sheet of City Banks and Other Financial Institutions   (Unit = ￥ billion)

Year-end	City Banks			Other Financial Institutions		
	1965	*1970*	*1975*	*1965*	*1970*	*1975*
Assets						
Central bank money	267.3	500.9	1,252.3	300.7	688.4	2,240.1
Call loans etc.	1.0	12.3	149.7	1,250.0	2,560.3	4,478.7
Investments	2,468.6	3,946.3	8,722.8	2,712.6	9,335.3	25,858.7
Loans	10,855.0	21,744.9	47,720.4	16,769.9	48,385.1	116,261.4
Liabilities						
Borrowing from BOJ	1,136.4	2,123.6	1,489.6	54.1	229.7	287.7
Call money etc.	1,327.0	2,567.3	6,624.4	170.0	34.2	382.1
Deposits	10,897.8	22,060.9	53,613.1	19,475.8	56,655.0	133,318.6
Others	230.7	102.5	−3,884.9	1,333.3	5,050.2	14,850.5
Net reserve assets	−2,195.1	−4,177.0	−6,712.0	1,326.6	2,984.8	6,049.0

Source: Bank of Japan, *Economic Statistics Annual.*
Notes: 1. Central bank money = Deposits at Bank of Japan + notes and coin (excluding checks and bills)

Call loans etc.   = Call loans + loans other financial institutions + bills sold
Call money etc.   = Call money + loans from other financial institutions + bills bought
Net reserve assets   = Central bank money + call loans etc. − loans from BOJ − call money

2. Financial Institutions includes the range of institutions covered in the "flow-of-funds accounts."

are normally net borrowers, a phenomenon not generally seen in Europe or the United States. For example, in the federal funds market in the United States, which is the money market of the commercial banks, there is no particular group of banks that is always lending, but for geographic, seasonal, or other incidental reasons, a bank that is normally a lender might temporarily become a borrower. The position of borrower or lender is therefore quite fluid. Also, the interbank markets of most other countries are generally for temporary lending or borrowing of central bank money or reserves within the banking system, and lenders and borrowers are not fixed. In the advanced countries of Europe and North America, the banking system is not normally divided between permanent lenders and permanent borrowers, but there often is such a relationship between the banks as a group and other financial institutions for the supply of short-term funds (as in the case of brokerage houses in the United States or discount houses in the United Kingdom). In these cases, the lending or borrowing relations may be viewed as transactions among dissimilar industries (short-term loans by the banking sector to the discount market or to capital market dealers). In Japan's case, there is a permanent lender-borrower relation between two different groups of banks.

This imbalance of bank liquidity first occurred historically during the Second World War, when the local banks, who had only a few clients in the munitions industries, were instructed to supply funds to the city banks, which bore the main brunt of financing the munitions industries.[6] However, the reason this feature has survived in its current form is to be found, in the same way as the origin of overloan, in the rapid growth policy pursued after 1955.

The phrase *imbalance of bank liquidity* suggests that, due to some exogenous conditions, the flow of funds becomes biased toward the noncity banks, with the result that city banks inevitably end up with negative reserve assets. For a time it was thought that these exogenous conditions were related to the regional supply and demand for funds associated with the regional bias of the Treasury Account with the private sector and banknote issue.[7] This view held that there was a tendency for the Treasury Account to be a net receiver of surplus funds in the cities and a net payer (in deficit) in the rural areas, while there was a net issue of banknotes to the cities and a net take-up of banknotes from the rural areas. Also, since the base for city banks' business was in the cities, there was a natural tendency for city banks to be short of funds. Conversely, since the local banks' base was in the rural areas, there was a tendency for local banks

6. For details on the development of the imbalance of liquidity among the banks during World War II, see Michisato Ishikawa [15].

7. See for example, Monetary System Research Council [21].

to have surplus funds, and hence the imbalance of bank liquidity. However, the reason for the net surplus on the Treasury's account with the cities and the net issue of banknotes there, related to the high rate of income growth in the cities, which produced both larger tax payments and a big demand for cash currency. But for the same reason, savings, the source of deposits, also grew rapidly. Conversely, the reason the fiscal system runs a net deficit in the regions and banknotes tend to be absorbed from the regional towns is that income growth in the regions is low and hence tax payments and the demand for cash are low. Consequently, savings and therefore deposits grow at a slower rate.

Obviously the net funds position of any particular area is not determined by its fiscal position and its demand for banknotes alone, but is even more greatly influenced by the flow of funds between regions, which is the counterpart of income-generating activity. It is because the income-generating potential in the big cities is greatest (and hence the deposit-base which forms the operating base for the city banks is most attractive) that competition among city banks has tended to cause the closure of their regional branches and an increase in the number of their branches in the big cities, such as Tokyo and Osaka.[8]

Despite the fact that city banks are favored with an urban deposit-base, the reason the city banks are continuously in an overloan situation is fundamentally due to their lending behavior. As we shall examine in more detail in chapter 2, the excess lending results from the Bank of Japan's credit-supply policy and the inherently strong demand for funds by city banks. To put it in extreme terms, as a result of the credit rationing which inevitably occurs due to the artificial low interest-rate policy, the relationship between the Bank of Japan and the city banks, and in their turn the city banks and the export-oriented, investing enterprises, is so inextricable that it preserves the overloaned position of the city banks and the imbalance of bank liquidity.

Parallel to this, as demonstrated in table 2.3 of chapter 7, section 1, there is a strong tendency for the loans of city banks (relative to local banks), to be dominated by the city bank demand for funds, while the loans of local banks (relative to city banks) are strongly influenced by their own fund positions (the level of their reserve assets). Because of this difference in behavior, there is a tendency for city banks to meet the loan demands of export-oriented or investment-related concerns irrespective of any deterioration in their own fund position and hence the corresponding surplus liquidity among the other banks.

---

8. For detailed theoretical and empirical analysis of the relation between regional economic activity and the flow of funds, see Yoshio Suzuki [41], References.

4. *The Predominance of Indirect Financing*

The predominance of indirect financing has been a distinctive characteristic of Japan's financial structure ever since Meiji times, and unlike overloan, the phenomenon has never even temporarily been eradicated.

The words *direct* and *indirect financing* indicate the route whereby funds flow from those sectors where savings exceed investment (e.g. the household sector in all countries, and the public sector in those countries where conservatively balanced budgets are the norm) to those sectors where investment exceeds savings (e.g. the corporate sector in most countries, and the public sector in those countries where large-scale government bond issues are the norm). "Direct financing" refers to the purchase of securities issued by the net investing (or deficit) sector in the securities market by the net saving (or surplus) sector. Conversely, the practice whereby the net saving sector deposits money with financial institutions (buys indirect financial obligations), and these financial institutions use those funds to invest in the net investing sector by buying the securities issued by that sector (or by other means) is referred to as "indirect financing."

As only Japan, the United States, and West Germany publish statistics of the financial assets for each sector in the economy, a comparison of the structure of financial assets in the personal sector, which accounts for most of the saving, is only possible for these three countries. According to table 1.7, which gives the comparison for the year-end 1974, indirect financing in Japan accounted for 87 percent and was the highest, with West Germany 84 percent and the United States only 48 percent. Of this indirect finance, the flow of funds through the banking sector (excluding insurance and pension money) accounted for 74.1 percent in Japan compared with 66.6 percent in West Germany and 28.0 percent in the United States. Therefore, the predominance of indirect financing in Japan may be interpreted in more extreme terms, not merely as the general predominance of financial intermediaries, but specifically of banks.

With the rise in income levels in recent years, the proportion of financial assets accounted for by insurance and pension schemes has been increasing, and therefore even in the United States the degree of indirect financing via financial intermediaries has been growing. Nevertheless, even with this trend the degree of indirect financing in the United States is far lower than in Japan. This has occurred despite the fact that the proportion of nonbank financial intermediaries in the United States is higher than in Japan, so that the overwhelmingly dominant position of the banking sector in Japan has resulted in creating a greater overall proportion of indirect financing.

In addition, the money collected from insurance and pension schemes in the United States is almost entirely invested in securities. In West Germany

Table 1.7   International Comparison of the Structure of Financial Assets in the Personal Sector (Year-end 1974)

	Amount			*Percentage Component*		
	Japan ¥ billion	*West Germany* DM billion	*United States* $ billion	*Japan* %	*West Germany* %	*United States* %
1. Currency and demand deposits	273,440	74.9	174.2	19.4	10.0	8.0
2. Time and savings deposits (incl. trust accounts)	779,682	435.9	695.3	55.1	57.9	31.8
3. Insurance, pensions	180,361	123.0	471.3	12.8	16.3	21.6
(*a*) Deposits, loans	90,627	92.1	31.6	6.4	12.2	1.4
(*b*) Securities	29,314	28.7	429.3	2.1	3.8	19.7
4. Financial debentures	49,837	–	–	3.5	–	–
Subtotal	1,283,320	633.8	1,340.8	90.8	84.2	61.4
Subtotal excl. 3(*b*)	1,254,006	605.1	911.5	88.7	80.4	41.8
5. Government bonds ⎫ 6. Corporate bonds ⎭	40,882	90.5	181.1 54.5	2.9	12.0	8.3 2.5
7. Equity shares (incl. Investment trust units)	70,048	26.0	523.2	4.9	3.5	24.0
8. Mortgages	–	–	39.3	–	–	1.8
Subtotal	110,930	116.5	798.1	7.8	15.5	36.6
Subtotal incl. 3(*b*)	140,244	145.2	1,227.4	9.9	19.3	56.2
Aggregate Total (incl. others)	1,414,103	753.0	2,182.6	100.0	100.0	100.0

Sources: Central Banks' Flow of Funds Tables.

also a large proportion is invested in securities. Thus, in both the United States and West Germany financial intermediaries tend to place individuals' savings in securities, instead of individuals buying the securities themselves. In contrast to this pattern, Japanese financial intermediaries specializing in insurance and pension schemes tend, like the banks, to use most individuals' savings as direct loans to companies.

These differences arise from the underdevelopment of Japanese securities markets which, at another level, results from the investment-led rapid growth policies, the artificial low interest-rate policy, and the lack of internationalization that we shall examine in more detail below. The item in table 1.7, "Subtotal incl. 3(*b*)" indicates how in Japan, when funds flow from the net saving sector to the net investment sector, only a miniscule proportion flows through the securities markets. Compared with 19 percent in West Germany and 56 percent in the United States, the proportion in Japan's case is far lower at 10 percent.

2 The Investment-led, Rapid Growth Policy and the Four Distinctive Characteristics

In this and the following chapter I shall examine the basic setting of the four distinctive characteristics of Japan's financial structure encountered in chapter 1.

1. *The Interdependence of the Four Distinctive Characteristics in Historical Perspective*

In examining the origins of the four distinctive characteristics the first thing to notice is that each is, in turn, a cause and an effect of the others, so that all four are deeply interrelated. For example, as we have already seen, overborrowing occurs, first, because Japanese companies depend heavily on external finance, and second, because of the large proportion of indirect bank-financing within external finance. In this respect, of the two causes of overborrowing, the second reflects the predominance of indirect financing within the flow of funds; but both are simply different facets of the same relationship.

Also, on account of the predominance of indirect financing, the government and corporate bond markets have remained underdeveloped, and therefore the Bank of Japan has been unable—at least until very recently—to conduct open market operations (operations whereby a central bank regulates the money supply through buying or selling bonds or commercial paper through a broker as an ordinary customer in the secondary bond market or in the discount markets for short-term government securities and commercial bills). The tendency has therefore been for Bank of Japan credit (i.e. central bank money) to be supplied through direct loans, and this has contributed to the persistence of overloan. Thus we find a mutual connection between overloan and indirect financing.

At the same time, since overloan derives primarily from Bank of Japan loans to the city banks, central bank credit is therefore a major factor contributing to the permanent overlending by the city banks within the banking sector—that is, in causing the imbalance of bank liquidity. Again, overloan and overborrowing are also extremely closely related. As we have seen, although these two characteristics are not by any means inevitably connected, nevertheless under the export-oriented, investment-led rapid growth policy, leading companies in these sectors tended to become over-burdened with debt, that is, indulged in overborrowing, and since this borrowing was concentrated on the city banks, there was a tendency for it to compound the problem of the imbalance of bank liquidity and the overloan situation.[1]

In this way the four distinctive characteristics of Japanese finance are closely interconnected in such a way that it is somewhat superficial, or at least an error of judgment, to say that any one is a basic cause or another a derivative result.

In terms of their historical evolution, overloan and the phenomenon of indirect financing go back as far as the promulgation of the National Bank Act of 1872. The background to this evolution is the fostering since Meiji times of a modern financial system centering primarily on indirect financing through the concentration of small savings in banks by offering favorable tax treatment for interest income, and by permitting borrowers of funds to write off interest payments from pretax profits. Under the Meiji slogan of *shokusankōgyō* ("encouraging industrialization and fostering the entrepreneurial spirit"), the accumulation of real physical capital before there were sufficient funds available from the build-up of privately held assets or from bank deposits, required the banks to become aggressive lenders, intensifying overloan and making it an integral feature of Japan's financial structure.[2]

As described in chapter 1, the predominance of indirect financing has been an unbroken phenomenon since the Meiji era, but overloan gradually became less conspicuous as government expenditure—financed partly by the central bank and partly by the indemnity received from China following the Sino-Japanese War in 1895—grew rapidly (see table 2.1). Indeed, overloan actually disappeared around the turn of the century. Overborrowing, on the other hand, did not exist in Meiji times, nor did the imbalance of bank liquidity, for in the Meiji and Taisho years, and the Showa years until 1934, government expenditures were the leading sector in the Japanese economy. As shown in table 2.1 private-sector plant and equipment investment did not constitute a high proportion of GNE (Gross National Expenditure), and corporate dependence on outside sources of funds was

1. The Monetary System Research Council [21] particularly stressed the interrelationships between overloan, overborrowing, and the imbalance of bank liquidity.
2. Toshihiko Yoshino [62] is representative of the school that emphasizes the historical, institutional, and social origins of overloan and the dominance of indirect financing.

Table 2.1 Estimates of GNP since the Meiji Era (Five-year Averages of Nominal figures at Annual Rates)

	Amount (Million Yen)							Component Ratios					
	C Personal Consumption	I_p Fixed Private Capital Formation	I_g Govt. Fixed Capital Formation	C_g Govt. Current Expenditure	E Exports	M Imports	V Gross National Product	$\frac{C}{V}$	$\frac{I_p}{V}$	$\frac{I_g}{V}$	$\frac{C_g}{V}$	$\frac{E}{V}$	$\frac{M}{V}$
1880–84	793.7		18.0	59.1	33.5	31.1							
1885–89	786.7		22.1	64.1	54.9	47.5							
1890–94	1,070.1	71.6	38.6	94.2	86.1	84.4	1,276.1	83.9	5.6	3.0	7.4	6.7	6.6
1895–99	1,756.2	62.3	101.5	178.8	162.7	205.7	2,055.5	85.4	3.0	4.9	8.7	7.9	10.0
1900–04	2,318.0	96.8	129.7	344.4	321.8	366.2	2,844.3	81.5	3.4	4.6	12.1	11.3	12.9
1905–09	2,921.0	157.0	243.6	470.4	533.9	618.2	3,667.6	79.6	4.3	5.6	12.8	14.6	16.9
1910–14	3,872.8	262.0	290.1	442.6	691.7	773.7	4,785.2	80.9	5.5	6.1	9.2	14.5	16.2
1915–19	6,728.6	529.4	451.7	724.9	2,193.8	1,561.1	9,047.3	74.4	5.9	5.0	8.0	24.0	17.3
1920–24	12,117.8	1,148.3	1,138.8	1,475.8	2,247.1	2,551.2	15,576.5	77.8	7.4	7.3	9.5	14.4	16.4
1925–29	12,773.7	1,016.4	1,247.8	1,606.8	2,715.9	2,875.5	16,484.9	77.5	6.2	7.6	9.7	16.5	17.4
1930–34	11,084.8	858.0	1,160.5	2,133.0	2,272.6	2,271.7	15,236.3	72.7	5.6	7.6	14.0	14.9	14.9
1935–39	15,547.1	2,495.7	3,053.8	4,779.8	4,128.6	4,354.3	25,650.6	60.6	9.7	11.9	18.6	11.1	17.0

Source: T. Nakamura, *Japanese Economic Studies* 1972, vol. 1, no. 1 (International Arts and Sciences Press).

low (see table 2.2), so that overborrowing did not exist. Moreover, since the big banks, which were the predecessors of today's city banks, had ample reserve assets after the elimination of overloan around the turn of the century, they were able to lend short-term funds in the form of call loans to the specialist foreign exchange banks such as the Yokohama Specie Bank, the Bank of Korea, and the Bank of Taiwan. The imbalance of bank liquidity, therefore, did not exist in the sense that it does today.

Overloan first began to appear simultaneously with the appearance of the imbalance of bank liquidity during World War II, as we saw in chapter 1. There it was noted that since funds were required to be loaned from local banks—which did not have the munitions industries as clients—to the city banks, an imbalance of bank liquidity evolved. Also, with the very rapid increase in private investment, especially by the munitions industries during these years, the degree of corporate dependence on external funds began to rise. However, even at this stage the degree of external financing was not enough to justify the term *overborrowing* (table 2.2).

The predominance of indirect financing since the Meiji era, together with the emergence of overloan and the imbalance of bank liquidity during the Second World War, continued throughout the immediate postwar reconstruction. Thereafter, overloan and the imbalance of bank liquidity declined markedly with the postwar recovery, even disappearing for a time in 1955 under the impact of a favorable balance of payments and a large surplus in the Special Food Account due to exceptionally good rice harvests.

Table 2.2   Trends in Component Shares of Sources of Corporate Finance

(Unit = Percent)

Year	Shareholders' Equity	External Funds		Total
			Loan Finance	
1914–20	70.9	29.1	–	100.0
1921–25	69.1	30.9	–	100.0
1926–30FH	58.9	41.1	–	100.0
1928–34	56.9	43.1	6.3	100.0
1935–40	57.7	42.3	5.4	100.0
1941–43FH	49.0	51.0	7.4	100.0
1950–54	35.7	64.3	28.1	100.0
1955–64	28.9	71.1	32.8	100.0

Source: Bank of Japan, "Main Economic Indicators in the Post-Meiji Era."
Note: Statistics are averages for years indicated; FH = first half of year.

Table 2.3 International Comparison of Flow of Funds, Expenditures, and Income by Sector

		Japan			United States	Britain	West Germany	France
		1961–65	1966–70	1971–74		1971–74		
		¥100m	¥100m	¥100m	US$100m	£m	DMm	Ff.100m
Sectoral Surplus/ Deficit (△)								
Amount	Personal	108,280	230,267	419,206	2,500	8,146	1,440	1,572
	Corporate	△ 94,100	△ 151,121	△ 273,176	△ 1,766	△ 3,679	△ 1,281	△ 2,954
	Public	△ 19,073	△ 56,680	△ 119,222	△ 963	△ 9,889	25	250
	Foreign	4,893	△ 22,466	△ 26,808	241	3,930	△ 382	397
		%	%	%	%	%	%	%
As proportion of	Personal	12.5	13.0	14.2	7.2	4.3	6.2	5.0
income share	Corporate	△ 51.4	△ 34.2	△ 57.5	△ 45.8	△ 18.6	△ 43.1	△ 60.5
	Public	△ 9.3	△ 14.2	△ 16.6	△ 9.4	△ 15.4	0.3	3.4
		%	%	%	%	%	%	%
Expenditures by sector	Personal	60.3	58.8	62.4	67.3	64.5	59.7	66.6
Component share	Corporate	22.1	22.7	18.4	11.1	9.4	15.6	17.7
	Public	17.9	17.5	18.5	21.4	26.8	22.1	15.5
	Foreign	△ 0.3	1.0	0.7	0.3	0.7	2.6	0.2
		%	%	%	%	%	%	%
Distribution of national	Personal	68.9	67.6	71.1	70.9	68.9	66.1	71.5
income by sector	Corporate	14.6	16.9	11.5	7.8	7.2	8.4	11.2
Component share	Public	16.4	15.3	17.3	20.9	23.4	23.8	16.6
	Foreign	0.1	0.1	0.1	0.4	0.5	1.6	0.7

Source: Bank of Japan, *International Comparative Statistics* and *Foreign Economic Statistics Annual*, various issues.
Note: Sectoral distribution of income (gross basis) is derived from national income statistics and income from sale of assets (land, etc.). Land purchases are therefore deducted from public sector income and added to the personal or corporate sector which sold the land.

The reasons these phenomena reemerged after 1956 and, together with the additional overborrowing became part of the distinctive characteristics of Japan's financial structure, are to be found in the particular conditions of the Japanese economy during these years. Under a regime of strict controls on trade and capital transactions, together with the maintenance of an artificially low rate of interest, the economy followed a path of investment-led growth. Three conditions—the rapid real growth rate, the artificially low interest-rate policy, and the lack of internationalization—formed the basic cornerstone of Japan's financial structure, along with the four characteristics mentioned earlier, from 1956 until recent years.

2. *Investment-led Growth and the Flow-of-Funds Structure*

2.1 *The Corporate Sector*

First we shall examine the significance that investment-led growth had for Japan's financial structure. The lower two panels of table 2.3 show an international comparison of the structural composition of GNE or GNP by expenditure and income shares for Japan, the United States, the United Kingdom, West Germany, and France. On the expenditure side, Japan's corporate sector accounted for an extremely high proportion—as high as 20–23 percent—of GNE, reflecting the fact that investment expenditures by Japan's private business sector were the driving force behind the policy of investment-led growth. To some extent West Germany and France exhibited investment-led growth characteristics but, as is clear from the component size of expenditures, there was still a marked discrepancy between them and Japan.

On the income side, the corporate income share in Japan is also high, and in this case the corporate income shares in West Germany and France are quite close to that of Japan. The high figure for Japan is due to (*a*) the existence of plentiful opportunities for investment given the background of investment-led growth and, reflecting this, the high rates of return of Japanese corporations (technically, the high marginal efficiency of capital); (*b*) the low level—by international standards—of corporate income tax; and (*c*) the high level of provisions for depreciation as a proportion of GNP reflecting the rapid rate of additions to the capital stock associated with investment-led growth. However, during the decade 1956–65 the corporate income share in Japan did not exceed those of Western Europe or the United States by as large a margin as the corporate expenditure share because, although there was a tendency for the corporate income share to rise under the policy of investment-led growth, wage increases and the continuous increase in the tax base provided incremental income to the personal and public sectors, so that the corporate income share could not rise disproportionately.

Thus, although the corporate expenditure share and the corporate income share were both rising during the investment-led growth period from 1955 onward, the rate of rise of corporate expenditures was higher so that the corporate sector overspent, so to speak, which resulted in a rapid increase in the absolute size of the corporate-sector deficit. The size of the corporate-sector deficit was 65 percent of gross corporate income in 1956–60, and 51 percent in 1961–65, both remarkably high figures compared with Britain, West Germany, or the United States. The corollary of the extremely large corporate-sector deficit relative to corporate income (i.e. retained earnings plus depreciation), of course, was that external financing as a source of corporate financing was exceptionally high. As we have already seen in table 1.5, this is one of the two factors which necessarily resulted in overborrowing. In this sense, overborrowing derives directly from the structure of the flow of funds which accompanied Japan's investment-led growth.[3]

After 1965, investment-led growth continued, and corporate sector expenditures continued to account for a sizable share of GNE. However, with the rise in the corporate income share due to the absolute increase in depreciation, the corporate sector's deficit as a proportion of its income share declined to around 34 percent, on a par with levels in Europe and the United States (see table 2.3). Nevertheless, as we saw in table 1.5, during this period the dependence of Japanese companies on external funds remained far higher than their European or American counterparts on account of the growth in the value of financial assets—mainly bank deposits —held by the corporate sector. Table 2.4 documents the statistical evidence.

Generally speaking, the ratio of internal funding by companies $\dfrac{Sg}{(Sg + B)}$ depends on $\left(\dfrac{Sg}{Ig}\right)$, the proportion of physical investment financed from internal sources and $\left(\dfrac{Af}{Ig}\right)$, the proportion of investment in financial assets relative to investment in physical capital. However, the reason for the low level of internal funding during the years 1966–69 was that, despite the proportion of physical investment funded from internal sources reaching about the same level as in Europe or the United States (see table 2.3 above), the ratio of investment in financial assets to investment in physical capital was about twice the level reached in the United States or in Europe, at 45 percent.[4]

Thus investment in financial assets by Japanese corporations was large mainly because the level of corporate-owned deposits was extremely

---

3. For the special characteristics of Japan's flow of funds, see Sadao Ishida [13].

4. The computations in table 2.4 were carried out by Kazuo Yasui of the Bank of Japan's Research Department.

Table 2.4 International Comparative Analysis of Corporate Financial Deficits (In Percent)

	Japan (Corporate Enterprises)			United States (Corporate Enterprises)			United Kingdom (Corporate Enterprises)			West Germany (All Industries excl. Housing)			France (All Industries)		
	1960-62	63-65	66-69	1960-62	63-65	66-69	1960-62	63-65	66-69	1960-62	63-65	66-69	1960-62	63-65	66-69
Percentage of physical investment financed from internal sources $\left(\dfrac{S_g}{I_g}\right)$	56.8	66.3	74.0	93.4	94.1	79.2	102.8	104.8	101.1	67.6	70.2	79.4	66.6	67.1	70.5
$\left(\dfrac{S_n}{I_n}\right)$	35.8	36.8	53.2	80.7	84.6	53.6	106.9	117.0	102.7	41.7	39.3	53.9	37.0	38.0	44.7
Corporate income shares $\left(\dfrac{S_n}{Y}\right)$	6.6	4.5	7.2	2.5	3.3	2.7	4.2	3.3	4.2	5.0	4.1	4.8	3.9	4.1	4.9
Corporate investment as % of national income $\left(\dfrac{I_n}{Y}\right)$	18.3	12.1	13.5	3.1	3.9	5.1	3.9	2.9	4.1	12.0	10.4	8.9	10.7	10.7	11.0
Internal financing as % of total funds employed $\left(\dfrac{S_g}{S_g + B}\right)$	39.5	41.0	51.1	70.2	72.1	63.7	75.1	72.4	75.0	64.2	64.7	68.6	60.8	62.7	64.4
Investment in financial assets as % of investment in physical plant and equipment $\left(\dfrac{A_f}{I_g}\right)$	43.7	61.9	44.7	33.0	30.5	24.4	36.9	44.7	34.9	5.4	8.5	15.8	9.5	7.0	9.5
$\dfrac{\text{Depreciation}}{\text{Net Savings}}\left(\dfrac{D_r}{S_n}\right)$	136.2	238.8	150.8	238.8	189.3	229.8	142.9	219.5	130.4	192.4	264.6	229.4	239.5	233.3	196.5

Notes: 1. Analytical formulae: (1) $\dfrac{S_n}{I_n} = \dfrac{S_n}{Y} \div \dfrac{I_n}{Y}$ (2) $\dfrac{S_g}{S_g + B} = \dfrac{S_g}{I_g} \div \left(1 + \dfrac{A_f}{I_g}\right)$ $S_g = S_n + D_r$

2. Symbols: S = savings; I = investment in physical capital; Y = national income; n = net; g = gross; B = external borrowing; A_f = financial investment (= increase in financial assets); D_r = depreciation.

high by comparison with Europe and the United States. This, as we shall analyze later, was closely associated with the policy of artificially low interest rates that forced down the published borrowing rates of companies to a low level and led to companies being compelled to place as compensatory deposits a proportion of the funds they had been loaned in order to raise the effective rate of interest. Companies were required to deposit up to 25 percent of their borrowings on average, independent of their normal cash-holding requirements. One particular feature about Japan, notably among large corporations, was the widespread practice of making substantial intercompany loans, which accounted for a substantial share of corporate holdings of financial assets. (The recipients of the corporate business sector's loans were the unincorporated individual businessmen in the service industries, in agriculture, forestry, and fishing.)

To summarize, the high degree of external financing by Japanese corporations that was one of the main causes of overborrowing resulted first from the large corporate-sector financial deficit which accompanied the investment-led growth, and second from the high level of investment in financial assets by the corporate sector due to the artificially low interest-rate policy.

2.2 *The Public Sector*

Next we examine the special characteristics exhibited by the public sector in contrast to the structure of the flow of funds in the corporate sector. First, with the exception of France, Japan's public-sector spending as a proportion of GNP is very low in comparison with other European and North American countries, as shown in table 2.3. This is because Japan's economic growth was not of the fiscal-led model as in Europe and North America, but had a strongly private investment-oriented character. On the other hand, the income share of the public sector was extremely low in Japan because the burden of taxation was less than in any major country in Europe or North America. Nevertheless, between 1956 and 1960 the extremely low proportion of government expenditures in GNE (see table 2.3) induced the public sector to match revenue and expenditure, allowing for a very small surplus each year. After 1960, government expenditure rose slightly, and because the taxation rate was marginally lower, the public sector switched into deficit, though the size of the deficit remained quite small. The column in table 2.3 for the years 1961–65 shows that the public-sector deficit appeared to grow quite considerably over the period, but this reflects the exceptionally large public-sector deficit in fiscal 1965. Taking the years 1956–65 as a whole, the public-sector deficit was generally small. This is clearly reflected in the sustained pursuit of a balanced-budget policy and in the fact that long-term government bonds were not issued until the final quarter of fiscal 1965. The growth in the volume of long-term government bonds in comparison with GNP as shown in table 2.5 from 1965 onward was quite similar in pattern to developments in Europe and in North America. However, in terms of the absolute amount outstanding, long-term government bonds (as a proportion of GNP) were, excluding France, lower than the level in Europe and America at least until 1970.

Table 2.5   International Comparison of Government Debt and Long-Term Government Bonds as Percentage of GNP

Calendar Year	Government Debt					Of Which, Long-Term Government Bonds				
	Japan	U. S.	U. K.	W. Ger.	France	Japan	U. S.	U. K.	W. Ger.	France
Amount Outstanding as % of GNP										
1961	6.6	57.0	110.1	8.7	26.7	2.3	47.6	83.1	7.3	7.4
1962	6.1	54.3	103.5	7.7	24.2	2.7	41.6	71.4	6.4	6.2
1963	4.8	52.4	98.7	7.8	21.8	2.4	41.8	77.2	6.5	5.8
1964	4.7	50.4	91.5	7.6	20.2	2.2	41.5	71.0	6.4	5.5
1965	5.4	46.9	87.1	7.2	17.3	3.0	38.1	67.0	6.0	4.7
1966	7.2	43.9	83.8	7.3	15.0	4.9	34.5	68.1	6.0	4.3
1967	8.8	43.3	84.4	8.8	15.8	5.9	34.5	64.6	6.4	4.0
1968	9.3	41.2	77.7	8.7	15.5	6.1	32.6	58.7	6.6	3.3
1969	9.2	39.4	70.7	7.5	13.9	6.0	30.7	55.2	6.6	2.7
1970	8.8	39.6	65.1	6.9	12.2	6.0	30.7	53.5	6.2	2.1
1971	9.6	39.9	62.7	6.4	10.7	6.9	30.7	52.3	5.8	1.8
1972	12.9	38.4	58.2	6.6	8.6	8.4	29.5	49.8	6.3	1.5
1973	11.8	36.0	55.1	6.6	7.5	8.4	27.7	44.2	6.1	2.6
1974	11.9	35.0	55.7	7.2	7.2	8.9	26.5	42.6	6.6	3.3
Amount of Increase as % of GNP										
1962	0.3	1.3	1.5	0.2	0.3	△0.1	△0.4	△0.5	0.1	△0.4
1963	△0.4	1.0	3.8	0.8	0.8	0.0	2.4	7.6	0.7	0.4
1964	0.6	1.4	1.1	0.3	△0.4	0.0	2.3	4.9	0.7	△0.0
1965	1.3	0.4	2.5	0.4	△0.6	1.7	△0.1	△0.1	0.5	△0.1
1966	2.4	1.1	1.7	0.5	△0.9	2.2	△0.3	5.2	0.3	0.0
1967	2.7	1.9	5.5	1.6	1.8	1.8	2.0	0.4	0.5	△0.1
1968	1.9	1.5	△0.5	0.7	1.1	1.1	0.9	△1.2	0.7	△0.3
1969	1.2	1.1	△1.8	△0.3	0.5	0.8	0.5	0.4	0.7	△0.2
1970	1.1	2.1	0.7	0.3	△0.2	0.9	1.4	3.1	0.4	△0.2
1971	1.7	3.3	4.2	0.2	△0.3	1.6	2.4	4.2	0.2	△0.2
1972	4.5	2.2	1.6	0.8	△1.0	2.3	1.6	2.6	1.0	△0.1
1973	1.3	1.6	4.4	0.7	△0.0	1.6	1.3	1.0	0.5	1.3
1974	1.9	1.5	7.0	1.1	0.7	1.9	0.7	3.4	0.8	1.1

Source: Various official government statistics, and Bank of Japan, *Foreign Economic Statistics Annual.*
△ = minus

Thus, throughout the period of investment-led rapid growth in Japan the public-sector financial deficit was small, even after long-term government bonds were issued in 1965, and in terms of volume, as a proportion of total government liabilities they remained very small. The question is, what impact did these circumstances have on the distinctive characteristics of Japan's financial structure?

In general, the public sector did not resort to short-term borrowing as a means of meeting its deficit, and financed its deficits mainly through the issue of long-term government bonds and public corporation debt. The fact that the public-sector deficit remained small until 1964 implies, firstly, that government and public corporation bonds were not issued in large quantities until that year, and secondly, that from 1965 onward the blocks of government bonds on the market were, in any case, small. From the standpoint of the development of a securities market this was disadvantageous, because for competitive pricing in both the bond-issuing market and the secondary markets it is necessary to have as many potential buyers and sellers of bonds as possible exchanging information about the bonds. In the United States and the United Kingdom, the bond markets do have this depth and breadth because large blocks of government bonds have been listed on public exchanges since the time of the First and Second World wars, so that these markets have been able to develop satisfactorily. In Japan, the small supply of government bonds available, the great variety in the quality and credit-worthiness of corporate issuers, together with the small size of issues in numerous categories, has meant that information concerning particular bonds is highly imperfect. Therefore, even with small changes in supply or demand there can be considerable movement in prices, and there is a widespread tendency for transactions involving the mutual consent of two parties to take place outside the market. For this reason the marketability and convertibility of bonds is a problem, and adequate development of an open, competitive market-price mechanism capable of encouraging an active and vigorous bond market has not occurred.

The development of direct forms of financing was hindered by the fact that the flow-of-funds structure which existed during the period of rapid investment-led economic growth meant that there was no large public-sector deficit or its counterpart, large issues of securities by the public sector, so that the large blocks of bond issues necessary for the development of a bond market were not available.

3. Supply of "Growth Money" for the Investment-led Growth Pattern

This section examines the relationship between sectoral surpluses or deficits and overloan. The large corporate-sector deficit and the small public-sector deficit meant that among the debts in the financial system, obligations of corporations accounted for the larger part, while government obligations (i.e. government obligations narrowly defined to exclude high-powered money) were small.

At the same time, the supply of money by the central bank necessarily implies the monetization of the internal debts of the financial system. For example, central bank discounting of commercial bills (which are liabilities of corporations) and purchases of commercial paper by the central bank are both processes of monetization. In addition, central bank purchases of government securities represent the monetization of government debt. Generally speaking, the kinds of debt which central banks choose to monetize are ultimately those which are the most marketable; it is not very desirable from the point of view of equity to monetize the less liquid obligations of particular private companies as a means of providing central bank money. More fundamentally, it is undesirable for the central bank to hold, as part of its assets, the long-term debt of any single corporation. Consequently, the monetization of government debt is generally deemed to be the most desirable.

However, under the investment-led, rapid growth policy, because corporate liabilities accounted for the larger part of the internal debts of the financial system and government liabilities were rather small, the provision of high-powered money necessarily required the monetization of corporate liabilities. Monetization was achieved either by discounting bills drawn by highly credit-worthy companies, by rediscounting foreign trade bills or loans with foreign trade bills as collateral, or by advances on promissory notes secured by corporate bonds. In effect, the supply of high-powered money was most likely to take the form of loans and so lead directly to overloan.

Of course, from a logical standpoint there is no reason why commercial paper or corporate bonds should not be acquired through central bank-buying operations on the open market. But in the 1950s and 1960s the commercial paper market and the secondary government and corporate bond markets in Japan were underdeveloped, and therefore it was impossible to supply high-powered money in a nondiscriminatory fashion when purchasing bills and bonds through brokers in the open market. From October 1962, with the start of the so-called New Scheme for Monetary Control, which was deliberately designed to avoid the build-up of an overloan situation, the Bank of Japan engaged in an active program of purchasing securities. But from the very beginning these operations were far from open-market-type operations and more on the basis of administered prices within a managed market, amounting to the purchase of bonds in exchange for loans by mutual consent (from 1967, those purchased were mainly long-term government securities, but initially government-guaranteed securities, financial debentures, and electricity corporation bonds were also acquired; for details, see part 3, chapter 11). In those economies where there is a large amount of government debt outstanding, it is much easier to develop a secondary market for the discounting of short-term government securities and medium- and long-term government bonds. In such cases it is relatively easy to supply high-powered money through the monetization of government debt by open-market operations in long- and short-term government bonds, and thus avoid overloan. In Japan's case, however, open-market operations in commercial bills, to be described in chapter 11, did not begin until 1972, after the start of the bills discount market in 1971.

Table 2.6 shows the type of debts which the central banks of some

Table 2.6 International Comparison of Composition of Assets of Central Banks (By Percentage Share)

		Foreign Assets	Credit to Central Government	Credit to Private Sector
Japan	1963	26.0	20.9	53.1
	1966	21.6	31.6	46.8
	1970	24.9	42.9	32.2
	1974	29.3	29.9	40.8
United States	1963	30.3	69.4	0.3
	1966	21.8	74.5	3.7
	1970	16.7	78.4	4.9
	1974	14.3	83.9	1.8
United Kingdom	1963	15.3	84.7	0
	1966	12.3	86.8	0.9
	1970	13.2	86.8	0
	1974	18.7	81.3	0
West Germany	1963	77.3	17.9	4.8
	1966	61.5	26.2	12.3
	1970	61.1	17.1	21.8
	1974	73.0	18.4	13.6
France	1963	41.1	19.4	39.5
	1966	47.2	19.4	33.4
	1970	30.7	13.0	56.3
	1974	28.0	7.5	64.5

Source: International Monetary Fund, International Financial Statistics, 1976.

leading nations monetized in order to provide high-powered money. Before the issue of long-term government bonds and the start of an active purchasing program in 1966, the monetization of private-sector debt in Japan was exceptionally high by international standards. But from 1970 purchases of long-term government debt increased so that the proportion of private debt monetized fell substantially. Nevertheless, the monetization of government debt in the United States, the United Kingdom, and West Germany was even higher. (The reason the monetization of private-sector debt in France was relatively high was that, up until the late 1960s, the corporate-sector deficit in France was extremely large and, correspondingly, the public sector had a cash surplus. West Germany's flow-of-funds structure was similar [see table 2.3], but in her case the balance of payments was in surplus during these years and the proportion of foreign government debt monetized in the supply of high-powered money was high and, correspondingly, the proportion of private debt monetized was low.)

Thus the structure of the flow of funds which accompanied the investment-led growth strategy in Japan restricted the ability of the authorities to supply high-powered money through the purchase of government bonds. There was therefore a strong tendency for high-powered money to be supplied either through the rediscounting of corporate debt (i.e. commercial bills or corporate bonds) or through loans and advances based on these as collateral—in other words, a strong tendency for overloan to emerge.

This tendency was at the same time closely associated with the continued existence of the problem of the imbalance of bank liquidity, because the type of securities which qualified for rediscount with the Bank of Japan were the bills of prime-quality companies or trade bills, and it was, of course, the city banks that held most of these types of instruments through their large, export-related corporate clients. Moreover, it was the city banks which held the largest share of electric utility bonds, corporate bonds, and financial debentures. Consequently, high-powered money tended to be supplied preferentially against city bank loans and in this sense was inextricably related to the imbalance of bank liquidity. Another point not to be overlooked in the relation between the imbalance of bank liquidity and the export-oriented investment-led growth pattern is that there were many large corporations in these industries and a distinct tendency for them to concentrate on the city banks to satisfy their demand for funds. For example, according to the "Short-term Economic Survey of Principal Enterprises" of the Bank of Japan, the ratio of exports among medium- and small-sized manufacturing industries as a proportion of sales was only 8.2 percent compared with 16.7 percent for larger corporations. (Both figures are averages for fiscal 1971.) Also because exports by manufacturing companies are concentrated among major corporations, medium- and small-sized businesses tend to deal through large trading companies. In

Table 2.7 Sectoral Classification of Industrial Production by Scale of Corporate Enterprise

	Composition of output by Scale of Enterprise (1965)			Composition of Industrial Sectors by Scale of Enterprise (1965)			Average Index in 1971 (1965 = 100)		
	Total	Large-Sized Enterprises	Medium & Small Enterprises	Total	Large-Sized Enterprises	Medium & Small Enterprises	Total	Large-Sized Enterprises	Medium & Small Enterprises
	%	%	%	%	%	%	%	%	%
Capital goods	29.4	29.3	29.7	100.0	74.8	25.2	277.0	295.5	224.5
Machinery, etc.	20.2	22.6	12.9	100.0	84.2	15.8	303.7	312.0	262.0
Plant	9.2	6.7	16.9	100.0	54.3	45.7	218.7	239.5	195.9
Consumer goods	31.7	29.4	38.6	100.0	69.7	30.3	195.4	214.0	156.2
Durables	9.4	10.7	5.6	100.0	85.1	14.9	293.2	311.7	194.9
Nondurables	22.3	18.8	32.9	100.0	63.2	36.8	154.3	158.5	149.6
Intermediate goods	38.9	41.3	31.7	100.0	79.7	20.3	213.9	231.4	186.2
Total	100.0	100.0	100.0	100.0	75.1	24.9	226.6	245.1	186.0

Source: Agency for Medium and Small Business Enterprises.

addition, the large trading companies' share of exports is so large that, for the financing of medium- and small-sized companies' exports, they tend to deal with the city banks. Furthermore, because the city banks were class A authorized foreign exchange banks, there was a widespread tendency for them to undertake export financing on behalf of the smaller businesses at a preemptive stage. Thus there was a tendency under export-led growth conditions for a large part of fund-demand to be focused on the city banks.

On the question of the number of major corporations in investment-related industries, table 2.7 shows the structural breakdown by size of corporation for specific components of the industrial production index. In terms of the overall industrial production index, large corporations account for 75 percent, and medium and small corporations for 25 percent. But in the capital goods sector, large corporations account for 84 percent while medium and small enterprises account for only 16 percent. Also, from 1966 to 1971 the rate of increase of output of capital goods over the six-year period was 3.1 times in the case of large corporations against only 2.6 times for medium and small enterprises. From these facts it is evident that the fund-demand by large corporations was very powerful and swelled the city banks' loan-demand. In fact, from 1965 to 1970 the demand from the leading city banks by large corporations in the investment-related industries was so large that the banks could not meet it. City banks were forced to reduce their share of total financing between about 1968 and 1970 and to permit large corporations to obtain financing from local banks, mutual loan and savings banks, and credit associations in order to satisfy the immense demand for funds.

In these ways, given the export-oriented, investment-led growth pattern, the demand for funds tended to focus on the city banks. Simultaneously, because high-powered money was supplied against the prime commercial bills, trade bills, and corporate bonds held by the city banks, it was the city banks that tended to become overloaned. In other words, the cause of the continuation of the imbalance of bank liquidity was firmly rooted in the interaction of these contributing elements.

5. Among the earliest to point out the close financial interrelationship between over-borrowing, the imbalance of bank liquidity, and overloan on the one hand, and the export-oriented and investment-related industries, the city banks, and the Bank of Japan on the other, were Tsuneo Iida [11] and Giichi Miyazaki [25].

3 The Maintenance of an Artificially Low Interest-Rate Policy and the Four Distinctive Characteristics

The previous chapter examined the relationship between the four special characteristics of Japan's financial structure and the export-oriented, investment-led growth policy. This chapter examines the relationship between the four distinctive characteristics and the artificially low interest-rate policy as well as the underlying barriers to internationalization.

1. *The Inflexibility of Interest Rates and Distortions in the Structure of Interest Rates*

1.1 *Causes of Inflexibility*
In postwar Japan, and particularly after 1955, the level of interest rates was kept low with the deliberate aims of reducing the cost of manufactured exports and stimulating investment. In order to see the impact the artificially low interest-rate policy had upon the structure of interest rates in Japan and their fluctuations, a statistical comparison of the coefficient of variation of average monthly rates for the ten-year period between January 1962 and December 1971 is presented in table 3.1.

In this analysis, five leading interest rates have been used: the official discount rate or bank rate, a short-term money-market rate, a bond-market yield, bank lending rates, and rates payable on bank deposits. The first conclusion is that the coefficient of variation (standard deviations divided by average rate) for these five kinds of interest rate shows that Japan's call rate had, by international standards, a high degree of flexibility, but that all other rates in Japan showed a far more rigid behavior than those in Europe and North America. (Since 1972 the bill discount rate has become the most representative rate for the short-term money market in Japan, but for the purpose of analysis in the period prior to this the call rate is used.)

First we examine why the four rates other than the call rate were so

Table 3.1 International Comparison of Interest Rates (1962–1971) (January 1962–December 1971, Monthly Data)

			Short-Term Money-Market Rate		Bond Market Yield		Bank Lending Rates		Deposit Interest Rates	
			Interbank Rate		Financial Debentures					
		Official Discount Rate	Unconditional	Over-Month-end	Issuing Terms	Market Yield	Overdraft Rate	All Banks' Average Contracted Lending Rate	Ordinary Deposits	1-year Fixed-Term Deposits
Japan	Average	5.992	7.716	8.884	7.338	8.240		7.182	2.550	5.589
	(Over-month-end call rate = 100)	(67.4)	(86.9)	(100.0)	(82.6)	(92.8)		(80.8)	(28.7)	(62.9)
	Coefficient of variation	0.092	0.202	0.255	0.002	0.084		0.040	0.004	0.002
	rate names →	Official Discount Rate	Federal Funds Rate	Treasury Bill Rate	Market Yield on Government Bonds	Yield on Corporate Bonds		Prime Rate (35 cities)	Fixed Deposits (for Small Deposits)	3-month C.D.'s
U.S.	Average	4.445	4.756	4.546	4.959	5.979		6.162	4.850	5.643
	(Treasury bill rate = 100)	(97.8)	(104.6)	(100.0)	(109.1)	(131.5)		(135.5)	(106.7)	(124.1)
	Coefficient of variation	0.222	0.402	0.287	0.186	0.243		0.204	0.086	0.266
	rate names →	Official Discount Rate	Overnight Rate	3-month Government Stock	Yield on Consols	Yield on Corporate Bonds	Over-draft Rate	Discount Rate on Commercial Paper	Sight Deposits (Inter-bank)	
U.K.	Average	6.143	5.090	5.718	7.217	8.195	7.475	7.383	4.107	
	(3-month government stock = 100)	(107.4)	(89.0)	(100.0)	(126.2)	(143.3)	(130.7)	(129.1)	(71.8)	
	Coefficient of variation	0.209	0.258	0.239	0.183	0.180	0.181	0.196	0.315	

France

	Official Discount Rate	Call Rate	1-year Finance Ministry Notes	Yield on Undated 5% Bonds	Yield on Ordinary Bonds	Over-draft Rate	Discount Rate on Commercial Bills	Fixed Deposits (3–6 Months)	Fixed Deposits (24–30 Months)
Average	4.744	5.564	3.188	5.887	7.462	7.887	5.143	2.406	3.777
(Interbank rate = 100)	(85.3)	(100.0)	(67.2)	(105.8)	(134.1)	(166.3)	(92.4)	(43.2)	(67.9)
Coefficient of variation	0.340	0.340	0.268	0.163	0.122	0.280	0.338	0.214	0.204

West Germany

	Official Discount Rate	Over-night Rate	60–90 Day Finance Ministry Notes	Yield on Public Corporation Bonds	Yield on Industrial Bonds	Over-draft Rate	Discount Rate on Commercial Bills	Savings Deposits (Regulated Rate)	Savings Deposits (over 12 Months)
Average	4.033	4.371	3.700	6.991	7.069	8.470	6.516	3.783	4.809
(Finance ministry notes = 100)	(109.0)	(118.1)	(100.0)	(188.9)	(191.9)	(228.9)	(176.1)	(102.2)	(130.0)
Coefficient of variation	0.328	0.470	0.370	0.127	0.125	0.147	0.194	0.155	0.169

Note: Coefficient of variation = $\dfrac{\text{Standard deviation}}{\text{Average}}$

inflexible. The coefficient of variation for Japan's official discount rate is less than half of those of other foreign countries, not because changes in this rate were fewer than those in other countries, but because the standard range of variation until 1969 was only 36.5 basis points compared with 50 or 100 basis points for European and North American countries. In addition, although it was calculated in terms of a daily rate, there ought to have been plenty of scope for it to move, but the fundamental reason for remaining within such a small range was that, given the artificially low interest-rate policy, there could be no official consensus in favor of large changes in the official discount rate.

Because changes in the official discount rate were of a small magnitude, the fluctuations in related discretionary lending rates and in all other standard rates of interest were, by international standards, very small. Consequently, the flexibility of Japanese lending rates was less than one-quarter of those prevailing in Europe and North America.[1]

Discretionary lending rates were set by mutual agreement of all banks with ceilings for various categories of loans in excess of ¥1 million with maturities of less than one year. Since the standard rates within these discretionary limits were generally adjusted to move exactly in step with the Bank of Japan's official discount rate, one has the strong impression that the contracted lending rate of all banks, principally the discretionary lending rates and all "standard rates" (i.e. the discount rate on commercial bills eligible for discount with the Bank of Japan, or the discount rate on bills of equivalent eligibility, and the commercial bank lending rates against those bills as collateral), fluctuated as if by regulation. Therefore in the past, prior to the official discount rate being raised, the contracted lending rate of all banks actually turned upward on two occasions only, specifically in August 1969 and March 1973, and there was no incident when the downturn in the contracted lending rate preceded declines in the official discount rate.

Apart from these institutional reasons for the low degree of flexibility in bank lending rates, another reason was that constraints were imposed by the rigidity of deposit interest rates and of the issuing conditions for government and corporate bonds which determined the cost of funds.

The coefficient of variation of Japanese government and corporate bond issuing conditions (yields) was negligible, and the coefficient of variation for the bond yield in the secondary market was also only half that of Europe and North America. This was because there was hardly ever any change in the issuing conditions for government and corporate bonds. Specifically,

1. A statistical analysis of the impact of changes in the official discount rate on fluctuations in the banks' lending rate and of the interrelationship between discretionary interest rates and the loan interest rate, call rate, and yields on government and corporate bonds is presented in chapter 7, section 2.2 below. (See also Y. Suzuki [43] and Bank of Japan Research Department [4].)

from 1960 to 1970 the issue terms for government-guaranteed bonds and local bonds were changed three times, corporate bonds four times, and financial debentures five times. Even when the rate *was* changed, it only moved 20 or 30 basis points.[2] As a result of the failure to change the government and corporate bond-issuing conditions, except on a few occasions, the secondary market yield on such government bonds from 1960 (with the exception of 1965–66 and 1971–72 when an easy-money policy was in force) far exceeded the yield available to initial subscribers. Needless to say, in Europe and North America bond-issuing conditions (coupon rate etc.) are revised in accordance with fluctuations in the market yield on such bonds (generally speaking, the yield to initial subscribers is set slightly above prevailing market yields), and, as shown in table 3.1, they tend to exhibit between 30 percent and 50 percent of the flexibility of the call rate, the tender rate for short-term government securities, and other short-term market rates.

Turning to the rates payable on deposits, the coefficient of variation is again negligibly small for Japan. Changes in deposit interest rates, like those for the issuing conditions of government and corporate bonds, were rare; in the ten years up to 1972 they were only changed twice: in April 1961 and April 1970. They were, in effect, pegged.[3] As a result, for example, the interest rates payable on one-year fixed deposits shown in chart 3.1 were, with the exception of the easy-money period from 1971 to 1972, consistently below the rates available in the call market and those on government and corporate bonds with repurchase agreements maturing within one year.

In the case of Europe and North America, the variability of the deposit interest rate lies halfway between those of short-term money rates and bond yields, there being an arbitrage relationship between the three. One reason for this, in addition to the relationship between deposit interest rates and the official discount rate, was that since 1967 in West Germany, from 1969 in France, and from 1971 in the United Kingdom, attempts were made at complete liberalization of deposit interest rates by breaking the almost mechanical relation between these rates and the official bank rate. Therefore the arbitrage relationship between long- and short-term market rates became even clearer. However, it should be noted that in the case of France it was only large-size long-term deposits which were liberalized. In the United States, on the other hand, due to Regulation Q, a relatively high interest-rate ceiling was placed on longer-term deposits in 1970–73, but since mid-1973 large denomination CDs have been exempt from the interest-rate ceiling,

2. After the easy-money period of 1971–72, the issuing conditions for government and corporate bonds began to be changed quite frequently.

3. The reduction of deposit interest rates in July 1972 and the subsequent raising of deposit interest rates in April, July, and October 1973, and January 1974 cannot be altogether dismissed as signs of return of some flexibility in the setting of interest rates.

**Chart 3.1 (1)   Differential between Medium- and Long-Term Bond Yields
in the New Issue and Secondary Markets (In Percent)**

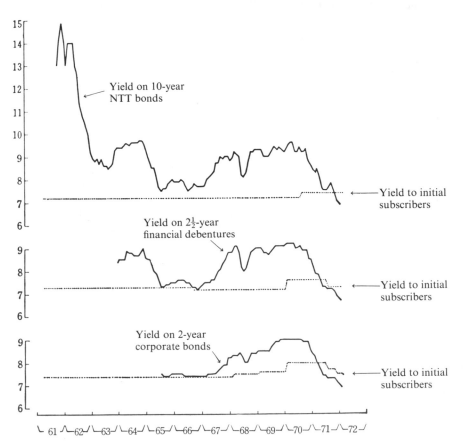

with the result that the yield on CDs and short-term market interest rates
have exhibited the same degree of flexibility.

1.2 *The Dual Structure of Interest Rates*

In general, if the fluctuations in interest rates faithfully reflect the supply
and demand for funds and there is rational arbitraging between related
financial markets, the variability of the shortest-term interest rates will be
the greatest, and next will be the rates on one- or two-year lending rates
or deposit interest rates, and the lowest degree of flexibility will be exhibited
by long-term lending rates in the yield available on bonds in the bond
market. However, because there is a very close relationship between the
official discount rate and short-term money-market rates, one would expect
to see a close relation between the variability of these two. In fact, as the

their customers, which justifies the term *dual structure*. In the dual structure, call rates and commercial bill rates (which are the interbank rates) are typically higher than the rates payable by bank customers on loans or received on deposits, but also the market yields on bonds in the secondary markets as determined by interbank sales and purchases are higher than the rates payable to initial subscribers who are customers of the banks (see chart 3.1). This may also be observed from the fact that interbank interest rates are higher than the rates payable to initial subscribers who are customers of the banks (see chart 3.1). A similar observation derives from the fact that interbank interest rates are higher than those received by bank customers on their deposits (in terms of fixed-term deposits the differential is between 0.75 percent per annum and 1.0 percent per annum).

Thus, in effect there are two sets of rates—that is, the call rate, bill discount rate, the rate on bonds with conditional repurchase agreements, and the yield available in the secondary bond market—all of which are interbank markets, on the one hand, and transactions with customers of a "regulated" variety (such as the official discount rate, interest rates payable on deposits, standard prime lending rates, long-term preferential interest rates, and the yield to subscribers on new issues of bonds), on the other. The former is a market structure which balances the supply and demand for funds by means of an equilibrating interest-rate mechanism; the latter structure is pegged artificially to a low average level. As a result, even for the same term, rates in the first group (such as the call rate or the bill discount rate) may be higher than the discount rate (second group); or again, the yield in the secondary market for one- or two-year bonds or the rate payable on bonds with a repurchase agreement (first group) may be much higher than fixed-term deposit rates payable for a corresponding term. Equally, the yields in the secondary bond market (first group) tend to be much higher than yields available to subscribers in the new issue market.

2. The Phenomenon of Excess Demand in Different Financial Markets

The fact that the call rate, which should be the lowest of the five rates of interest, has become the highest rate reflecting variations in the demand for funds in turn reflects the fact that all of the other four interest rates— those belonging to the second group of regulated interest rates—have been fixed at subequilibrium prices. Since the rates have been set at nonequilibrium levels, the price mechanism cannot do its job, so that in the market for funds there is naturally an excess demand situation.

2.1 *The Bank Loan Market*
In the bank loan market, if we exclude periods of easy money, there was a

persistent excess demand for funds with—to use a Japanese expression—
banks always taking the seat of honor (i.e. it was a seller's market). As a
result, the banks practised a kind of credit rationing, selecting the most
desirable clients on the basis of comparative profitability and growth rate
among those seeking loan funds. What the banks paid particular attention
to was the average level of compensatory deposits placed with the banks
against loans. From every company that borrowed funds, the banks required
a certain average-size deposit and monitored this so-called deposit-loan
ratio for each customer. In making new loans, banks would check the ratio,

Chart 3.2   Returns from City Bank Lending

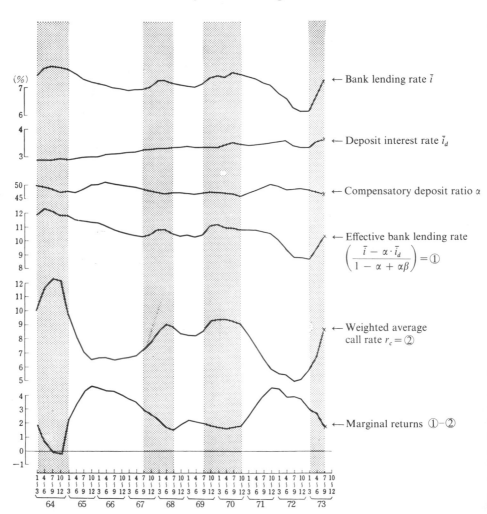

allocating more credit to those companies whose average level of compensatory deposits against loans was higher.[5] In other words, the effective rates of interest were highest for those with the largest compensatory deposits. Loans would also be granted because these customers imposed least strain upon the bank's own liquidity position (i.e. the banks' credit-creation multiplier was maximized), and also there was an ample safety margin for rolling over the loans. Of course, on the company's side also, attention was paid to the volume of deposits left with the bank and the ex post effective borrowing rate, so that, for instance, at its trough during the easy-money period in 1972 the rate was around 9 percent (see charts 3.2 and 3.3). Also it is interesting to note that at this time the rates on intercorporate credit, particularly rates applied to trade receivables in the form of long-term deferred credits extended by large companies were just about 9 percent. These particular rates seem to reflect ex post effective borrowing rates.

Although what has been said above emerges quite clearly from discussions with financial directors of large corporations or with credit department personnel in major banks, an attempt was also made at empirical verification of the effective borrowing rate by means of regression analysis on the current deposits owned by the corporate sector.[6]

5. Compensatory deposits against bank loans are taken as the average amount required to be deposited in an ex post sense. Because there is an excess demand for funds in the loan market, Japanese corporations do not like to repay their loans by reducing their deposits, but prefer to prepare for a period when their borrowing may be restricted in the future and hold the surplus funds on deposit. In extreme cases, there are companies that hold cash or deposits in excess of 100 percent of their loans.

6. The statistical results introduced in this section were published in the *Chōsa Geppo* (November 1971) of the Bank of Japan Research Department, under the title, "Concerning the Recent Relaxation in Corporate Finance." In note (1) of that paper, it was reported how a questionnaire was sent out to companies inviting them to describe the criteria upon which they based their current cash position. The results, recorded below, show that the majority judged their cash and deposit balances in relation to their outstanding borrowings. Also, among those companies replying that they judged their cash and deposit balances "strictly on the basis of the amount of cash and deposits in hand," or "cash and deposits in hand plus securities negotiable on demand," some probably used a ratio relative to their outstanding borrowings when judging the *relative* level of their cash and deposit balances.

Results of Questionnaire to 435 Leading Companies (October 1969)
  (Percentages are those of the number of companies responding)
  Most important indicators in judging cash position:
  1. Liquidity in hand/borrowings   28.7
  2. Strictly on the basis of the amount of cash deposits in hand   27.8
  3. Liquid assets/accounts payable   17.9
  4. Cash and deposits in hand and securities negotiable on demand   12.9
  5. Liquidity in hand/monthly sales   11.7
  6. Other measures   0.9

Note: Liquidity in hand denotes current bank balances and includes securities negotiable on demand.

Chart 3.3(1)   Returns from Local Bank Lending

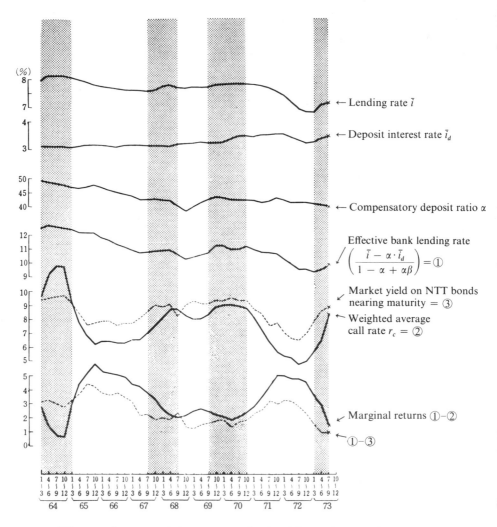

The results quoted here were obtained by estimates from regression analysis (using data from "Quarterly Corporate Enterprise Statistics," a survey of companies capitalized at over 2 million yen) covering different industrial groups, with levels of corporate deposits as the unexplained variable and with the following as explanatory variables: (1) quarterly expenditures or the value of accounts payable as a proxy for the transactions motive; (2) the adjusted sales forecast rate as a proxy for the precautionary motive (this statistic is compiled so that downward revisions indicate an increase in uncertainly about the future when the precautionary motive may

Chart 3.3(2) Returns from Credit Association Loans

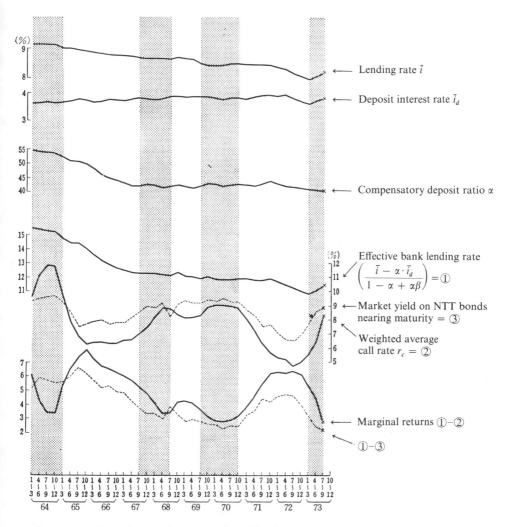

be expected to rise, and conversely); (3) the corporate profit rate is taken to show the asset holding motive; (4) the average contracted bank-lending rate for all banks is included as a proxy for unintended changes in cash currency and deposit holdings associated with the ease or difficulty of borrowing from the banks; and finally (5) the volume of borrowed funds.

Judging from the values given in parentheses, each of the explanatory variables is significant at the 5 percent level except for variable (3). This supports the hypothesis that the level of corporate deposits is affected by the (*a*) transactions, (*b*) precautionary, and (*c*) asset motives, as well as (*d*) unintended changes in levels of cash balances reflecting the difficulty or ease of obtaining funds from the bank, and independently by (*e*) the volume of outstanding borrowing from financial institutions.

The parameter values for total borrowings (0.225 and 0.266) show that apart from the three motives for holding money and the need to guard against the possibility of unforeseen fluctuations in borrowing capacity, Japanese businesses hold about 25 percent of their borrowings in the form of cash or deposits. Put the other way round, this implies that only 75 percent of their borrowings are actually used, and their effective borrowing rate is therefore the nominal borrowing rate divided by 0.75. As shown in table 3.1, the average lending rate over the last decade has been 7.2 percent and the a priori effective lending rate has been 9.6 percent ($= 7.2\% \div 0.75$).[7]

This 9 percent level is not in itself unnaturally high when one considers that the average overdraft rate in West Germany was 8.5 percent (shown in table 3.1). To judge from the experience of the last decade of investment-led rapid economic growth in Japan, the rate of return on real capital (the so-called natural rate of interest) was even higher than in West Germany, and consequently a 9 percent lending rate in Japan was not unreasonable compared with the average equilibrium lending rate in West Germany of 8.5 percent. (Since the latter is an overdraft rate, nominal and effective rates are identical.)

In this way, there was a tendency for banks to allocate credit more willingly to those companies which kept large deposits with the bank, and the fact that companies have reckoned to keep at least 25 percent of their borrowings on deposit independent of their motives for holding money meant that, in spite of the rigidity of published interest rates, the price mechanism was in fact brought into effect—at least to some extent—through variations in the effective lending rate. Even institutionalized compulsory compensatory deposits do not flout the most fundamental laws of economics. However, it would be going too far to regard these effective lending rates as established by perfect competition and fulfilling an adequate price-mechanism function. In addition to the inadequacy of information about the effective lending rate, the price mechanism for the effective lending rate is

7. In addition to the method of calculating effective rates of interest in this chapter, other methods are also conceivable. The interest rate paid on the unutilized portion of deposit balances could be deducted. According to this method, if the average rate of interest on deposits is 4 percent, the effective interest rate on loans is $[7.2 - (4.0 \times 0.25)] \div 0.75 = 8.3\%$.

However, if one regards the effective interest rates paid by companies as "ex post," then the ex post marginal deposit requirement is not 25 percent, but as much as 40 percent. Therefore, even if the deposit interest rate received is included, the effective lending rate is 9.3% ($= [7.2 - 4 \times 0.4)] \div 0.6$). In the author's experience, the effective lending rates calculated by bank credit departments and corporate finance departments tend to be this latter, ex post type. In charts 3.2 and 3.3, above, these ex post effective lending rates in 1972 are shown to be slightly under 9 percent for city banks, just over 9 percent for local banks, and 11 percent for credit associations.

extremely imperfect, because when companies are under extreme pressure the banks are often obliged to permit companies to withdraw the money they have deposited, thus lowering the effective lending rate.

2.2 *The Government and Corporate Bond Markets*

Next we examine the phenomenon of excess demand in the government and corporate bond markets. In tight-money periods, as we saw previously in chart 3.1, a big gap of around 200 basis points opened up between the yield in the secondary market and the yield available to initial subscribers in the government and corporate new-issue market, so that as the absorption of new issues became less and less attractive the new-issue market was effectively frozen. In less extreme circumstances, bond issues were parceled out, mainly among the city banks, by a kind of credit-rationing process.

Excess demand in the public and corporate new-issue markets, and the credit-rationing process which accompanies it, appears in an explicit form in the regular revisions of quality ratings for corporate bonds. These revisions are conducted by the *Kisai Chōsei Kyogikai* (Council for the Regulation of Bond Issues), which is comprised of the leading banks and underwriters, and the company making the flotation is classified in advance as either *A*, *A'*, *B*, *C*, or *D*. This classification is determined on the basis of criteria such as the capital and net assets of the issuing company, its dividend rate, the net asset to capital ratio, the equity ratio, and the rate of return on capital. The council also determines the amount to be issued by category for each fiscal year and for each month, as well as the number of issues per year and the issue terms. In addition, the issue schedule for companies which have received classifications is arranged within the framework of the overall plan for each category. The classification process and the revision of quality ratings is simply a mechanism designed to allocate credit in such a way as to deal with the excess supply of corporate bond issues generated by setting the yield to initial subscribers at a subequilibrium level.[8] Corporate bond issues ranked in this way are purchased mainly by the city and local banks (see table 3.2). The reason why city banks are able to absorb a certain amount of corporate bonds at subequilibrium yields is that a number of these companies are loan clients of the banks themselves. The banks can therefore regard these bond purchases as simply loans in a different guise and take them into account when computing the required compensatory deposits to give the effective interest rate. This is well illustrated by the fact that an overwhelming proportion of electrical utility bonds—which themselves accounted for nearly half of total corporate bond issues—is absorbed by the city banks.

---

8. The various rules regarding the setting of bond-issuing conditions were slightly altered during the easy-money period of 1971–72. The discussion here is restricted to the rules prevailing before 1970.

Table 3.2 Bond Purchases by Type of Financial Institution

(Unit = %, ¥ billion)

| | Overall Market Share (Percent) | | Percentage of New Issues Purchased | | | | | | | | | | | | |
| | | | Government Bonds | | Government-Guaranteed Bonds | | Local Government Bonds | | Corporate Bonds | | Of Which Electric Utility Bonds | | Financial Debentures | |
	31/12/65	31/12/71	FY1965	FY1971	65	71	65	71	65	71	65	71	65	71
City banks + long-term credit banks	42.3	41.2	57.0	58.7	50.8	48.6	68.4	63.0	46.4	34.8	68.6	50.5	59.2	37.1
Local banks	20.0	18.6	22.7	21.3	24.5	21.4	3.8	4.7	27.8	27.8	16.6	19.7	17.2	16.2
Trust banks	2.3	2.5	4.0	4.0	3.6	3.1	1.2	2.8	5.0	8.6	2.5	6.9	0.4	0.3
Insurance companies	5.9	7.1	4.0	4.0	5.4	5.4	6.1	3.6	0.9	3.9	0	2.4	3.1	6.2
Nōrinchūkin Bank and credit federations of agricultural cooperatives	10.3	10.9	4.3	4.0	5.2	8.1	13.1	14.0	9.9	7.0	3.9	1.8	2.1	4.3
Shoko Bank and credit associations	10.1	11.6	4.1	4.0	5.2	6.9	5.8	10.6	7.2	14.1	6.7	13.5	8.6	19.7
Mutual banks	9.1	8.1	4.0	4.0	5.2	6.5	1.8	1.3	2.8	3.8	1.7	5.2	9.4	16.2
Total	100.0	100.0	100.0 (96)	100.0 (838)	100.0 (288)	100.0 (303)	100.0 (50)	100.0 (84)	100.0 (323)	100.0 (452)	100.0 (110)	100.0 (119)	100.0 (442)	100.0 (1,153)

Notes: 1. Bond purchases by individuals and others are excluded.
2. The market share of each group of banks is defined as the percentage of total deposits plus bank debentures accounted for by that group.

Arrangements for the flotation of long-term government bond issues and agreements on the underwriting terms are concluded between the underwriting syndicates (viz. city banks, long-term credit banks, local banks, trust banks, mutual banks, credit associations, the Norinchukin Bank—a specialized bank for agriculture and forestry—life insurance companies, securities companies, and, from 1972, non-life insurance companies) and the Bank of Japan. These syndicate groups underwrite the full amount of the issue—being required to take up any residual—and sales outside the syndicate are handled only by securities companies, their share being fixed at 10 percent. However, even among the syndicate group, the proportion of total funding accounted for by the city banks is very substantial (see table 3.2), and there appears to be a considerable element of rationing amongst them. For government-guaranteed bonds almost exactly the same system applies, and a large share of the issue tends to be taken up by the city banks. Although these long-term government bonds and government-guaranteed bonds are issued at subequilibrium yields, the reason why the city banks are so willing to subscribe is that these securities can be sold to the Bank of Japan "by mutual consent," since they are eligible instruments for obtaining Bank of Japan credit. Hence they are obviously extremely useful despite their low yield.

Turning to the issue of short-term government bills (ministry of finance securities, foreign exchange bills, and food bills), superficially these are floated by a public subscription system. However, since their yield at issue falls far below the call rate—and they are hardly ever altered—even though they have comparable sixty-day maturities, the greater part of these short-term bills is taken up by the Bank of Japan itself, with industrial corporations only subscribing in exceptional circumstances because they cannot participate in the call market.

The financial institutions that issue bank debentures (long-term credit banks, the Central Bank for Commerce and Industry, the Nōrinchūkin Bank, and the Bank of Tokyo) all arrange the flotation procedures themselves and also organize direct subscriptions or sales of the bonds, but securities companies also participate in the retailing of issues. One of the reasons local banks and the financial institutions for medium and small industries subscribe for a sizable amount of these issues is that, by doing so, they are in effect able to take over, as agents, part of the loans which would otherwise have been financed by the issuing institutions. Also, the reason city banks subscribe is that many of the companies which receive long-term loans from the long-term credit bank are, of course, companies to which they themselves are lending. By purchasing some of these debentures the city banks provide a lead for other financial institutions to subscribe. The result is that additional funds become available via the long-term credit bank to meet the demand from city bank clients which the city banks themselves would be unable to supply independently. Conversely, with the decline in the demand for funds for plant and equipment investment by corporate businesses after the April–June quarter of 1966, the city banks greatly reduced their acquisitions of bank debentures (table 3.2). In this they were motivated by the reduced need to give a lead to debenture purchases by other financial institutions. In the tight-money period around 1970, when the city banks became unable to meet the fund demand from their own large corporate clients, they negotiated for their clients directly with financial institutions for medium and small business.

Local government bodies issue two kinds of local bonds: publicly placed bonds that are subscribed to by the general public after underwriting by financial institutions or by securities companies, and privately placed bonds underwritten by financial institutions in the locality. The largest holders of both types are those financial institutions which are depositaries for the revenues of local public-sector bodies. (Since table 3.2 only covers publicly subscribed local bonds, the share accounted for by city banks is high and that by local banks is low; but if the privately placed bonds were to be included, most would be accounted for by local banks.) If one takes into account the size of the deposits placed by local governments with these financial institutions, the effective yield paid on local bonds turns out to be extremely high. The purchase of local government bonds by these financial institutions is therefore exactly analogous to the city banks' practice of making preferential loans to those clients that keep large deposits with them.

To summarize, public- and corporate-sector bond issues are sold at subequilibrium yields and therefore tend to be allocated among those financial institutions which have an interest at stake. As a result, Japan's financial structure reflects numerous consequences of this system.

First, because the new-issue market is a place where credit is allocated primarily among financial institutions which have special interests at stake, it cannot grow in a regular and orderly fashion and, as a market, it has remained underdeveloped. (By implication this is one of the major causes of the predominance of indirect financing.)

Second, in the case of corporate bonds, because credits were allocated among a large number of companies with numerous classifications, the bond market consists of a huge variety of issues spaced at short intervals and in small lots, conditions unfavorable to the development of a secondary market. (In this connection, whereas in Japan no less than 18 percent of all companies issuing bonds in 1971 had more than three issues during the year, in the United States from 1957 to 1971 an average of only 1.6 percent of companies that issued bonds in any one year had more than one issue per year.) To repeat, it is an essential condition of competitive price formation in a market where both sellers and buyers have adequate information that the bond lots must be large.

Third, from the standpoint of the banks, even though the same considerations of credit rationing in a situation of excess demand apply to purchases of corporate bonds, they naturally prefer making loans (where they have a high degree of maneuverability) to buying corporate bonds. As a result there is a bias in the external financing of corporations away from bond financing in favor of bank borrowing, and clearly this has intensified the overborrowing situation.

Fourth, the proportion of public and corporate bonds taken up by the city banks has constituted a substantial share of total funds and further contributed to the continuation of the imbalance in bank liquidity. This bias was evidently reflected in the secondary market for government and corporate bonds in Japan in the late 1960s when the city banks were consistently sellers and the financial institutions for medium and small businesses were consistently buyers, creating essentially a one-way market.

Fifth, because short-term government securities were almost entirely underwritten by the Bank of Japan, no secondary market for treasury bills evolved; instead, for short-term financing an active market (known as *gensaki*) developed in the purchase and sale of medium- and long-term government and corporate bonds with repurchase or resale conditions attached. Because the buying and selling rates spelled out in the conditions attached to these instruments approximated the overmonth call rate, the overall yield in the government and corporate bond market tended to be distorted, both on the upside and on the downside, by movements in the call rate (see chart 3.1 above). In principle, of course, the prices for government and corporate bonds with resale or repurchase conditions ought to have been related to short-term rates, and therefore they should not have been used in determining over-the-counter prices or yields for medium- and long-term bonds. In fact, however, because there was a very active repurchase market in long- and short-term bonds, the time pattern of the market yield curve was distorted, and this undoubtedly hindered the healthy development of the medium- and long-term bond markets. In particular, the fact that medium- and long-term yields showed the same degree of fluctuation as short-term interest rates in periods of tight money further aggravated the restricted nature of the new-issue market. This unquestionably contributed to and was reflected in the lack of development in the market.

2.3 *The Deposit Market*

In examining the phenomenon of excess demand for funds in the loan market or in the bond-issuing market, we found that the banks were in a suppliers' market. By contrast, because of their excess demand in the deposit market, the banks appear in the role of fund-takers. That is to say, the level of interest rates payable on deposits in Japan was below the level required to balance the supply and demand for deposits, so that the banks were prepared to spend in excess of these rates in order to attract deposits. As a result, banks increased the number of their branches as much as possible, lavishly decorated their customer reception rooms, gave gifts such as matches or towels to their depositors, and also tried to collect deposits by sending out salesmen or representatives to visit people at their homes and companies. From the banks' point of view, excess demand in the deposit market occurred because the maximum permitted rate payable on deposits was much lower than the effective lending rate or the call rate, so that by attracting primary deposits and utilizing the funds to finance loans, call loans, or to repay call money borrowings, they could enlarge their spread and hence profit very considerably. Similarly, such actions as expanding their branch network, redesigning the interior of their customer reception halls, giving gifts, or hiring public relations staff to go out and solicit deposits in person were all highly profitable operations.

An estimate of the marginal return to a bank for soliciting an additional unit of primary deposits, which I have estimated in a separate publication,[9] showed that, given deposit interest rates around 4 percent on average and a variable cost per unit of deposit-raising activity of less than 1 percent, it was approximately 4 percent cheaper for the banks to raise funds through deposits than in the money markets.

Thus, as deposit interest rates were fixed at a low level around 4 percent compared with rates of 8 percent in the short-term money market (see table 3.1) or an effective lending rate of around 9 percent, fierce competition for deposits in order to obtain these spreads emerged in the form of a competitive expansion in the number of bank branches and intensified nonprice competition. Because they attracted the savings of households and self-employed businessmen to the banking system, these factors were a major cause of the persistence of indirect financing. By comparison, when the securities houses sold securities to households or self-employed businessmen, they only received a limited commission income and therefore, compared with financial institutions, their motivation for branch expansion and public relations work was weak.

Although deposit interest rates and the yields on government and corporate bond issues were both fixed at artificially low subequilibrium levels within the framework of regulated interest rates, both were in an approximately similar range—allowing for the different length of terms—(see table 3.1), and therefore, judged on the basis of interest rates alone, there was no special motivation for an individual to prefer deposits. Nevertheless, indirect financing has continued to play a dominant role in Japan because, apart from institutional factors prevalent since the Meiji Era and the small average size of savings, there was a fundamental difference between the

9. See Yoshio Suzuki [41], part 1, chapter 2, section 4, "The Marginal Benefits of Deposit-Raising Activities—Theory and Estimation."

profitability to financial institutions of attracting savings (in the form of deposits or bank debentures) and the profitability to be derived by securities houses—and hence the difference in the zeal with which these two kinds of institutions pursued their fund-raising activities.

Conversely, if deposit interest rates, loans rates, and public and corporate bond-issuing conditions were to be liberalized so that both call rates and other market interest rates would be in equilibrium, a unified structure could be established and the dual structure of interest rates abolished. Even if there were still a close relationship between deposit interest rates and the issuing conditions for government and corporate bonds, the level of deposit interest rates relative to both the effective lending rate and the rate of interest in the short-term money market would be much higher, and as a result the activities of financial institutions in opening new branches and in the promotional area would be more limited. Sooner or later this would cause some diminution in the role of indirect financing.

2.4 *Bank of Japan Credit*

Next we examine the phenomenon of excess demand in the market for Bank of Japan credit. Once again banks were in the position of seeking funds in a market where there was excess demand. In chapter 1, section 1.1, we saw how banks' reserve assets were negative due to their borrowings from the short-term money market and their heavy borrowing of central bank credit. Consequently, banks could arbitrage directly among loans from the central bank at the official discount rate and the other short-term money-market rates (the call rate, bills discount rate, commercial bill rate, and Treasury bill rate), at least to the extent that free market transactions were possible, and no wide gap opened up among these rates.

Table 3.1 showed how the official discount rates in the United Kingdom and West Germany were only slightly higher than the equivalent of the call rate in those countries, and how in the United States it was almost exactly the same level. In Japan and France, by contrast, the discount rate was lower than the call rate, and decisively so in the Japanese case. However, in the United Kingdom and West Germany banks that were unable to make up their negative reserves in the short-term money markets were forced to borrow from the central bank at penal rates. In these countries the official discount rate was set slightly higher than the short-term money-market rate, but central banks did not in principle refuse to lend funds to those banks which were prepared to pay the penalty rate. Thus, those central banks passively accommodated the demand for loans except in periods of deliberate credit squeeze. In these countries the phenomenon of an excess demand for funds did not exist in the same way, and the official discount rate enabled the supply and demand for central bank credit to meet at an equilibrium interest rate.

In contrast, the official discount rates in Japan and France were below the short-term money-market interest rates, and therefore banks that were seeking to make up their negative reserve assets would, whenever possible, try to borrow directly from the central bank at a cheaper rate rather than resort to the relatively more expensive short-term money markets. As a result, there was a strong demand for central bank borrowings and a willingness to pay the official discount rate. However, the Bank of Japan and the Bank of France did not accommodate this demand to the full extent: in other words, they rationed credit. Consequently, there was a persistent excess demand for central bank credit, and the banks were forced to make up their negative reserve asset positions by paying high rates of interest in the short-term money markets.

In the United States the principle is essentially the same as in the United Kingdom and West Germany, but during periods of monetary squeeze the Federal Reserve temporarily rations credit, so that sometimes the discount rate and the average short-term money-market rates are at the same level (see table 3.1). When the Federal Reserve rations credit, the federal funds rate exceeds the discount rate so that even an outsider can easily judge when credit rationing is occurring.

In the British and West German systems, banks generally try to repay their high-cost borrowings from the central banks as soon as possible. But if central bank loans are only extended at this penal rate, at some stage short-term money-market rates will approach the level of the official discount rate. Therefore, when the central bank does not deliberately want to squeeze, it must supply funds to the market either by open market purchases or by reducing reserve requirements, thus enabling the banks to repay their central bank borrowings. Also, when the central bank wants to impose a squeeze it raises its official discount rate again, further strengthening the motivation of banks to repay loans to the central bank. In each case, neither the commercial banks nor the central bank have any motivation to maintain large central bank lendings permanently on their books: in other words, the overloan situation does not arise.

In the Japanese and French patterns, however, there is no motivation for banks to reduce the level of their low-cost borrowings from the central bank or to repay them, since the alternative implies dependence upon higher-cost short-term money-market funds. Also, because there is almost no cost effect due to the subequilibrium official discount rate, these central banks seek to effect their policy through quantitative allocations of central bank credit. (On this point see part II, chapters 5 and 6 and part III, chapters 9 and 10 for details.) But equally, if there are no central bank loans and advances outstanding, it is clearly impracticable to operate this mechanism. In this way the Japanese and French patterns do not provide any incentive either on the banks' side or on the central bank's side to eliminate central bank loans. Where the official discount rate is set at a lower level than that required to balance the demand for central bank credit, such credits to the banking system will tend to persist in very large volume; in other words, "overloan" will emerge, and this is the fundamental explanation for it.

After 1971 the overloan situation in France was solved, and thereafter the official discount rate followed the British and West German patterns, being set at a level above short-term money-market interest rates. However, as one can see in the case of the United States, when a strict tight-money policy was enforced, the volume of central bank lending was reduced through credit rationing—as, for example, in West Germany or in France after 1971—and as a result short-term money-market rates temporarily exceeded the official discount rate. The only place where such a phenomenon did not occur was in Britain, notably after October 1972, when a "minimum lending rate" (MLR) was substituted for "bank rate." Since MLR was always set one-half of 1 percent above the leading short-term money-market rate (represented by the yield on treasury bills), the penal character of the Bank of England's lending rate was never superceded by episodes of credit rationing.

In this section some international comparisons have been made in order to explain the relationship between the excess demand for Bank of Japan credit and overloan. To conclude, the root cause of overloan is that the official discount rate is set at a level below the equilibrium price.[10]

3. *The Noninternationalization of Japanese Finance*

In the preceding sections we have seen how the driving force of an artificially low interest-rate policy, along with the investment-led rapid growth policy described in the previous chapter formed the fundamental background to the four distinctive characteristics of Japan's financial structure. I shall now show how the relationship between the artificially low interest-rate policy and the four distinctive characteristics of the financial structure was protected by the noninternationalization of Japan's financial system.

During the late 1960s, especially until the revaluation of the yen in 1971, the Japanese economy was essentially cut off from international economic influences through trade and exchange controls, and its money markets were no exception to this rule. In terms of corporate finance, fund-

---

10. The earliest authors to point out that the fundamental cause of overloan was to be found in the artificially low interest-rate policy and the setting of the official discount rate below equilibrium, and hence that "normalization of monetary policy" essentially consisted of liberalizing interest rates or increasing their flexibility so as to restore them to their proper functions, were Tachi and Komiya [54], Tachi [51] [52], Ryūtarō Komiya [23], and Motohiko Nishikawa [31]. An earlier reference that mentions it as one of the causes is Toshihiko Yoshino [61].

raising operations by Japanese corporations on foreign money markets by impact loans (loans raised abroad by Japanese corporations for unspecified use in Japan), foreign bond issues, and long-term trade financing, were all regulated by the Foreign Exchange Control Law. In other words, through the medium of foreign exchange control, credit rationing was being imposed on any financing arranged abroad. Equally, the purchase of new or outstanding equity shares on Japan's capital markets by nonresidents was also subject to ceilings determined under the Foreign Exchange Control Law.

These restrictions were justified on the grounds that they were designed either to prevent the undermining of a tight-money policy, or to prevent takeovers of Japanese corporations by foreign capital, and no doubt in themselves were appropriate methods of foreign exchange control at any particular moment. However, as a result of these overall controls, any reduction in overborrowing by corporations through an inflow of funds from abroad was prevented; and, to that extent, the regulations definitely operated in such a way as to preserve the special characteristics of Japan's financial structure.

In the government and corporate bond markets, on the other hand, nonresidents were not permitted to float yen-denominated bonds until the first issue by the World Bank in June 1971. In the past, the issuing terms in the government and corporate bond markets, as table 3.1 makes clear, were by no means cheap or easy by international standards; so that even though Japan was suffering repeated balance of payments deficits and the yen was a weak currency during the period, there was some demand for the flotation of yen-denominated bonds. However, in order to protect the balance of payments, no internationalization of the bond market was undertaken. This meant that the opportunity to issue bonds according to market conditions as in Europe or the United States—a custom which might have been introduced into the Japanese government and corporate bond markets through the flotation of yen-denominated bonds by nonresidents—was stifled. Thus, the failure to internationalize Japan's financial markets worked to the detriment of the development of the domestic government and corporate bond markets and also helped to preserve the predominance of indirect financing.

For the Japanese foreign exchange banks, their ability to borrow funds in the Eurodollar market was initially controlled through restrictions on the rate of interest payable for Eurodollars, and subsequently through regulation of the amount that could be borrowed. Also from 1965 onward, as the international credit-worthiness of Japanese banks began to grow and they began to accumulate deposits and other funds, the inflow of capital to Japan was restricted by means of yen conversion restrictions. The prevention of short-term capital inflows of this kind was necessary as a measure to stop the international movement of funds having a disruptive influence on the domestic economy; but at the same time, one cannot overlook the fact that these regulations hindered the disappearance of overloan through the supply of short-term funds from overseas.

Moreover, although the branches of foreign banks in Japan were permitted until February 1972 to supply funds to the domestic call market, they were forbidden to borrow funds from the call market or from the Bank of Japan. These kinds of restrictions on the forms of permissable banking activity were a legacy from the past policy of trying to protect the balance of payments, but again the ultimate effect was to operate so as to preserve the imbalance of bank liquidity that we have identified as one of the special characteristics of Japan's financial structure.

The noninternationalization of Japanese finance, specifically as evidenced in measures such as the protection of the balance of payments and the domestic economy from the impact of disruptive short-term international capital flows each of which had its own deliberate objectives, was entirely natural given the policy in force at that particular phase in Japanese economic history. However, the end result was that, apart from their immediately intended effects, the measures functioned to maintain the peculiar characteristics of Japan's financial structure. From 1971 to 1972 these characteristics associated with the lack of internationalization gradually began to change; but we shall leave the description of those facts and an evaluation of their influence on the financial structure to part V.

4 Role and Limitations of the Financial Structure

1. *Origins of the Four Distinctive Features of the Financial Structure*

Chapters 2 and 3 examined the cause-and-effect relationship between the three observed traits in the Japanese economy between 1955 and 1970—export-oriented, investment-led growth, the artificially low interest-rate policy, and the noninternationalization of the financial system—and the four distinctive features of the financial structure: overloan, overborrowing, the imbalance of liquidity in the banking system, and the predominance of indirect financing. This chapter offers a recapitulation of these topics.

1.1 *Overloan*
Overloan, a by-product of the method adopted for supplying high-powered money, was a consequence of the policy environment which promoted export-oriented, investment-led growth and which entailed the pursuit of artificially low interest rates. Given the rapid rate of economic growth, the growth in demand for high-powered money would necessarily have been very high, but in order to balance the demand for Bank of Japan credit due to requirements for high-powered money with the supply of an appropriate volume of Bank of Japan credit from the standpoint of maintaining external equilibrium and domestic price stability, it would have been necessary, during tight-money periods, to set the official discount rate or the rate used in Bank of Japan money market operations at over 10 percent. Given the policy environment in favor of low interest rates, there was no consensus that would have regarded such a level of the official discount rate or purchasing rate for Bank of Japan operations as justifiable.

In response to the greater potential demand for Bank of Japan credit at the lower official discount rate or Bank of Japan buying rate, the Bank of Japan was therefore compelled to conduct its monetary stabilization by rationing the appropriate amount of Bank of Japan credit and through administrative guidance of the day-to-day funding of its client banks. Since Bank of Japan loans were the best means of regulating the marginal element of credit rationing, such loans became a permanent feature of the system, resulting in the perpetuation of overloan. However, since a cumulative increase in loan volume was undesirable, from 1962 onward the Bank of Japan introduced limits on the amount of these loans for city banks with large outstanding loans, thus inaugurating the New Scheme for Monetary Control, which was intended to supply Bank of Japan credit corresponding to an appropriate growth of high-powered money and matching the growth rate of the economy (for details, see chaps. 10 and 11). After 1962 Bank of Japan credit was adjusted at the margin through loan policy, and excess loans were avoided by means of purchases of bills and securities.

From the technical standpoint, since there was an abundance of corporate liabilities and a shortage of government liabilities in the export-oriented, investment-led flow-of-funds structure, the supply of high-powered money rested heavily on the monetization of corporate debt, implying a bias toward rediscounts of commercial bills or loans against commercial bills or other corporate debt as collateral—namely, overloan. Also, since the repayment of Bank of Japan borrowings from foreign receipts was prevented by the blockage imposed on short-term inflows from abroad, the banks were unable to unwind their overloan positions.

The perpetuation of overloan meant that the city banks lost any incentive to cast off the stigma of permanent dependence upon the Bank of Japan in their modus operandi and tended, on the contrary, to seek to expand their loans with an even more deliberate dependence on the Bank of Japan, thus intensifying overloan. Also, since the low interest-rate policy meant that the official discount rate was below the call rate, there was no financial incentive for the banks to borrow call money and repay Bank of Japan loans.

1.2 *The Imbalance of Bank Liquidity*

The imbalance of bank liquidity had two basic sources: (1) the concentration, associated with export/investment-led growth and the low interest-rate policy, on city banks for financir~; and (2) overloan. First, since there were many firms in the export and investment sectors that were customers of the city banks, not only was there a tendency for fund demand to be concentrated here as a result of the growth process, but given the low interest-rate policy, corporate bonds—issued at regulated yields below market rates—were mostly allotted to city banks. Second, since overloan meant that the city banks were permanently in debt to the Bank of Japan, these banks did not have to observe the normal prudential requirements of restricting lending within the range permitted by their deposits and capital. Also, since they were supplied with cheap Bank of Japan loans rather than expensive call money, it was more profitable to be overloaned.

As documented in detail elsewhere,[1] many institutional and historical factors helped to explain the imbalance of bank liquidity; the main point to be emphasized here is that it was more profitable, given the concentration of fund demand on the city banks and the preferential loans available to the city banks from the Bank of Japan, for the city banks to be overlent, while it was more profitable for the local banks to be underlent.[2]

1.3 *Overborrowing*

The basic reasons for overborrowing were: (1) the high degree of dependence on external finance by the corporate sector due to the policies of investment-led growth and artifically low interest rates; and (2) the predominance of indirect financing. Investment-led growth, as we saw in chapter 2, meant that the corporate sector's financial deficit was consistently expanding. Also, since the low interest-rate policy dictated that published lending rates must be pegged, the effective rate on bank loans had to be raised by increasing the amount of compensatory deposits required: the rise in corporate deposits (financial assets) in turn meant that firms were made more dependent on external sources of finance. The fact that bank borrowings were a far more common form of external financing than the issue of debt or equity securities reflects the preference for indirect financing. The restrictions on foreign issues of Japanese companies and the restraints on nonresident acquisitions of Japanese equity stock inhibited the elimination of overborrowing through inflows of foreign capital.

1.4 *The Predominance of Indirect Financing*

The continuance of indirect financing as the dominant form of financing between the Meiji Era and the 1950s was largely due to the structure of the flow of funds, the artificially low interest rates, and the noninternationalization of finance that were associated with investment-led growth. Since the flow of funds under investment-led growth did not permit any large-scale issue of public-sector bonds for government projects, and since artificially low interest rates froze the yield available to subscribers of public and corporate bonds at subequilibrium levels, while noninternationalization restricted yen-denominated issues overseas, these were major factors behind the lack of development in the bond market. Also, because deposit interest rates were pegged below the effective bank lending rate or the call rate, banks competed fiercely (through nonprice competition) for highly profitable deposits, thus diverting household savings from the capital markets toward the banks and preserving the predominance of indirect financing.

---

1. Yoshio Suzuki [41], pt. 1, chap. 1.6.
2. On the relation between bank profits and the imbalance of bank liquidity, see part II, chapter 6, section 2.4 below.

2. *Historical Role of Four Distinctive Characteristics*

Between 1965 and the early 1970s the four distinctive characteristics of Japan's financial structure—overloan, overborrowing, the imbalance of funds, and the predominance of indirect financing—were essentially determined or supported by the three observed traits in the economy which characterize this period: investment-led growth, the promotion of artificially low interest rates, and the noninternationalization of the economy. Conversely, the four special characteristics of the financial structure contributed to the investment- and export-led growth pattern of this period; in fact, because they enabled this growth pattern to function, they are the hallmark of the financial structure during the period.

Consider, for example, the predominance of indirect financing. Because the immediate postwar inflation had disastrously diminished the value of financial assets, and because from 1955 to the early 1960s the income level in Japan was still very low, the accumulated savings of households in this period were minute in comparison to other developed countries. It was clearly better that these tiny individual units should be removed from the family treasure chest and placed collectively at the disposal of financial institutions for safe corporate investment purposes. Also, whereas indirect financing enables very small sums to be deposited, investment in securities for direct financing requires a substantial amount of money. In addition to such securities being of larger denomination than deposits (for example, the minimum denomination for fixed-coupon securities was ¥10,000, ranging up to ¥1,000,000), the capital value is at risk through fluctuations in the price of the securities, so that it is also necessary to hold a number of different securities in order to spread the risk. Again, this requires a substantial accumulation of funds. Consequently, one may say that indirect financing was an appropriate financial device for an era of small-scale funds.

Looked at from the viewpoint of the supply of credit too, indirect financing was well-suited to an investment-led economy. Enthusiastic entrepreneurs made aggressive investment plans and actually carried them through; but compared with an impersonal capital market it was more appropriate for money to be loaned through a bank which, knowing the individual, could distinguish between the real entrepreneurial spirit and blind recklessness. In the capital market it is easy for an already reputable firm to raise money, but normally "growth companies" cannot obtain funds so readily. In a financial system which is primarily an open capital market, neither reckless firms nor those with true entrepreneurial spirit can raise funds, so that under such a system a brake is applied to investment-led growth.

Also, to ensure that export-oriented companies obtained sufficient funds, indirect financing was advantageous. Without bank credit supplied at low interest rates and without preferential treatment for every export contract from the production stage through collection (pre-export advance bill system) to loading and export (system for loans against foreign exchange assets), the whole process would have been much more difficult.

In this light, the predominance of indirect financing and the existence of its counterpart—overborrowing—as the means of corporate financing provided the most appropriate financial structure for the investment-led growth of this period. Typically, combinations of groups of companies and a bank, or effective competition between such groups, were given financial backing through the predominance of indirect financing and overborrowing.[3]

Overloan and the imbalance of funds contributed to this type of bank behavior because the demand for funds by firms in the investment and export sectors tended to be concentrated on the city banks, which received funds from other financial institutions—thanks first to the peculiarities of the imbalance of funds, and second to advantageous Bank of Japan credit that was the basis for their overloan position. City banks were therefore permanently in a situation with excess loans extended to supply a steady stream of funds to firms in the export and investment sectors.[4]

The Bank of Japan, for its part, utilized the overloan and fund imbalance situations to influence bank behavior, and the banks utilized the overborrowing situation of firms powerfully to influence their behavior, thereby enhancing the effectiveness of monetary policy in relation to aggregate demand and prices.

3. Distortions Due to the Four Distinctive Characteristics

Thus, while the four distinctive characteristics assisted in the development of the investment-led pattern of economic growth in Japan between 1955 and 1970, it would be an overstatement to claim that everything worked out perfectly. For example, the close relationship between banks and business enterprises associated with indirect financing or its counterpart, overborrowing, played a significant part in stimulating investment in export-related and capital goods industries. At the same time, because an excessive amount of funds was channeled in this direction, in the early 1960s bottlenecks began to appear in consumption and retail distribution, contributing to the rise in consumer prices.

Moreover, from around 1970, when on the one hand the surge in Japanese exports began to cause concern abroad, on the other hand over-

3. Giichi Miyazaki [25] emphasizes this point.
4. For an early appraisal of the positive benefits of overloan and overborrowing from the point of view of growth, see Tsuneo Iida [11].

investment in steel, petrochemicals, and textiles at home was reflected in a conspicuous lack of investment in antipollution equipment, social welfare facilities, and leisure-related industries. The strong ties between the banks and business enterprises tended to result in an excess flow of funds to existing industries even at times when major structural changes were either actually in progress or were desirable, and conversely, created a shortage of funds in the newly developing industries so that bottlenecks occurred. From the standpoint of stablization policy, too, the motivation of businesses to carry out investment projects voluntarily and rationally in the light of their own financial position was undermined, while on the other hand city banks were deprived of the incentive to lend only within the limits set by their capital and deposits. Hence, competition to invest by firms was superimposed upon competition to lend by banks, adding to the amplitude of fluctuation on the upswing. The estimation results shown in table 7.1 of part II, chapter 7, confirm that there was a particularly strong tendency for city banks to be attracted by the corporate demand for funds when the call rate was raised during tight-money periods even though the marginal profit on loans was deteriorating. In such instances, the Bank of Japan was to some extent obligated, under the overloan system, to accommodate the city bank demands. From a macroeconomic perspective, the amount of credit rationing which the Bank of Japan can actually restrict in the short term is very limited, because such restrictions simply show up as an increase in defaults on commercial bills and a breakdown in credit discipline. Therefore, given a tight-money policy which operated through the overloan → overborrowing route, its ultimate effects were very powerful, but during a mild tight-money period or at the beginning of such a period, the tendency of banks to be encouraged to make loans by the growth in loan demand eventually resulted in the amplification of cyclical fluctuations.[5]

Along with this structural fault in the financial system, the fundamental background was aggravated by the policy of maintaining artificially low interest rates. For example, the consumption and distribution bottlenecks of the 1960s and 1970s mentioned earlier had their origins in a misallocation of funds, which in turn was a consequence of either the negation of free market interest rates or the deliberate rationing of credit. Similarly, the phenomenon of excess demand for funds in different markets suggests a failure of the interest-rate mechanism properly to allocate funds, because in rationing credit through nonmarket methods there is some margin for noneconomic, irrational judgments, and to that extent there is a possibility of further distortion in the allocation of financial resources. To express this in the most extreme terms, the reason why direct financing is preferable to

---

5. The Monetary System Research Council [21] emphasizes this problem. See also chapter 14, section 3.1 below.

indirect financing is that funds are then allocated through the interest-rate mechanism by competition, whereas the policy of artificially low interest rates in Japan prevented the development of competitive government and corporate bond markets, and thus the allocation of funds was to a greater or lesser extent affected by the four distinctive characteristics.

Moreover, there are grounds for doubting whether the basic objective of artificially low interest rates—reducing the cost of funds to firms in order to stimulate exports and investments—was in fact achieved. Because loan rates were effectively raised through methods described earlier, corporate deposits increased, intensifying the need for overborrowing. Since the dependence on borrowed funds was high despite the low nominal interest rates, the total interest burden of businesses was not reduced at all. This finding is confirmed by many international comparative analyses of Japanese corporate statistics.

Though the policy failed in its objective of lowering the cost of funds to firms, it had the side-effect of widening the spread available to financial institutions and protecting the inefficient ones. Since the interest rates paid on deposits and debentures (which were their sources of funds) were pegged at low rates, and the rates on loans (which were their use of funds) could be raised through higher effective rates, and in addition the call rate and the yield on bonds in the secondary market were flexible upward, the management of a financial institution that was a regular lender in the call market or the bond market was relatively easy. Unlike other industries, price competition was restricted among financial institutions, and in this sense the criticism that they were excessively protected is not entirely wide of the mark. The policy of artificially low interest rates thus fostered a misallocation of resources between the financial sector and the nonfinancial sector.[6] Also, as a result of the dual structure of interest rates produced by the policy, there was a maldistribution of income between the city banks that could borrow on preferential terms at the low-level official discount rate, and other financial institutions—and also between those large financial institutions and firms that were able to lend funds at the higher repurchase market rates or in the secondary bond market, and individual holders of smaller funds who only had access to low-interest deposits or the yields available in the new-issue market.

As we have seen, the four distinctive characteristics of Japan's financial structure were shaped or maintained by the investment-led, export-oriented growth of the economy and its concomitant low-interest policy and deliberate noninternationalization from 1955 through the late 1960s. Simultaneously,

---

6. On the distortions produced by artificially low interest rates, see also chapter 14, section 3 below.

these characteristics fostered this pattern of development but produced numerous distortions. From a historical perspective, because these flaws were not fatal, one may say that, from an overall point of view, Japan's financial structure fulfilled a useful historical role. However, as the economy has developed, and as it enters a new era, the distortions which could hitherto be overlooked, could now become a barrier to further development. In the domestic Japanese economy of the future, reallocation of new resources and redistribution of income will become major topics of debate with the attempt to raise welfare, improve social capital, prevent pollution, extend social security, and economize on resources and energy. Moreover, the internationalization of the Japanese economy is now made obligatory by the need to maintain equilibrium in the balance of payments, to intensify cooperation with other nations, to liberalize the import of commodities and capital, to lower tariffs, to expand overseas investment, and to extend aid to developing countries.

There can be no doubt that at such a historical turning point a new dimension is required for Japan's financial system. In order to carry out this new role, the existing distortions, in particular the faults in the functioning of interest rates, must inevitably be closely examined as a potential cause of trouble.

PART II
Japan's Monetary Mechanism

Part II takes the financial structure examined in part I and develops an analysis of how the Japanese monetary mechanism functions.

The model of bank behavior presented, and the theory of the effects of policy based on the model, are basically the same as those used to explain Japan's financial mechanism in my book, *The Effects of Monetary Policy— The Theory and Measurement of Bank Behavior* (see [41]). However, I believe that certain points in that work concerning the analysis of credit rationing and the function of interest rates were ambiguous. Here a more clear treatment is given. My debt for these revisions is due to the many people from whom I received comments following the publication of the book, in particular Ryūichirō Tachi, Shinji Moriguchi, and Mazakazu Royama.[1] Also, the model of bank behavior estimated and presented in the previous publication has since been examined by the Bank of Japan's Statistics Department, and its sophistication improved. It was included in the "Bank of Japan Econometric Model," published in the fall of 1972.[2]

1. The author found many useful suggestions in Tachi [53], Tachi and Hamada [56], Moriguchi [26], and Rōyama [35], [36], and [37].
2. For details of the Bank of Japan Statistics Department financial model, see [6].

5   A General Equilibrium Model

1. *The Inapplicability of a Simple Keynesian Model*

In making a positive analysis of the financial mechanism according to the methods of modern economics, one of the first tools that springs to mind is Keynes's $IS = LM$ model. However, the distinctive characteristics of Japan's financial structure that we analyzed in part I are decisively different from the assumptions of the Keynesian $IS = LM$ model. Consequently, in any analysis of Japan's financial mechanism by a Keynesian model the criticism of excessive simplification will be almost inescapable.[1]

Keynes's $IS = LM$ model assumes the following simplified hypotheses:

(1) The financial accounts of a one-country economy can be summarized as being comprised of *money* and *fixed-interest securities*.

(2) The economic units or agents comprising the one-country economy and their actions may be simplified in the following way:

(*a*) The net *asset-owners* (households) engage in asset portfolio selection (i.e. express their liquidity preference) between money and fixed-interest securities.

(*b*) There are *investors* (business enterprises) which issue fixed-interest securities in order to invest in real goods.

(*c*) There is a *central bank* which supplies money through open market operations in fixed-interest securities.

(3) The *yield* on fixed-interest securities fluctuates in the market to give a simultaneous equilibrium between the three economic agents and the supply and demand for financial assets in the two markets.

---

1. On the inapplicability of basing an analysis of the effects of Japan's monetary policy, or, more broadly, an analysis of Japan's financial mechanism on the Keynesian $IS = LM$ model, see Yoshio Suzuki [40], chapter 5, "The Equilibrium of Demand and Supply for Money in Japan," published in 1964. The same caution had already been expressed at that time in S. Tsuru's "The Meaning of Modern Economics" (Keizai Seminar no. 82, May 1963). More recently the problem has been explicitly stated by Masakazu Rōyama [37].

Table 5.1   Money-Flow Accounts for a Keynesian Model

	Central Bank	Firms	Households	Total
High-powered money	$-M$		$+M_h$	0
Fixed interest securities	$+B$	$-B_b$	$+B_h$	0
Real goods		PK_b		PK_b
Total	0	0	$M_h + B_h = W_h$	$PK_b = W_h$

Note: Sign conditions applying to financial assets:
          + implies asset of the economic agent
          − implies liability
Symbols: M = High-powered money (nominal)
           W = Wealth (nominal)
           P = At current prices
           K = Physical capital or real goods
           B = Fixed-interest securities (nominal)

These three hypotheses can be expressed in the form of money-flow accounts, shown in table 5.1. In this table the central bank holds fixed-interest securities B on its asset side, and money M on its liabilities side. Households hold money, M_h, and fixed-interest securities B_h as assets, which together give their savings W_h, while business enterprises hold real goods PK_b, as assets, and fixed-interest securities B_b, as liabilities. In this model the central bank determines, through a policy decision, the amount of high-powered money $\bar{M}$ (equal to the amount of fixed-interest securities B which it purchases through open-market buying operations). Households determine the amount they will save on the basis of the yield on fixed-interest securities r, the price P (the price level) of real goods, and their real income y. They also decide how much of their savings will be held in the form of money or in the form of fixed-interest securities. Business enterprises decide the amount of the increase (investment) in stocks of real goods I, and the amount of fixed-interest securities B_b they will issue according to the yield on fixed-interest securities, prices, and real income.

In this way the equilibrium between the three economic agents and the equilibria of supply and demand in the three markets for money, fixed-interest securities, and real goods are simultaneously determined by the variations in the yield on fixed-interest securities r, and in the level of real income y for any given price level.

By Walras's law, one of the three market equilibrium equations giving the simultaneous attainment of equilibrium among the agents and the markets is not independent, so if we here suppress the equation in the market for fixed-interest securities, we are left with the equilibrium equations for money and real goods, or Keynes's $IS = LM$ model. In other words, the equilibrium equations for money and real goods are:

$$\text{(A)} \quad \frac{\bar{M}}{P} = L(r, y) \qquad\qquad \text{Equilibrium for money}$$

$$\text{(B)} \quad I(r, y) = S(r, y) \qquad\qquad \text{Equilibrium for real goods}$$

where $\bar{M}$ is the supply of central bank money (nominal); P is the price level; L is the demand for money by households, or their liquidity preference (real); I is the amount of investment (real), or, using the symbols of table 5.1. ΔK: S is the amount of savings (real), or, in the symbols of table 5.1. $\Delta \left(\frac{W}{P} \right)$; r is the yield on fixed-interest securities; and y is real income.

However, in order for the simple Keynesian $IS = LM$ model to correspond to the actual financial mechanism of the real world, the three assumptions given above must be reasonably appropriate simplifications of the actual economy. But in present-day Japan there are several conspicuous differences between the actual financial system and the Keynesian model.

First, the predominance of indirect financing and overborrowing in the Japanese financial structure must be taken into account. To treat the financial accounts of Japan as if they were composed of only money and fixed-interest securities would indeed be an extreme simplification of reality. Among the financial assets of the personal sector (shown in table 1.7 of chapter 1), negotiable securities held either directly or indirectly through financial intermediaries only account for 9.9 percent of the total in Japan (compared with 56.2 percent in the Unites States and 19.3 percent in West Germany). In Japan the major form of households' financial assets are

2. When prices are given in the $IS = LM$ model, equilibrium is attained through variations in the interest rate r, and real income y. However, in the whole Keynesian structure, P is an endogenous variable. By adding the three following equations to the two equations (A) and (B) developed in the text, an entire Keynesian model can be developed with P endogenized.

$$\text{(C)} \quad y = y(N) \qquad \text{Production function}$$

$$\text{(D)} \quad N = f\left(\frac{w}{P} \right) \qquad \text{Demand for labor}$$

$$\text{(E)} \quad w = \bar{w} \qquad \text{Nominal wages}$$

where

N is the volume of employment
w is the nominal wage level
$\bar{w}$ is the nominal wage level as determined by wage-bargaining.

If in the three equations (C), (D), and (E) and the two in the main text (A) and (B), the quantity of high-powered money $\bar{M}$ and the nominal level of wages $\bar{w}$ are all given, then the unknowns are r, y, P, N, and w. Since there are five equations, the system is uniquely determined. The reader is referred to L. R. Klein [22] for a mathematical description of Keynesian models.

deposits that are claims on the banking system. Conversely, as shown in table 1.5, the external financing of business enterprises through the issue of securities only accounts for 11.0 percent, while the remaining 89.0 percent of external funds is borrowed from financial institutions, primarily banks. Consequently, one must regard enterprises as economic units that accumulate real goods not through the issue of fixed-interest securities but through borrowing from the banks.

Second, it is not appropriate to say that the Bank of Japan supplies money through open-market operations in fixed-interest-rate securities. From 1962 onward the amount of money supplied by buying securities gradually increased but, from the point of view of the overall monetary system, the main method of control was through the extension of quasi-permanent loans to the banking system—namely, overloan. Moreover, the banking system was divided into one group of banks whose reserve assets were permanently negative (city banks) and another group whose reserve assets were permanently positive (local banks, mutual banks, and credit associations, hereafter summarized as "other banks"). The established pattern among these two groups has been that city banks have been net borrowers and other banks have been net lenders in the call market (which is taken to include the bill discount market after 1971), that is, the phenomenon of the imbalance of bank liquidity.[3]

2. *A Theoretical Financial Model of Japan—A Revision of Keynes's Model*

Given these features of Japan's financial structure, a theoretical model designed to analyze the financial mechanism must at least include the following economic units and financial assets.

First, in addition to the economic units or agents specified in the Keynesian model—that is, the central bank, business enterprises, and households—banks must also be included, but they in turn must be divided into city banks and other banks as two separate economic agents. Turning to financial assets, fixed-interest securities are eliminated, and in their place

3. In 1971 the bills discount market was started. Here the city banks were predominantly sellers, other banks predominantly buyers. But from June 1972, over-month transactions in the call market were abolished and the only remaining transactions were for overnight and unconditional money. Lending and borrowing transactions for periods of one to three months began to be switched to the bills discount market. Apart from the time period for the loans and borrowings, the bill discount market is essentially the same as the call market. From the standpoint of the theoretical treatment in this book, where no specific reference is given, the words *call market* refer to the short-term interbank money market (broadly defined), which includes the bill discount market after 1971. For details of the evolution of the bill discount market, see chapter 11, section 1.3.

Table 5.2 Simplified Money-Flow Accounts for the Japanese Economy

	Bank of Japan	City Banks	Other Banks	Firms	Households	Total
High-powered money	$-M$	$+M_1$	$+M_2$		$+M_h$	0
Bank of Japan loans	$+C$	$-C_1$				0
Call loans		$-C_{l1}$	$+C_{l2}$			0
Bank loans		$+L_1$	$+L_2$	$-L_b$		0
Deposits		$-D_1$	$-D_2$	$+D_b$	$+D_h$	0
Physical capital				PK_b		PK_b
Total	0	0	0	0	$M_h + D_h = W_h$	$PK_b = W_h$

Note: See notes to Table 5.1
C = Bank of Japan loans
C_l = Call loans
L = Bank loans
D = Deposits

deposits, commercial bank loans to business enterprises, and Bank of Japan loans must be added. Finally, call loans within the banking system must be included.

These revisions to economic units and financial assets enable us to build the money flow table shown in table 5.2, which includes the four distinctive characteristics of Japan's financial system. In this table the Bank of Japan has, on its assets side, Bank of Japan loans, and on its liabilities side, money (i.e. cash currency; more strictly, central bank money including deposits of financial institutions with the Bank of Japan, that is, high-powered money). This encapsulates the overloan situation. City banks and other banks have loans (on their assets side), and deposits (as liabilities) in common, but in addition the city banks have borrowings from the Bank of Japan and call loans as liabilities, whereas the other banks have call loans on their assets side. This, of course, reflects the phenomenon of the imbalance of bank liquidity. Households save by acquiring the liabilities of financial institutions, holding cash currency and bank deposits as assets, which expresses the predominance of indirect financing. Finally, business enterprises hold deposits and real goods, which they obtain by borrowing from banks on their liabilities side, thus expressing the condition of over-borrowing.

These modifications to the economic units and financial assets overcome the problem of excessive simplification in the Keynesian $IS = LM$ model, but they require some reexamination of the underlying assumptions of the general equilibrium model. For, in order to postulate this expanded model of Japan's financial mechanism, we must examine which variables the various economic units take as given in achieving their subjective equilibrium and how overall market equilibrium will be attained in the markets for financial assets and real goods.[4]

In this respect, the most difficult aspect of the theoretical treatment is that Japanese interest rates—with the exception of the call rate—are unusually rigid, and as a result there is credit rationing in several of the markets. In other words, in a theoretical model we are faced with the major obstacle that, in the Keynesian $IS = LM$ model, equilibrium among economic units and economic goods is hypothesized to be simultaneously obtained through the fluctuations of a variable rate of interest. In Japan's financial structure, because interest rates are rigidly fixed at subequilibrium levels, excess demand exists in the three markets for Bank of Japan loans, commercial bank loans, and commercial bank deposits. (In the government and corporate bond market there is also excess demand, but, given the predominance of indirect financing and the existence of overborrowing, issuing bonds is essentially the same as borrowing from a bank, and the sale or purchase of a bond is essentially the same as any call market transaction, and we can therefore omit the government and corporate bond market.) In these markets we shall therefore approach the problem of the three economic units receiving credit allocations by indicating the degree of credit rationing as a, b, and c. (As a, b, and c become larger the degree of credit rationing intensifies, diminishing the availability of this kind of credit.)

First, in the market for Bank of Japan loans, the amount of Bank of Japan credit (i.e. discounts and advances) C, and the official discount rate r are both given, so that excess demand exists and credit rationing is in force. In this instance the level of the official discount rate $\bar{r}$ together with a, the degree of Bank of Japan credit rationing, affect the portfolio selection of city banks. Therefore, the demand function of city banks for Bank of Japan credit depends on the variable $[a : \bar{r}]$, which consists of the official discount rate $\bar{r}$ and the degree of Bank of Japan credit rationing as felt by the city banks.[5] The variable $[a : \bar{r}]$ represents the availability and cost of Bank of Japan credit as indicated by the daily fund-position guidance imposed by the Bank of Japan on the city banks. (The degree to which they feel this availability basically depends upon the gap between the actual discount rate and the equilibrium rate.) Fluctuations in this variable affect both the

---

4. Attempts to return to the fundamentals of general equilibrium analysis and to construct a general equilibrium theory with several assets were made by J. Tobin [58], Tobin and Brainard [60], and Brainard [7]. These constitute the Yale Approach, and the theory given here owes much to these authors. However, because the Keynesian $IS = LM$ model has been revised in the theoretical model adopted here, the treatment of equilibrium on the real side is different from the Yale Approach.

5. This kind of treatment of Bank of Japan credit allocations in a theoretical model is suggested in Rōyama [35] and specifically spelled out in Rōyama [36] and [37]. Also, Bunji Kure [24] expressed the concept of availability, a, in terms of the degree of bank loan restrictiveness.

willingness of city banks to resort to call money borrowings and their attitude in lending to business enterprises.

Second, in the bank lending market, bank lending rates $\bar{i}$ fluctuate to some extent, and the *effective* rate of interest (which takes into account compensatory deposits) fluctuates to an even greater degree. However, it would be factually inaccurate to pretend that equilibrium in the loan market is attained through the effective bank lending rate.[6] Banks make their optimum portfolio selection of assets on the basis of the cost and difficulty of obtaining Bank of Japan credit allocations shown by the variable $[a : \bar{r}]$, the call rate r_c, the rather rigid bank lending rate $\bar{i}$ (which is institutionally related to the official discount rate), and the difficulty and cost of attracting deposits, which is shown by the variable $[c : \bar{i}_d]$, to be described below. The total volume of bank loans decided through this subjective equilibrium process is then rationed among business enterprises. In this way, business enterprises that receive credit allocations are simultaneously affected in their asset portfolio selection by the bank lending rate $\bar{i}$ and by the difficulty of obtaining bank loans (i.e. by the availability of bank credit as viewed by the companies) shown by b;[7] hence the demand function of business firms for bank loans is expressed in the variable $[b : \bar{i}]$.

Finally, in the bank deposit market, because the interest rate payable on bank deposits $\bar{i}_d$ is almost entirely institutionally pegged, the banks take as given the amount of deposits determined by the portfolio selection process (= subjective equilibria) of businesses and households. In this case, the banks are influenced in their portfolio selection behavior by the interest rate on deposits $\bar{i}_d$, and the difficulty of deposit-raising activities indicated by the symbol c. (Banks normally express this in terms of an improvement

6. Ryūtarō Komiya [23] brings demand and supply into equilibrium through the effective interest rate on loans. However, to the author's knowledge, although it is widely known that the credit departments of city banks and the loan chiefs always check on the effective interest rate, it is flying in the face of facts to think that the bank lending market is brought into equilibrium by means of fluctuations in the real interest rate. In the decision to grant a bank loan, many factors relating to the borrower's credit-worthiness, such as degree of familiarity with the client, are considered, and not all requests for loans are necessarily granted. It is therefore not possible to say that loans are granted up to an equilibrium point determined by the relation between the effective level of interest rates and the lending cost (including the risk of default).

In chapter 7, section 2.2, actual fluctuations in the lending rate are analyzed by regression analysis. Although the supply and demand for funds is found to have a significant impact on the fluctuation in lending rates, the general tone of interest-rate levels is decided by changes in institutionally regulated interest rates such as the voluntarily regulated rates and prime long-term lending rates that move directly in sympathy with the official discount rate. In chapter 3, charts 3.2 and 3.3 show the ex post relationship between these rates and the effective interest rates.

7. To the author's knowledge, Motohiko Nishikawa's [30] was the earliest study to point out the importance of bank credit availability in Japan's financial mechanism.

or deterioration of the "deposit environment.") Together these two factors give us the variable $[c : \bar{i}_d]$ as a component of the banks' demand for deposits function.[8]

Given the attainment of equilibrium in the three markets where credit rationing occurs consistent with the variables $[a : \bar{r}]$, $[b : \bar{i}]$, and $[c : \bar{i}_d]$ in the respective demand functions, simultaneous equilibrium will be achieved in the six markets as a result of the asset selection process of the five economic units among the six types of assets (see table 5.2).

Using the symbols of table 5.2 and omitting the supply and demand for money equation following Walras's law, the theoretical model developed above may be presented in general equilibrium form as follows:

$$\bar{C} = C_1([a : \bar{r}], r_c, \bar{i}, [c : \bar{i}_d]) \qquad \text{Equilibrium for Bank of Japan loans}$$
$$C_{12}(r_c, \bar{i}, [c : \bar{i}_d]) = C_{11}([a : \bar{r}], r_c, \bar{i}, [c : \bar{i}_d])$$

$$\text{Equilibrium in the call market}$$
$$L_1([a : \bar{r}], r_c, \bar{i}, [c : \bar{i}_d]) + L_2(r_c, \bar{i}, [c : \bar{i}_d]) = L_b([b : \bar{i}], \bar{i}_d, P, y)$$
$$\text{Equilibrium in the commercial bank loan market}$$
$$D_b([b : \bar{i}], \bar{i}_d, P, y) + D_h(\bar{i}_d, P, y) = D_1([a : \bar{r}], r_c, \bar{i}, [c : \bar{i}_d])$$
$$+ D_2(r_c, \bar{i}, [c : \bar{i}_d])$$
$$\text{Equilibrium in the deposit market}$$
$$I([b : \bar{i}], \bar{i}_d, P, y) = S(\bar{i}_d, P, y) \qquad \text{Equilibrium in the real goods market}$$

where y is real income; P is the price level; I is the amount of investment (real), or ΔK_b in the symbols of table 5.2; S is the amount of savings (real), or $\Delta \left(\dfrac{W_h}{P} \right)$ in the symbols of table 5.2.

In this general equilibrium system, if the volume of Bank of Japan credit $\bar{C}$, the official discount rate $\bar{r}$, the institutionally rigid bank lending rate $\bar{i}$, the interest rate on deposits $\bar{i}_d$, and the price level P are given,[9] the solution for the five equations is uniquely obtained by the five endogenous

8. In this book, the words *demand* and *supply* are widely used in connection with funds to the effect that banks are "demanders" of deposits. In this sense, note that the use is different from normal usage, where banks are usually regarded as suppliers of deposits.

9. The price level in this model could, of course, be endogenized, just as the employment level could be, by adding the three equations of the Keynesian model as in note 2 above. The theoretical model here uses the minimum revisions necessary to adapt the $IS = LM$ model to the analysis of Japan's financial mechanism. Consequently, in theoretical terms it is simple to develop a more complex model for application to the Japanese economy. For example, K_{b-1} could be added to the investment function so as to explain the stock adjustment process, and private wealth W_{h-1} could be added to the saving function so as to pursue the wealth effects. The public sector, too, could be expanded, and fixed-interest securities could be added as a financial asset. However, such revisions are not absolutely essential for consideration of Japan's financial mechanism from 1955 to the late 1960s, particularly for considering the effects of monetary policy.

variables: the call rate r_c ; the cost and availability of Bank of Japan credit as experienced by the city banks $[a : \bar{r}]$; the cost and availability of bank credit as experienced by business enterprises $[b : \bar{i}]$; the cost and availability of deposits as felt by the banks $[c : \bar{i}_d]$; and real income y.

This structure adapts the fixed-interest securities market in Keynes's $IS = LM$ model to the special characteristics of Japan's financial structure, dividing it into four markets: the call market, Bank of Japan loan market, the commercial bank loan market, and the deposit market. Similarly, the rate of interest in the Keynesian model is split into four market rates: the call market, the cost and availability of Bank of Japan loans, the cost and availability of commercial bank loans, and the cost and availability of deposits. If the three equations (C), (D), and (E) given in note 2 to this chapter are added to the five equilibrium equations, a theoretical explanation can be given for the mechanism by which adjustments in the volume of Bank of Japan credit C, changes in the official discount rate $\bar{r}$, together with the institutionally rigid bank lending rate $\bar{i}$, and the deposit interest rate $\bar{i}_d$, affect the ultimate policy objectives of the real economy—namely, the real income level y, the price level P, and the employment level N.

6 The Theory of Bank Behavior

Chapter 5 explained how, with minimum revisions, the Keynesian $IS = LM$ model could be adapted from the first principles of general equilibrium analysis to analyze the monetary mechanism of Japan so as to incorporate the distinctive features of the Japanese financial structure examined in part I. The market equilibrium between financial assets and real goods in the theoretical model incorporated the subjective equilibrium of the different economic units. This chapter presents a theoretical examination of the central element of the financial mechanism of the model, namely, the behavior of the banks and their subjective equilibrium.[1]

1. *Profit Maximization and the Constraints on Bank Behavior*

The simplified balance sheet of city banks and other banks as presented in table 5.2 of the previous chapter can be rewritten in the following form.

$$[\text{City Banks}] \quad M_1 + L_1 \equiv C_1 + (-C_{l1}) + D_1 \tag{1}$$
$$[\text{Other Banks}] \quad M_2 + C_{l2} + L_2 \equiv D_2 \tag{2}$$

Call money is defined as the negative of call loans and has a minus sign.

Deposits are composed of derived deposits from bank loans L and primary deposits unrelated to L. (Japanese banks generally distinguish between these deposits, designating them as "debtors' deposits" and "genuine net deposits.") In terms of the theoretical model, an additional simplification of the hypothesis is permissible to the effect that all derived deposits are corporate deposits, and all primary deposits are those allocated

---

1. For the theory of bank behavior presented here, the author is indebted to J. Tobin [59].

to the banks as a result of the asset portfolio selection of households. Primary deposits of households deposited with city banks and other banks will be designated D_1^* and D_2^* respectively. (For the portfolio selection behavior of households which determines D^*, see chapter 2.) If the ratios of derived deposits to loans at city and other banks determined as a result of the corporate portfolio selection process are designated α_1 and α_2 respectively, the following relations must hold:

$$[\text{City Banks}] \quad D_1 \equiv D_1^* + \alpha_1 L_1 \tag{3}$$
$$[\text{Other Banks}] \quad D_2 \equiv D_2^* + \alpha_2 L_2 \tag{4}$$

(For a description of the portfolio selection behavior of corporations which determines α, see table 6.1 and chapter 8, section 1.)

If high-powered money M in equations (1) and (2) maintains a stable ratio β to deposits D, the relation between high-powered money and deposits can be expressed as follows:

$$[\text{City Banks}] \quad M_1 \equiv \beta_1 D_1 \tag{5}$$
$$[\text{Other Banks}] \quad M_2 \equiv \beta_2 D_2 \tag{6}$$

(β depends on the level of reserve requirement ratios, on the amount of vault-cash banks require in order to meet customers' deposit withdrawals, and on the interest rate in the call market. Since the amount of cash currency or high-powered money held by Japanese banks appears to be rather inelastic to the level of interest rates, the assumption that β is relatively stable seems quite realistic.[2]

Substituting equations (3) and (5) into (1), and (4) and (6) into (2), and rearranging, we obtain:

$$[\text{City Banks}] \quad (1 - \alpha_1 + \alpha_1 \beta_1)L_1 - (-C_{l1}) \equiv (1 - \beta_1)D_1^* + C_1 \tag{7}$$
$$[\text{Other Banks}] \quad (1 - \alpha_2 + \alpha_2 \beta_2)L_2 + C_{l2} \equiv (1 - \beta_2)D_2^* \tag{8}$$

The expressions on the left-hand sides of equations (7) and (8) show the constraints on the banks' asset portfolio section behavior as a choice between bank loans and call loans (call money borrowings for city banks and call loans for other banks). When D^* and α are given as a result of the portfolio selection process of households and firms, and borrowings from the central bank C are determined by the Bank of Japan, the overall range of choice available to banks between loans L and call loans C_l is seen to be highly constrained.

2. On the inelasticity of cash currency held by Japanese banks relative to interest rates, see Suzuki [41], chapter 3.

Table 6.1 Estimation Results for Corporate Cash and Deposits Function

Dependent variable	Explanatory Variables						Constant Term	Multiple Correlation Coefficient	Durbin-Watson Statistic
	Total Expenditures by Business Enterprises	Trade Credit or Accounts Payable	Corporate Profit Rate	Bank Loans	Interest Rate	Rate of Forecast Revision			
Cash currency and deposits	0.017 (2.035)		$(-)$1,559.099 $([-]$1.773)	0.255 (4.090)	$(-)$10,662.811 $([-]$8.476)	$(-)$403.285 $([-]$2.730)	122,244.402	0.9996	0.7794
Cash currency and deposits		0.100 (1.959)	$(-)$ 579.075 $([-]$1.214)	0.266 (7.296)	$(-)$10,311.564 $([-]$8.934)	$(-)$350.266 $([-]$2.524)	110,693.607	0.9995	0.6416

Notes: 1. Total expenditures and accounts payable by business enterprises correspond to the transactions motive. Since there is multicollinearity between the two, they cannot be used as explanatory variables simultaneously.

2. The corporate profit rate is the rate of return on fixed assets, and the interest rate is the average of all banks' contracted lending rate.

3. The rate of forecast revision is taken from the Bank of Japan's Short-Term Economic Forecast and uses a comparison with the forecast in the previous period, thus: $\dfrac{\text{Value of sales forecast in previous quarter for current quarter}}{\text{Value of sales forecast 2 quarters previously for current quarter}} \times 100$

4. Estimating period: 1962:I–1970.IV

5. The regression equation was published in the Bank of Japan's Monthly Research Report (*Chōsa Geppō*) for November 1971.

6. 't' values are shown in parentheses; all variables except the corporate profit rate are statistically significant at the 5 percent level.

If the net returns from bank loans L are shown as a function of L, $R(L)$; if the cost of Bank of Japan loans C is shown as the product of the official discount rate and the volume of such loans $\bar{r}C$; and if the returns from call loans C_l are expressed as a function of C_l, $R_c(C_l)$; then the net earnings of banks E may be expressed by the following equations:

$$[\text{City Banks}] \quad E_1 = R_1(L_1) + R_{c1}(C_{l1}) - \bar{r}C_1 \qquad (9)$$
$$[\text{Other Banks}] \quad E_2 = R_2(L_2) + R_{c2}(C_{l2}) \qquad (10)$$

The objective of bank behavior is to maximize E in equations (9) and (10) subject to the constraints of equations (7) and (8).[3]

2. Graphical Analysis of the Point of Profit Maximization

Next we shall consider the characteristics of the banks' profit-maximization point and its main determinants, explaining by means of graphs the banks' net returns E subject to the constraints outlined above.

2.1 Net Return on Bank Loans Function
We start with an examination of the net returns on bank loans function $R(L)$ in equations (9) and (10). Net returns on bank loans result from the difference between the cost of funds used to make loans and the income derived from loans. The costs of loan funds are of two major kinds: administrative expenditures associated with the operations of bank credit departments (inspection, etc.), and the payment of interest on derived deposits created when new loans are extended.

Putting the net returns on bank loans $R(L)$ on the vertical axis and the volume of loans L on the horizontal axis, the graph of the net return on bank loans in the upper section of chart 6.1 slopes upward and to the right from the origin, with a convex upward slope. The upward slope implies the rate of return on bank loans function is an increasing function of the volume of bank loans due to the fact that interest received on bank loans increases more rapidly than the cost of loans.

---

3. The profit-maximization hypothesis for the behavior of Japanese banks which the author proposed in Suzuki [41] in 1966 does not seem to require any modification, even today. In particular, the trend from 1965 onward, when city banks began to pay particular attention to loans to medium and small businesses and to individuals, can be entirely explained on the basis of profit-maximization principles. On this point, see Bank of Japan Research Department [5]. The profit motivation of banks was greatly strengthened by the so-called Kōritsuka Gyōsei ("Efficiency Administration") enforced by the Ministry of Finance in the early 1960s. As explained in chapter 1, note 1 above, maximization of market share by city banks is one expression of profit-maximization behavior under controlled interest rates.

Chart 6.1   Net Return on Bank Loans Curve

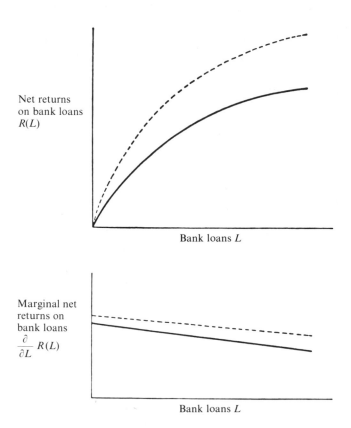

For two main reasons, the upward sloping convex curve gives a successively diminishing marginal rate of return on bank loans $\frac{\partial}{\partial L} R(L)$, as in the lower section of chart 6.1. First, since one method of increasing loan volume is to extend loans to higher risk enterprises, such loan increases suggest a greater probability of suspension of interest payments or even default on the principal. Since this implies either a continuous reduction in marginal revenue from its expected value, or a continual increase in business expenses associated with provisions for bad debts or the disposal of collateral, the net return on loans would continuously decrease. Second, in order to develop new loan outlets, marginal expenditures would inevitably rise continuously with the various costs associated with extra public relations or liaison work, conference and entertainment expenditures, inspection expenses, and general office expenses. Further, with the expansion of loan volume, the average size of loan must inevitably diminish, so that in this respect there would also be a continuous increase in the various expenses per unit of loan money leading to a continuous decline in the marginal net returns on loans. For these reasons the net return on bank loans function is upward sloping to the right with diminishing slope.

Next we consider some factors that would lead to a shift in the curve. First, a rise in the lending rate will increase the slope of the curve so that it shifts from the solid line to the dashed line in chart 6.1; similarly, lower interest rates would lead to a shift from the dashed line to the solid line. Other factors causing the same pattern of shifts in the curve would be any improvement or deterioration in the profits of business enterprises (through raising or lowering the possibility of suspension of interest payments or business failures), or any change in wages or prices affecting the administrative costs of loans, or any decrease or increase of interest payments on derivative deposits. Finally, movements of the curve from the solid line to the dashed line could be caused by technological innovations leading to a decline in lending costs.

2.2 *Net Return on Call Loans Function*
Next we examine the net return on call loans function $R_c(C_l)$ in equations (9) and (10). Since there is a fundamental difference between the net return on call loans function for city banks and for other banks, it is necessary to treat them separately. For convenience of explanation, the net return on call loans function of other banks will be taken first.

2.2.1 *Other Banks*
Since call loans are interbank transactions, the funds supplied cannot return to the lending banks in the form of derivative deposits. Call loans must be drawn either entirely from the deposits of lending banks with the Bank of Japan, or from deposits with an affiliate bank, and transferred to the account of the borrowing bank either at the Bank of Japan or with an affiliate. Consequently, the net returns on call loans do not require consideration of the costs of interest payable on derived deposits, as in the case of the net return on bank loans function. The net return on call loans is equal to total interest income on call loans less the associated transactions costs.

Chart 6.2 illustrates the graph of the net return on call loans function. The curve slopes upward to the right from the origin in the first quadrant. In other words, the net return on call loans increases with the increase in the volume of call loans because interest revenue on call loans exceeds costs. Unlike the case of an increase in bank loans to business enterprises, the possibility of nonrepayment of principal or suspension of interest payments rarely arises, and marginal costs do not grow, so that the factors causing a continuous decline in returns in the case of ordinary loans would be insignificant in the case of call loans.

Chart 6.2   Net Return on Call Loans Curve for Other Banks

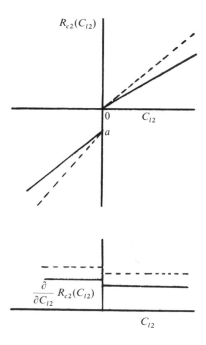

Next, in the third quadrant of the net return on call loans chart, the curve begins below the origin at point a and slopes downward to the left. The movement of call loan volume C_{12} from zero to minus represents a resort to call money borrowings when a bank experiences a shortage of cash for payment to customers after all second-line reserve assets such as call loans have been used up. Therefore, the absolute value of returns $R_{c2}(C_{12})$ is given by the (negative) sum of interest rates paid on call money borrowings and the costs of call market transactions.

The reason why the curve in the third quadrant does not start at the origin 0 but at the point a is that, exactly as in Europe or North America, if a noncity bank runs short of vault-cash, has persistent excess liabilities and negative payment reserves, this imposes various costs on the bank. For example, in the case of local banks, mutual banks, credit associations, and credit cooperatives, if the general public were to know that the bank was in difficulties through shortage of vault-cash, they would steer clear of that bank. Also, in such a case fund-position guidance by the Bank of Japan would be intensified, and probably there would be more energetic bank inspection by the Bank of Japan and the Ministry of Finance. The resulting loss of prestige and standing in the eyes of the public, combined with stricter guidance from the Bank of Japan and Ministry of Finance, may be regarded as the imposition of higher fixed costs, associated with the shift of C_{l2} from positive to negative. In chart 6.2 the distance $0a$ shows the size of these fixed costs. The curve slopes downward to the left because, as call money borrowings $(-C_l)$ increase, the amount of interest payable also increases.

Since there is a brokerage fee to be paid to money-market brokers of 0.125 percent or 0.25 percent on all transactions in the call market, the interest received on call loans (or on bills bought in the bills discount market) is not identical to the interest paid on call money borrowings (or on bills sold). This explains why, for equal positive and negative values of C_{l2} in the lower part of chart 6.2, the marginal return on call loans $\dfrac{\partial}{\partial C} R_{c2}(C_{l2})$ is smaller for call loans (C_{l2} positive) than for the same numerical value of call money borrowings (C_{l2} negative).

2.2.2 City Banks

The preceding section explained the net return on call loans function for other banks in terms of chart 6.2. The net return on call loans function for city banks—that is, for C_{l1} positive—would be the same shape as that drawn in the first quadrant, and therefore the analysis would be the same as for other banks. The difference between the two groups of banks occurs in the negative region.

Chart 6.3   Net Return on Call Loans Curve for City Banks

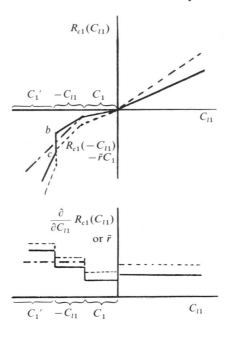

Chart 6.3 shows the graph of the net return on call loans function for city banks, including in this case not only $R_{c1}(C_{l1})$ but also $-rC_1$, the cost of borrowings from the Bank of Japan. The first quadrant is the same as the first quadrant in chart 6.2. In the third quadrant there are the following three differences. First, the origin and point a coincide so that fixed costs $0a$ do not exist, and the curve starts from the origin 0. Second, shortly after call loans C_{l1} have turned negative in the range C_1, the marginal returns are extremely small. Third, after call loans have moved well into negative territory, fixed costs bc (corresponding to fixed costs $0a$ for other banks) appear.

The first difference implies that even if payment reserves of the city banks run short and call loans C_{l1} turn negative, the city banks themselves do not regard this as a loss of prestige or face, and in fact there is no decline in their standing or credibility in the eyes of the public. As discussed in detail in part I, during the post–World War II recovery the city banks consistently had negative payment reserves, and this habit became well established with the regularization of overloan and the imbalance of bank liquidity. Prior to World War II, the city banks, like other banks today, maintained sizable prudential reserves on their own responsibility, and it was considered shameful for a bank to depend on Bank of Japan credit even to tide over a temporary shortage of payment reserves. However, as a result of almost ten years of overloan and the imbalance of bank liquidity, as well as on account of government intervention in funding for the postwar recovery in the early 1950s, the city banks forgot their loss of face over a lack of payment reserves. The public at large also began to feel no particular uneasiness about the persistent excess liabilities of the city banks.

The second difference between city banks and other banks arises because when city banks' second-line reserves C_{l1} become negative, they are able to receive Bank of Japan credit allocations C_1. As we saw in part I, the interest rate on Bank of Japan loans, namely, the official discount rate, is lower than the call rate, the bill discount rate, and other short-term money-market interest rates, except in periods of extreme monetary relaxation. Thus the marginal net returns are smallest in the range where Bank of Japan credit C_1 is being allocated, as shown in the lower section of chart 6.3.

When external liabilities (negative reserve assets) exist in addition to Bank of Japan loans C_1, these are made good by call money borrowings $(-C_{l1})$, as in the case of other banks, so the curve in this range is basically the same as that shown in the third quadrant of chart 6.2 for other banks. However, when $-C_{l1}$ increases again, a third difference arises: the appearance of fixed costs bc. This is the point where external liabilities are already large, and borrowings from the Bank of Japan C_1 are so substantial as to result in borrowings in excess of the limit set by the Bank of Japan, C_1'. Details of the consequences of borrowing in excess of Bank of Japan loan limits will be dealt with in chapter 10, section 2.3, but it may be mentioned in passing that such limits are imposed on the ten largest city banks which borrow from the Bank of Japan, and generally speaking this loan limit is inviolable.

In extreme cases where loans do exceed the limit, a penal rate of 4 percent p.a. over the discount rate is charged in order to accelerate repayments. This system was initiated on November 1, 1962, and up to now (1977) there has been no case of any bank exceeding its borrowing limits. Under these conditions, if one bank were to exceed its limits and penal rates were to be imposed, that bank's position vis-à-vis other city banks would undoubtedly be damaged and it would experience a loss of prestige. Moreover, since special pressure for loan repayment would be brought to bear by the Bank of Japan, this situation would surely give rise to the kind of fixed costs suggested earlier. These fixed costs are indicated by *bc*, and in the range to the left of *bc* the slope of the curve becomes very steep, reflecting the 4 percent rate and any other special pressures brought to bear.

2.2.3 *A Shift in the Curve*
The previous subsections examined the net return on call loans function for each of the two groups of banks. We now turn to the effects of a shift in the net return on call loans curve. The first cause of a shift in the curve is a change in the call rate. Also, in the case of city banks, a change in the discount rate would also cause a shift in the curve. In charts 6.2 and 6.3, the dashed lines indicate the situation after a rise in the call rate (in the discount rate for the city banks) leading to a shift in the curves. These shifts cause the slopes of the curves to increase about the origin. Conversely, when either the call rate or the bill discount rate is lowered, the curves shift from the position of the dashed line to the solid line in each case (the slopes about the origin are reduced).

Next we shall examine the effects of a change in the volume of Bank of Japan loans for the city banks. In chart 6.3 the solid line illustrates the case where a bank has borrowed up to the limit specified by the Bank of Japan and has further received loans in excess of the limit, although in practice Bank of Japan loans cease within this limit. Such a case would be represented by the intermediate line (dots and dashes). Given the ceiling on Bank of Japan loans, the curve in the third quadrant beyond the range of Bank of Japan loans C_1 would continue just like the curve in the third quadrant of chart 6.2 for other banks. Under such conditions, a change in the volume of Bank of Japan loans would lead to a horizontal shift (i.e. no change of slope) in the curve as shown by the dotted and dashed line. In other words, a decrease in Bank of Japan loans would cause a rightward shift in the curve, and an increase in Bank of Japan loans would cause a leftward shift in the curve. Now if Bank of Japan loans were to continue to increase, so that the amount outstanding exceeded the limit (i.e. the dotted and dashed line coincided with the solid line) the curve would change so as to incorporate fixed costs bc.

2.3 *Net Return on Call Loans Function as the Opportunity Cost of Bank Loans*

The preceding sections have explored the net return on call loans function, subject to the constraints in equations (7) and (8) where the volume of call loans C_l was related to the volume of bank lending. Rewriting equations (7) and (8) in terms of the volume of call loans we have:

$$C_{l1} \equiv (1 - \beta_1)D_1{}^* + C - (1 - \alpha_1 + \alpha_1\beta_1)L_1 \qquad (7)'$$
$$C_{l2} \equiv (1 - \beta_2)D_2{}^* - (1 - \alpha_2 + \alpha_2\beta_2)L_2 \qquad (8)'$$

These equations state that if the total loan volume L increases by one unit, the quantity of call loans C_l must decrease by the amount $(1 - \alpha + \alpha\beta)$. Consequently, a unit increase in loans brings about an increase on the one hand in the net return on loans, and on the other hand leads to a reduction in call loans of $(1 - \alpha + \alpha\beta)$, leading in turn to a reduction in the net return on call loans. The net return on call loans R_c is therefore the opportunity cost of bank loans. Thus, to express the net return on call loan function as the opportunity cost of bank loans $R_c{}^*(L)$, we can substitute the net return on call loans functions $R_{c1}(C_{l1})$ and $R_{c2}(C_{l2})$ in equations (7)' and (8)', which gives $R_{c1}{}^*(L_1)$ and $R_{c2}{}^*(L_2)$:

$$R_{c1}(C_{l1}) = R_{c1}[(1 - \beta_1)D_1{}^* + C - (1 - \alpha_1 + \alpha_1\beta_1)L_1] = R_{c1}{}^*(L_1)$$
$$R_{c2}(C_{l2}) = R_{c2}[(1 - \beta_2)D_2{}^* - (1 - \alpha_2 + \alpha_2\beta_2)L_2] = R_{c2}{}^*(L_2)$$

The shift parameters of the function $R_c{}^*(L)$ are the official discount rate $\bar{r}$, the call rate r_c, and the amount of Bank of Japan loans C—all of which are important shift parameters in the function $R_c(C_l)$—and, in addition, the amount of primary deposits D^*, the ratio of compensatory deposits α, and the reserve requirement rate β.

Chart 6.4 shows the net return on call loans function as the opportunity cost of loans in graphical terms. For the city banks, the net return on call loans curve $R_{c1}{}^*(L_1)$ is inclusive of the cost of Bank of Japan borrowings $(-\bar{r}C)$, exactly as in chart 6.3. It is assumed that Bank of Japan borrowings C_1 do not exist in the range where C_{l1} is positive, but exist only where C_{l1} is negative. For city banks, the solid line describes the case where a bank has borrowed up to its full limits from the Bank of Japan and, in addition, having borrowed a certain amount of call money $(-C_{l1})$, it borrows in excess of those limits. The dotted and dashed line describes the case where borrowings from the Bank of Japan cease within the prescribed limit. The

Chart 6.4 Net Return on Call Loans Curve as the Opportunity Cost of Bank Loans

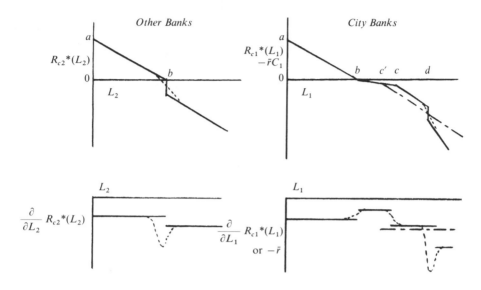

point where these curves intersect the vertical axis, a, shows the net return on call loans $R_c^*(0)$, equal to $R_c((1-\beta)D^*)$ when bank loans L are zero.

The point where these curves cross the horizontal axis b, indicates the volume of bank lending when call loans are zero. From equations (7)' and (8)' the volume of bank lending at this point is

$$\frac{(1-\beta)D^*}{1-\alpha+\alpha\beta}.$$

For city banks, the range where their loans increase backed by borrowings from the Bank of Japan loan allocations is bc or bc'. The size of this range, from equation (7)', is equal to $\dfrac{C_1}{1-\alpha_1+\alpha_1\beta_1}$, and the net returns in this range are equal to $(-\bar{r}C_1)$. The range beyond c or c' possesses the same characteristics as the range beyond the point b for the other banks, but where Bank of Japan borrowings C_1 exceed the permitted limit at point d, the same kind of fixed costs as occur for other banks beyond point b are incurred for city banks.

Among the shift parameters of the function, the derived deposit rate α and primary deposits D^* are determined by the asset portfolio selection of households and business enterprises, and the call rate r_c, the official discount rate $\bar{r}$, the volume of Bank of Japan borrowings C, and the reserve requirement-related rate β all depend upon the Bank of Japan lending policy, Bank of Japan bond and bill-buying policy, and Bank of Japan policy with respect to reserve requirements. Therefore, from the point of view of the banks, these shift parameters are dependent upon unpredictable elements, best regarded in terms of a probability function with a certain distribution. As a result, the curve for the net return on call loans as the opportunity cost of lending in the region of b for other banks and d for city banks does not actually have a kink, as shown by the solid line, but may be thought of as being continuous, as shown by the dotted line in chart 6.4.

The influence of the shift parameters on the curve may be broadly divided into three categories. First, those which make the curve shift horizontally (without changing the slope): changes in primary deposits, changes in Bank of Japan loans C, and Bank of Japan operations in buying and selling securities. An increase in deposits D^* shifts the whole curve to the right, and a decrease shifts the whole curve to the left. An increase in Bank of Japan loans C beyond the point C' causes a horizontal shift to the right for the curve in the region of C or beyond it for the city banks, and a decrease similarly causes a shift to the left. (The leftward and rightward horizontal movements are shown by the dotted and dashed section.) Finally, Bank of Japan operations in securities cause the same kind of shift as that produced by changes in primary deposits. Assume, for example, that the Bank of Japan had bought securities equal to the amount S. Since bank loans L are broadly defined to include bills discounted as well as investment in securities, the volume of loans L may be thought to have diminished by the amount S. In the case where banks themselves reduce their volume of loans by the amount S, it is clear from equations (7)′ and (8)′ that the call loans will increase by the amount $(1 - \alpha + \alpha\beta)S$, but where Bank of Japan operations cause a decrease equal to S, the entire amount S enters the call market so that call loans increase by the amount S. In contrast to the case where banks themselves restrict their loans L by the amount S, when this amount of securities is sold to the Bank of Japan, call loans are increased by the additional amount $S - (1 - \alpha + \alpha\beta)S = (1 - \beta)\alpha S$.[4]

This amount is equal to the increase in the budget line of banks shown above in equations (7) and (8), $(1 - \beta)D^*$ (for the city banks, when $C_{l1} < 0$, $(1 - \beta)D_1^* + C_1$). In terms of the increase in primary deposits, it is as if D^* had increased by the amount αS. Therefore the impact on the curve R_c^* of Bank of Japan buying operations S would lead to a similar horizontal shift to the right in the curve as increases in D^* equal to the amount αS.

4. Since commercial banks in Japan do not hold government deposits, no problem of compensatory deposits arises when commercial banks sell long-term government bonds or government-guaranteed securities to the Bank of Japan. Thus, investment of an amount S in government securities leads to an equal reduction in available funds. Similarly, the sale of such securities S to the Bank of Japan implies an equal increase in available funds S equal to the amount by which the banks have reduced their investments in securities, so there is no shift in the curve R_c^*.

Conversely, selling operations of the amount S would have the same effects as a horizontal shift to the left in the curve due to a decrease in D^* of αS.

Second, movements in the call rate r_c and the official discount rate $\bar{r}$ would cause a shift leading to a change in the slope, point b remaining fixed. A rise in the call rate or discount rate obviously leads to steepening of the slope, and a fall in these rates reduces the gradient of the slope.

Third, changes in reserve requirement ratios leading to a change in β would simultaneously result in a horizontal shift of the whole curve and a change in the slope of the curve. A rise in reserve requirements (increase in β) would cause the slope to steepen as the curve moved to the left, and a relaxation of reserve requirements (a decline in β) would lead to a rightward shift in the curve and a reduction in its slope.[5]

5. The reasons for these three kinds of shifts can be checked mathematically. First, the net return on call loans function R_c may be approximated by the following linear function:

$$R_c = (r_c - e)\, C_l - \bar{r} C \tag{1}$$

where e is the cost of call market transactions. Writing the net return on call loans function R_c^* as the opportunity cost of loans enables us to substitute C_l in the above equation (1) with equations (7)′ or (8)′ from the main text:

$$R_c^* = (r_c - e)\,\{(1 - \beta)D^* - (1 - \alpha + \alpha\beta)L\} - \bar{r} C \tag{2}$$

and $\dfrac{\partial}{\partial L} R_c^*$ which determines the slope of the curve is given by

$$\frac{\partial}{\partial L} R_c^* = -(r_c - e)(1 - \alpha + \alpha\beta) \tag{3}$$

Since neither D^* nor c are included in equation (3), it is clear that even if there are variations in the volume of primary deposits D^* and Bank of Japan loans C, the slope of the curve does not change.

It is also clear from (2) that variation ΔD^* in D^* shift point a by the amount $\Delta D^*(r_c - e)$ $(1 - \beta)$, and point b by the amount $\dfrac{\Delta D^*(1 - \beta)}{1 - \alpha + \alpha\beta}$, so that the curve is moved horizontally. Changes in the volume of Bank of Japan loans ΔC also cause a shift in the point c for city banks $\dfrac{\Delta C}{1 - \alpha + \alpha\beta}$, and affect the horizontal location of the curve (for example, in chart 6.4, movements from the solid line to the dashed line, or conversely). Next, since movements in call rate r_c have no effect on point b, that is, on the value of $\dfrac{(1 - \beta)D^*}{1 - \alpha + \alpha\beta}$, they only change the slope of the curve around point b, shifting point a by the amount $\Delta r_c(1 - \beta)D^*$. Changes in the slope of the curve at this point will be

$$\frac{\partial}{\partial r_c}\left(\frac{\partial R_c^*}{\partial L}\right) = 1 - \alpha + \alpha\beta < 0.$$

Changes in the official discount rate $\Delta \bar{r}$ will affect the city banks' curve by changing the slope of the curve around b in the range bc by $\Delta \bar{r}$ and the slope of the curve around d to the right of d by $\Delta \bar{r}$.

**Chart 6.5   Shifts in the Net Return on Call Loans Curve and the
Opportunity Cost of Bank Loans**

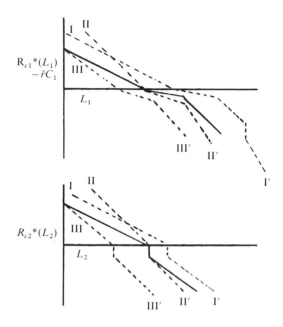

The above three categories of change are shown in chart 6.5. Starting
from the solid line, an increase in primary deposits, an increase in Bank of
Japan borrowings, and buying operations by the Bank of Japan—all
leading to horizontal shifts in the curve—are shown by a shift from the
solid curve to the dashed curve I–I', increases in the call rate and the official
discount rate leading to an increase in the slope of the curve are shown by
the shift to II–II', and a rise in the reserve requirement ratio leading to both
a shift in the position of the curve and a change in its slope is shown by
III–III'. Opposite shifts in the curve are, of course, shown by movements
from the dotted line back to the solid line. When I discuss the effects of
monetary policy in part III, changes in bank behavior resulting from changes
in the profit-maximization point due to the first type of shift will be called
liquidity effects, and changes in bank behavior resulting from changes in
the profit-maximization point due to the second type of shift will be called
cost effects. Shifts of the third type produce a combination of the liquidity

---

Finally, movements in the reserve requirement ratio β affect both point a, that is, $(r_c - e)$
$(1 - \beta)D^*$, and point b, that is $\dfrac{(1 - \beta)D^*}{1 - \alpha + \alpha\beta}$, and while simultaneously causing these to change
location, change the slope of the curve by the amount $\dfrac{\partial}{\partial \beta}\left(\dfrac{\partial R_c^*}{\partial L}\right) = \alpha(r_c - e) < 0$.

effect and the cost effect. Also in the discussion in part III, shifts in the curve R_c^* shown by chart 6.5 will be considered again, so it is important to understand fully the meaning of the shifts at this stage.

2.4 *Determination of the Profit-Maximization Point*

Substituting for $R_c(C_l)$ in equations (9) and (10) with $R_c^*(L)$ which we examined above, the equation for banks' net earnings E may be rewritten as follows:

$$E_1 = R_1(L_1) + R_{c1}^*(L_1) - \bar{r}C_1 \qquad (9)'$$
$$E_2 = R_2(L_2) + R_{c2}^*(L_2) \qquad (10)'$$

Equations (9)′ and (10)′ show that banks' net returns E are a function of their loans L. We can therefore draw E as a function of L to show the profit-maximization point for banks. In chart 6.6 the net return on loans

Chart 6.6   Profit-Maximization Point for Banks

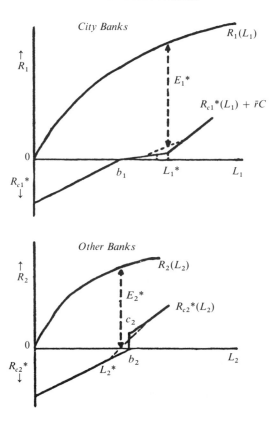

curve $R(L)$ is drawn in the first quadrant and shows diminishing marginal returns, slightly less steep in the case of the city banks. This is due to the fact that the loan clients of city banks are generally large-scale, stably managed, superior companies. In addition, city banks enjoy more advantageous lending opportunities because they can find safe and profitable lending outlets through their domestic branch network and foreign branches as authorized foreign exchange banks. In contrast, other banks are restricted to specific regions inside Japan, and in addition, there are restrictions on large-scale loans by mutual banks, credit corporations, and credit associations. Moreover, financial institutions for agriculture and forestry are restricted in the type of client they may lend to, so that by comparison with city banks their lending opportunities are less profitable, and therefore the slope of diminishing marginal returns for them may be thought to be steeper than that for the city banks. The net return on call loans R_c^* is shown in chart 6.6 on an inverted scale vertically below the origin. Consequently, banks' net earnings E are shown by the length of the dashed line between the curve $R(L)$ and the curve $R_c^*(L)$ (shown in chart 6.6 by the arrowed line labeled E^*.)

It is clear from an examination of chart 6.6, that in the range where R_c^* is positive (i.e. R_c^* corresponds to L in the range where C_l is positive—in terms of chart 6.6, that part drawn below the horizontal axis in the fourth quadrant) there is no great difference between the city banks and other banks. But in the range where R_c^* is negative (i.e. R_c^* corresponds to L in the range where C_l is negative, implying that call money borrowings are being made —in terms of chart 6.6, that part drawn above the horizontal axis in the first quadrant), they are very different in shape for reasons we have already examined.

The vertical line E_1 (arrowed in chart 6.6) between R_{c1}^* and R_1 reaches a maximum at the point E_1^*. Since the degree of diminishing marginal returns for the curve R_1 is small, and the range for marginal losses $b_1 c_1$ in the curve R_{c1}^* is small, the amount of loans necessary for city banks to maximize E_1 is to the right of c_1. In other words, city banks are fortunate in having both more profitable lending opportunities than other banks, and, because they can obtain preferential Bank of Japan loans at the official discount rate (which is cheaper than the call rate), they try to borrow as heavily as possible from the Bank of Japan. Hence, any situation where they can continue to lend, but only borrow on a small scale from the call market (to the right of the point c_1) is the range that yields profit maximization.

In contrast, the situation for other banks is shown by curve R_{c2}^*. As long as L_2 is in the range from 0 to b_2 (loans are being extended but borrowings from the call market C_{l2} are zero), the shape of the curve is the same as that for the city banks' curve R_{c1}^*, but at point b_2 fixed costs $b_2 c_2$ come into existence. Unlike the city banks, other banks must observe the normal rules of financial discipline—just as banks in Europe and North America—and hold prudential payment reserves on their own responsibility. A bank that ought to be pursuing this discipline and yet has to borrow money from the central bank because of a shortage of reserves, or is constantly borrowing in the money market, must suffer a form of loss of prestige.

In the range to the right of c_2 where these fixed costs emerge, the shape of the curve R_{c2} is basically the same as that of the city banks' curve R_{c1} in the range to the right of c_1. However, whereas in the case of city banks there exists a point d (see chart 6.4) representing borrowings from the Bank of Japan in excess of a permitted limit, no such point exist for other banks.

Thus the vertical line $E_2{}^*$ (in chart 6.6) reaches a maximum to the left of b_2. This is due to the two conditions that the degree of diminishing marginal returns for the curve R_2 is large and that fixed costs b_2c_2 come into effect at the point b_2. In other words, compared with city banks, there is a constraint imposed upon the lending ability of other banks, and since in addition they are unable to obtain Bank of Japan credit allocations and must observe certain standards of financial discipline, profit maximization must occur in the range where call loans are positive.

It is precisely this difference in the locations of the volume of loans L^* that maximizes profits for city banks and other banks which is the fundamental cause of the imbalance of bank liquidity discussed in part I.

3. *Bank Lending Behavior*

Finally let us examine the determinants of the location of the profit-maximizing loan volume of banks explained graphically above. As described in the theoretical model of the previous chapter, the equation for the behavior of city banks and other banks is as follows:

$$L_1 = L_1([a : \bar{r}], r_c, \bar{i}, [c : \bar{i}_d]) \tag{11}$$
$$L_2 = L_2(r_c, \bar{i}, [c : \bar{i}_d]) \tag{12}$$

The variable $[a : \bar{r}]$, which shows the availability and cost of Bank of Japan loans, appears only in the city bank equation. The other three variables, the call rate r_c, the bank lending rate $\bar{i}$, and the difficulty and cost of collecting deposits $(c : \bar{i}_d]$ are common to the equations for both sets of banks.

First, the availability and cost of Bank of Japan loans $[a : \bar{r}]$ is related to the part b_1c_1 of the curve $R_{c1}{}^*$ in chart 6.6 for city banks. The availability of Bank of Japan credit a affects the amount of credit $\bar{C}_1$ that city banks can expect in the future, and therefore the size of b_1c_1. The cost of Bank of

Japan loans $\bar{r}$ affects the marginal losses (the positive upward slope) of $R_{c1}{}^*$ in the range $b_1 c_1$. With a reduction in the availability of Bank of Japan loans, point c_1 shifts to the left, causing the volume of loans which maximize E_1 to shift to the left (and conversely). In contrast, a rise in the cost of Bank of Japan loans increases the upward slope of $R_{c1}{}^*$ in the range $b_1 c_1$, but it does not affect $L_1{}^*$ unless the increase in this slope becomes so large that $L_1{}^*$ shifts into the range $b_1 c_1$, or even to the left of b_1. (A profit-maximizing loan volume with $L_1{}^*$ to the left of b_1 implies positive secondary reserve assets similar to the situation that exists for other banks.) Consequently, changes in the official discount rate normally do not have any "cost effect" on bank behavior: they warn of a change in the availability of Bank of Japan loans and show up in the call rate r_c and in the resulting changes in institutionally related lending rates $\bar{i}$, so that the more tangible effects of policy on bank behavior are in this area.

From the above, the following condition may be deemed to hold:

$$\frac{\partial L_1}{\partial [a : \bar{r}]} \leq 0.$$

The major effect on bank lending derives from the "liquidity effect" which accompanies a change in the availability of Bank of Japan credit.

Next we examine the remaining three variables common to both city banks and other banks. Since marginal losses from the curve R^* in chart 6.6 increase throughout its range (except in the range $b_1 c_1$), a rise in the call rate will increase the slope of the curve $R_c{}^*$, causing a leftward shift in the volume of loans L^* which maximizes E. Therefore, in equations (11) and (12) the following conditions obtain:

$$\frac{\partial L_1}{\partial r_c} < 0 \qquad \frac{\partial L_2}{\partial r_c} < 0.$$

The effects on L_1 of changes in the call rate are "cost effects."

Since changes in the bank lending rate $\bar{i}$ affect the slope (marginal returns) of curve R in chart 6.6, we have in equations (11) and (12):

$$\frac{\partial L_1}{\partial \bar{i}} > 0 \qquad \frac{\partial L_2}{\partial \bar{i}} > 0.$$

Also, the slope of the net return on bank lending curve R is greatly affected by lending opportunities, which in turn are affected by corporate profits and the bank lending rate $\bar{i}$. As explained in chapter 1, the bank lending rate $\bar{i}$ is not an equilibrium interest rate, and because of its strong, institutionalized rigidities, the determinants of the slope of curve R clearly must include the trend of safe lending opportunities (which basically depends on the corporate profits situation). If the corporate profit rate P_r is expressed as a shift parameter of functions L_1, L_2 in equations (11) and (12) above, we have:

$$\frac{\partial L_1}{\partial P_r} > 0, \qquad \frac{\partial L_2}{\partial P_r} > 0.$$

Finally, we consider the impact of cases where the difficulty and cost of soliciting deposits shown by $[c : \bar{i}_d]$ increases. In the case where deposit collecting becomes more difficult (c increases), banks consider that the volume of primary deposits D^* to be collected in the future decreases (dynamically speaking, the expected rate of growth of D^* declines). In other words, given a certain level of Bank of Japan borrowings—and this applies to city banks only—banks find that their budget line for asset selection between loans, L, and call loans, C_l, has been reduced. As we saw in chart 6.5, this caused the curve R_c^* to shift to the left, and as a result, points b and c in chart 6.6 shift to the left so that the profit-maximizing loan volume L^* also shifts to the left. However, a rise in the deposit interest rate $\bar{i}_d$ has no direct impact on the banks' choice of assets (i.e. on the choice between loans and call loans) because $\bar{i}_d$ is always set at a subequilibrium level. However, if the interest rate payable on derivative deposits from loans increases, the net returns on bank lending function decrease and therefore the slope of R (in chart 6.6) would be reduced, shifting the profit-maximizing loan volume L^* to the left. Consequently, for the variable $[c : \bar{r}_d]$ in equations (11) and (12), we have

$$\frac{\partial L_1}{\partial [c : \bar{i}_d]} < 0 \text{ and } \frac{\partial L_2}{\partial [c : \bar{i}_d]} < 0.$$

The change in the profit-maximization of loan volume accompanying a change in primary deposits D^* is, of course, the "liquidity effect." As we explained in section 2.3 and in chart 6.5, the same kind of change could occur through Bank of Japan operations in securities (excluding government bonds or government-guaranteed bonds—see note 4 above).

Although not shown in equations (11) and (12), when reserve requirements are changed, β, which is one of the shift parameters for the bank lending function, produces both "cost effects" and "liquidity effects" and causes a change in the profit-maximizing loan volume L^*. Thus, if β is expressed as a shift parameter for equations (11) and (12), we have

$$\frac{\partial L_1}{\partial \beta_1} < 0 \text{ and } \frac{\partial L_2}{\partial \beta_2} < 0.$$

From equations (11) and (12), and using chart 6.6, we have examined the determinants of the profit-maximization point for banks; but we can express these determinants more generally by saying that the factors that affect bank loan behavior are (1) interest rates, (2) the volume of available funds, and (3) lending opportunities.

Starting with (1), the official discount $\bar{r}$, the call rate r_c, the bank lending rate $\bar{i}$, and the interest rate payable on deposits $\bar{i}_d$, all have some effect, but the most significant interest rate is that with the largest range of variability, namely, the call rate r_c. These interest rate effects are called "cost effects" because, in terms of chart 6.6, the effects of monetary policy operate on bank behavior through changing the slopes of the curves and hence shifting the banks' profit-maximization point.

Changes in (2), the volume of funds, are produced by variations in primary deposits D^*, variations in Bank of Japan credit C, and Bank of Japan operations in bills and securities. In terms of charts 6.5 and 6.6, monetary policy operates on bank lending behavior by causing the curve R_c^* to move horizontally to the right or to the left, thus altering the point of profit maximization. When monetary policy has its effects through this kind of route, we call this the "liquidity effect."

Lending opportunities (3) means the volume of profitable and safe lending which shows up in changes in the volume of loans reflecting the relative demand for funds. As we saw in part I, since loans in Japan are made at a rate below that which equilibrates supply and demand, banks must ration loans among customers, and in such circumstances the number of profitable and safe lending opportunities affects the slope of the net return on bank lending curve R in charts 6.1 and 6.6 and causes shifts in the profit-maximization point in chart 6.6. It is the shift in the profit-maximization point which determines the volume of loans that banks have available to allocate among customers. In saying that the volume of bank lending changes in response to the demand for funds, we imply that banks are constantly watching for changes in safe and profitable lending opportunities and vary the amount of credit they grant accordingly. When monetary policy operates on bank lending through this route, there is an "announcement effect" whereby changes in monetary policy have a psychological impact on what banks think will be the future course of the business cycle and hence future lending opportunities.

The above three are the fundamental factors affecting the behavior of Japanese banks. In addition, there is an intensely Japanese sense of rivalry among city banks. This is a form of conscious attempt to secure at least as large a share of the volume of bank loans as any other similar-sized city bank. The acute awareness that city banks have of the actions of others in their lending behavior is due to the enormous influence that Bank of Japan credit has on the shape of the net return on call loans curve (in the case of Bank of Japan loans) and on shifts in the curve (in the case of Bank of Japan purchases of securities), and therefore on the profit-maximization point (see charts 6.4, 6.5 and 6.6).

Thus, since Bank of Japan loans and purchases of securities have such a big influence on the profit-maximization point of city banks, they are aware that they will incur losses if they do not receive an adequate allocation of Bank of Japan credit C_1. On the one hand, in order not to incur loss and not to be treated disadvantageously relative to other banks of similar size, they will try to obtain Bank of Japan loans. On the other hand, since Bank of Japan lending policy and securities-purchasing policy operate through the restriction of Bank of Japan loans to those banks which have been excessively aggressive in loan expansion, in determining any one city bank's lending volume, the lending activities of other banks of similar size are an extremely important criterion. Bank of Japan "window guidance," as we shall explain in part III, is to a great extent effective because it cleverly utilizes this sense of rivalry in the lending behavior of city banks.[6]

6. One author who has particularly emphasized the "sense of rivalry" as a basic principle of bank lending behavior is Bunji Kure [24]. However, as pointed out in chapter 1, note 1, this sense of rivalry has arisen because the attempt to increase market share consistent with profit maximization is the natural consequence of profit maximization under controlled or regulated interest rates, and therefore can be explained by the hypothesis of profit maximization.

7 The Measurement of Bank Behavior

Based on the assumptions about the theory of bank behavior presented in chapter 6, this chapter presents some results of estimating bank lending and interest rates, and an interpretation thereof.

1. Estimation of Bank Loan Behavior

1.1 Marginal Returns from Bank Lending

The theory of bank behavior presented in the previous chapter showed that banks extend loans L so as to maximize their net earnings function E.

$$E_1 = R_1(L_1) + R_{c1}*(L_1) - \bar{r}C_1 \tag{9$'$}$$

$$E_2 = R_2(L_2) + R_{c2}*(L_2) \tag{10$'$}$$

Where E is maximized, the following equations will hold:

$$\frac{\partial E_1}{\partial L_1} = \frac{\partial}{\partial L_1}R_1(L_1) + \frac{\partial}{\partial L_1}R_{c1}*(L_1) = 0 \tag{13}$$

$$\frac{\partial E_2}{\partial L_2} = \frac{\partial}{\partial L_2}R_2(L_2) + \frac{\partial}{\partial L_2}R_{c2}*(L_2) = 0 \tag{14}$$

Since it is difficult to deal statistically with the marginal costs of loan transactions and call transactions, it is hard exactly to estimate movements in the marginal net return on bank loans $\frac{\partial}{\partial L}R(L)$ and the marginal cost of lending opportunities $\frac{\partial}{\partial L}R_c*(L)$ in equations (13) and (14). However, if in place of the marginal net returns on loans we are willing to take the

104

marginal gross returns before deducting the marginal cost of loan transactions, estimation is substantially simplified. Also, in place of the marginal net opportunity cost we can use the cost of raising funds prior to adding in the marginal costs of call transactions, that is, we may take the marginal gross opportunity costs. We may now estimate the marginal gross returns on bank lending, and the marginal gross opportunity cost, and compare their actual trends.

If loans are increased by the amount ΔL, then net returns are increased by the product of the nominal interest rate paid on those loans and the volume of loans $\Delta L \cdot \bar{i}$. At the same time, if compensatory deposits are created in the ratio α for every additional unit of loans, derivative deposits of $\Delta L \cdot \alpha$ will be created and interest has to be paid on these at the rate $\Delta L \cdot \alpha \bar{i}_d$. Consequently, gross returns are:

$$\Delta L \cdot \bar{i} - \Delta L \cdot \alpha \cdot \bar{i}_d = \Delta L(\bar{i} - \alpha \cdot \bar{i}_d).$$

Note that when loans are actually increased, equations (7)′ and (8)′ in the preceding chapter make it clear that there is a simultaneous decrease in the amount of call loans C_l equal to $\Delta L(1 - \alpha + \alpha\beta)$. Conversely, the marginal gross returns on bank lending compared with the marginal gross opportunity cost of lending (equal to the call rate r_c) is the amount $\Delta L(\bar{i} - \alpha\bar{i}_d)$ divided by $\Delta L(1 - \alpha + \alpha\beta)$, that is:

$$\frac{\Delta L(\bar{i} - \alpha \cdot \bar{i}_d)}{\Delta L(1 - \alpha + \alpha\beta)} = \frac{\bar{i} - \alpha \cdot \bar{i}_d}{1 - \alpha + \alpha\beta} \tag{15}$$

In other words, having made loans of ΔL, this is the ex post actual interest rate obtained on the funds utilized. Hereafter we refer to this rate as the "effective loan interest rate."

Charts 3.2 and 3.3 (1) and (2) show the results of estimating the effective loan interest rate for city banks, local banks, and credit associations from 1964 onward.[1] Equation (15) is made up of the nominal bank lending rate $\bar{i}$, the deposit interest rate $\bar{i}_d$, the compensatory deposit ratio α, and the reserve requirement rate β. But since the latter two appear as the product $\alpha\beta$, their impact on the effective bank lending rate is negligible. Consequently, in charts 3.2 and 3.3 (1) and (2), the reserve requirement rate β is omitted, while trends in the nominal lending rate $\bar{i}$, the deposit interest rate $\bar{i}_d$, and the compensatory deposit ratio α are plotted at the top of each chart, and the computed effective interest rates are shown immediately below them. It is clear from the charts that movements in the effective rate of interest

1. This estimate was computed by Haruhiko Terada and Kuniki Sato of the Bank of Japan Research Department.

are mainly determined by fluctuations in nominal bank lending rates $\bar{i}$ and the compensatory deposit ratio α.

Next, a weighted average of the call (or bill discount) rate r_c representing the marginal opportunity costs of loans is deducted from the effective bank lending rate to arrive at an estimate of marginal net returns from bank lending. These two series are illustrated in charts 3.2 and 3.3 (1) and (2). Also in chart 3.3, the calculation is carried out for local banks and credit corporations using the yield in the bond market (represented by the yield on maturing NTT bonds). Looking at charts 3.3 (1) and 3.3 (2), it is at once clear that the marginal gross return on bank lending declines sharply in tight-money periods such as 1964, 1970, and 1973, but improves rapidly during easy-money periods such as 1965–66 and 1971–72. The marginal gross income during these periods of decline is in the range 0–2 percent for city banks, 1–2 percent for local banks, and 3–4 percent for credit corporations. (In the period up to January–March 1974, when the call rate and the bill discount rate reached the 12 percent level, despite the fact that the effective bank lending rate also reached 12–13.5 percent, the marginal gross return for all types of banks was in the range $-1\% \sim +1\%$.) If the difference between the marginal cost of loans transactions and the marginal cost of call transactions were higher, the net marginal returns from loans in tight-money periods would actually be negative. Since there is quite a wide distribution of marginal net returns from individual loan transactions, even if the average for marginal net returns in a tight-money period were not negative, the number of loss-making loans would certainly increase. In practice, because it takes time for banks to adjust their loan volume, it is unlikely that the loan volume would be such as to make the marginal net earnings $\dfrac{\partial E}{\partial L}$ exactly zero, and it is appropriate to think of banks as being in the process of adjusting their loan portfolio to this level. Consequently, there is nothing unusual in an increasing number of loan losses (i.e. the marginal return on loans becoming negative) in tight-money periods, balanced by positive marginal returns in times of easy money.[2]

If the marginal gross returns on loans are included as an explanatory variable in regression analysis of the level of bank lending L, we arrive at the significant conclusion that when marginal gross returns improve, the volume of loans L rises very rapidly, but conversely, when the marginal gross returns deteriorate, loans are restrained. The equations set out below show an example of such a relationship (Estimating period: 1963 III–1972 I).[3]

2. The method and results of estimating the marginal returns on bank lending given here are basically the same as those used in table 1.3 of Suzuki [41], with some modifications.

3. This regression equation was computed by Haruhiko Terada, economist at the Bank of Japan Research Department.

$$\frac{\Delta L_1}{I - S} = -98.831 + 7.807\,\Delta E_{g1} - 0.898\,(-\dot{C}_{11}) + 11.357\frac{EX}{Y}$$
$$\phantom{\frac{\Delta L_1}{I - S} = -98.831 +}(4.16)\phantom{\,\Delta E_{g1}}(-1.00)\phantom{\,(-\dot{C}_{11}) +}(2.72)$$

$$\bar{R}^2 = 0.617 \qquad d = 1.795$$

$$\frac{L_2}{D_2} = 14.927 + 0.188\,\Delta E_{g2} + 1.128\,P_r + 0.169\frac{I - S}{D_2}$$
$$\phantom{\frac{L_2}{D_2} = 14.927 +}(3.71)\phantom{\,\Delta E_{g2} +}(2.94)(7.38)$$

$$+\,0.339\left(\frac{C_{12}}{D_2}\right)_{-1} + 0.773\left(\frac{L_2}{D_2}\right)_{-1}$$
$$(3.92)\phantom{\left(\frac{C_{12}}{D_2}\right)_{-1} +}(11.05)$$

$$\bar{R}^2 = 0.917 \qquad d = 2.078$$

Key to symbols:
ΔL_1 = Increase in quarterly average of city bank loans (SA)
$I - S$ = Corporate sector's financial deficit (flow-of-funds data, SA)
ΔE_{g1} = Marginal gross returns on city bank loans (shown in chart 3.2)
$(-\dot{C}_{11})$ = Rate of change in city banks' external liabilities from preceding quarter
$\dfrac{EX}{Y}$ = Exports as a proportion of GNP (SA)
L_2 = Quarterly average of local bank loans (SA)
D_2 = Average volume of local bank deposits (less checks and bills) (SA)
ΔE_{g2} = Marginal gross returns on local bank loans (shown in chart 3.3)
P_r = Rate of return on assets of corporate enterprises (corporate enterprise statistics, all industries, SA)
C_{12} = Net surplus fund position of local banks (SA)
SA = Seasonally adjusted data

It is clear from the t values in parentheses that the variable marginal gross earnings on loans E_g has an extremely high statistical significance. The regression equation confirms the finding, stated at the end of the preceding chapter, that the fundamental factors affecting bank lending behavior are (1) interest rates, (2) the volume of available funds, and (3) lending opportunities. Thus, marginal gross earnings E_g is a variable which effectively represents (1), interest rates; $(-\dot{C}_{11})$, $\dfrac{EX}{Y}$, D_2, and C_{12} are proxies for (2), the volume of available funds; and I–S and Pr are proxies for (3), lending opportunities.

1.2 An Equation for Bank Lending Behavior
The preceding section provided a regression analysis of bank lending behavior, using the marginal returns from bank lending. Next we shall try

to estimate a function for bank lending behavior directly from equations (11) and (12) above, that is:

$$L_1 = L_1([a:\bar{r}], r_c, \bar{i}, [c:\bar{i}_d]) \tag{11}$$

$$L_2 = L_2(r_c, \bar{i}, [c:\bar{i}_d]) \tag{12}$$

First, we start with an earlier example of this estimation from Suzuki's "Effects of Monetary Policy" [41], chapter 2, section 3, where $\hat{L}$ is defined as $\hat{L} = \dfrac{\Delta L}{L_{-1}}$:

$$\hat{L} = 0.771 + 0.2260\,P_r - 0.2600\,r_c + 0.7520\,\hat{L}_{-1}$$
$$\quad\;(0.74)\quad\;(1.96)\qquad\;(-3.80)\qquad(7.37)$$

$$\bar{R} = 0.8460 \qquad d = 2.2758$$

$$\hat{L} = -0.6897 + 1.5541\,\frac{P_r}{r_{c-1}} + 0.6850\,\hat{L}_{-1}$$
$$\quad\;(-1.21)\qquad(4.19)\qquad\quad\;(9.99)$$

$$\bar{R} = 0.8717 \qquad d = 2.093$$

This estimate uses quarterly data from 1954 III to 1964 IV. Under the hypothesis that actual bank loans are constantly in the process of being adjusted toward the profit-maximizing loan volume, this equation was estimated so as to include a distributed lag in equations (11) and (12). Compared with equations (11) and (12) in chapter 6, the estimating equation has the special characteristic that it combines the equations for city banks and local banks. Second, the variables $[a:\bar{r}]$ and $\bar{i}$ are not included; third, in order meaningfully to capture the rapid increase in the volume of available funds in $[c:\bar{i}_d]$, the unexplained variable ΔL is divided by L_{-1} (that is, L in the previous period) and the equation is estimated for $\hat{L}$. Fourth, the corporate profit situation, which is a shift parameter of the net return on bank lending function $R(L)$, is captured by adding in the corporate profit rate P_r as an explanatory variable.

The most significant aspect of this estimating equation is that the key variable of Japanese banks' lending behavior is empirically found to be the call rate, r_c.

The Bank of Japan econometric model, published in the fall of 1972 (Estimating period: 1958 II–1971 I) contains the following estimating equations, which can be derived from the theoretical model of bank behavior given in this book.

City Banks

$$\Delta LB1P = \underset{(-1.10)}{-199.9} + \underset{(2.65)}{0.3190\Delta}\left[\sum_1^4\left(\frac{1}{4}\right)(D^\nabla B1 + SEC^\nabla B1)_{-t}\right]$$

$$\underset{(-3.10)}{-1.1577\Delta}\left[\sum_0^1\left(\frac{1}{2}\right)\left(\frac{RLNC - RLB1}{100}\right)_{-t}\right.$$

$$\left.\cdot \sum_1^4\left(\frac{1}{4}\right)(D^\nabla B1 + SEC^\nabla B1)_{-t}\right]$$

$$+ 2.5 \times \underset{(3.32)}{0.2152}(IF + II - SC - DF) + \underset{(3.17)}{0.4420\Delta LB1P_{-1}}$$

$$+ \left[\underset{(-5.60)}{-1.1319QQ1} - \underset{(-2.12)}{0.3976QQ2} + \underset{(3.43)}{0.5715QQ3}\right]\cdot\frac{LB1P_{-1}}{100}$$

$$+ \left\{LBTSP - 0.4420LBTSP_{-1} - \left[0.3190 - 1.1577\sum_0^1\left(\frac{1}{2}\right)\right.\right.$$

$$\left.\left.\cdot\left(\frac{RLNC - RLB1}{100}\right)_{-t}\right]\cdot\sum_1^4\left(\frac{1}{4}\right)D^\nabla BTS_{-t}\right\}$$

$$\bar{R}^2 = 0.935 \qquad d = 1.695$$

Other Banks

$$\Delta LB2P = \underset{(-1.08)}{-202.1} + \underset{(3.26)}{0.4913\Delta}\left[\sum_1^4\left(\frac{1}{4}\right)(D^\nabla B2 + SEC^\nabla B2)_{-t}\right]$$

$$\underset{(-3.43)}{-0.5739\Delta}\left[\sum_0^3\omega_t\left(\frac{RLC - RLB2}{100}\right)_{-t}\cdot\sum_1^4\left(\frac{1}{4}\right)\right.$$

$$\left.\cdot(D^\nabla B2 + SEC^\nabla B2)_{-t}\right] + 2.5 \times \underset{(1.49)}{0.1012}(IF + II - SC - DF)$$

$$+ \underset{(2.73)}{0.4385} \times \Delta LB2P_{-1} + \left[\underset{(-7.68)}{-2.3933QQ1} - \underset{(-2.38)}{0.6409QQ2}\right.$$

$$\left.+ \underset{(6.30)}{1.4566QQ3}\right]\cdot\frac{LB2P_{-1}}{100} - \left\{LBTSP - 0.4385LBTSP_{-1}\right.$$

$$- \left[0.4913 - 0.5739\sum_0^3\omega_t\left(\frac{RLC - RLB2}{100}\right)_{-t}\right]\cdot\sum_1^4\left(\frac{1}{4}\right)$$

$$\left.\cdot D^\nabla BTS_{-t}\right\}$$

$$\bar{R}^2 = 0.971 \qquad d = 2.184$$

Key to symbols:

$LB1P$ = Increase in city bank loans to private sector
$LBP2$ = Increase in other banks' loans to private sector
$D^\nabla B1$ = Deposits of private and public sector at city banks
$D^\nabla B2$ = Deposits of private and public sector at other banks
$SEC^\nabla B1$ = Debenture issues by city banks
$SEC^\nabla B2$ = Debenture issues by other banks
$RLNC$ = Interest on external liabilities of city banks (weighted average of call rate and official discount rate)
RLC = Call rate
$RLB1$ = Average contracted lending rate on city bank loans
$RLB2$ = Average contracted lending rate on other bank loans
IF = Amount of new investment in secondary and tertiary industries, II: inventory investment in secondary and tertiary industries
SC = Corporate saving
DF = Capital consumption provisions by private-sector corporations
$QQ1 \sim QQ3$ = Seasonal dummy, $LBTSP$ in {} allows for the change in status to city bank of the Taiyo and Saitama banks
ω_t = Weighting of the distributed lag ($\omega_0 = 0.4$, $\omega_1 = 0.3$, $\omega_2 = 0.2$, $\omega_3 = 0.1$)

This estimating equation is extremely sophisticated in comparison with the author's earlier equation. The main differences are: first, city and other banks are estimated separately; second, although the variable $[a : \bar{r}]$ is not included in either, the variable $\bar{i}$ (bank lending rate) is included and the official discount rate $\bar{r}$ is included for the city banks, using a weighted average of $\bar{r}$ and the call rate, r_c ; third, the variable $[c : \bar{i}_d]$ is included by using the total of ordinary deposits, government deposits, and the volume of debentures issued; fourth, the condition of business enterprises, which is a shift parameter of the net returns from bank lending $R(L)$, is included so as to represent the amount of "excess" investment by the corporate sector.

In this estimating equation all the variables of equations (11) and (12) except $[a : \bar{r}]$ are therefore effectively included as explanatory variables, but, as explained later, $[a : \bar{r}]$ strongly determines the call rate r_c, and therefore $[a : \bar{r}]$ and r_c have a multicollinear relation, so that the inclusion of both of these in the bank loan equation would present a problem. The estimating equation reveals an extremely interesting fact concerning the difference in behavior between city banks and other banks. Although the bank lending behavior equation is nonlinear, it can be converted to approximate linear form and the elasticities of the various explanatory variables can be cal-

Table 7.1   Elasticities of Explanatory Variables for Bank Loans

	Rate of Adjustment to Desired Loan Level during Quarter	Elasticity with Respect to:		
		Funds Employed	Interest-Rate Spread*	Loan Opportunities
Increase in city bank loans to private sector	56%	0.299 (0.535)	0.226 (0.405)	0.353 (0.633)
Increase in loans of other banks to private sector	56%	0.570 (1.015)	0.211 (0.376)	0.110 (0.196)

Note: Figures in parentheses are long-run elasticities.
*Spread between lending rate and cost of funds.

culated, as presented in table 7.1. Concerning the speed of adjustment toward the profit-maximizing loan volume and the elasticity relative to the differential between the call rate (a weighted average of the call rate and the official discount rate for the city banks) and the bank lending rate, there is little difference between city banks and other banks. However, for the elasticity with respect to loan volume, that for other banks is the larger of the two, while the elasticity with respect to lending opportunities is larger for the case of the city banks.

To see the meaning of this result, it is extremely interesting to return to chart 6.6. The volume of loans L_2^*, which maximizes profits for other banks, is dominated by the existence of fixed costs $b_2 c_2$ and cannot be to the right of point b_2. Consequently, even if there is a change in the slope of the curve R_2 with a change in lending opportunities, this will not have very much effect in altering L_2^*. Rather, a shift to the right by point b_2 as a result of an increase in primary deposits D^* (represented by the volume of available funds in the estimating equation) causing a shift in the curve R_{c2}^* would have a far greater influence on L_2^*. In contrast, since for the city banks there is no fixed cost element $b_2 c_2$, a change in their lending opportunities leading to a change in the slope of the curve R_1 (through its relationship with the curve R_{c1}^*) would have a far greater effect than in the case of other banks on the profit-maximizing loan volume L^*. Conversely, a shift to the right in the curve R_{c1}^* due to an increase in primary deposits D_1^* would not have such an expansive influence on the profit-maximizing loan volume of city banks L_1^* as the same shift would have in the case of the other banks, where such a situation would be close to a corner maximum. Officers in the banking field have pointed out that, whereas city banks passively follow the demand for funds, other banks observe certain standards of monetary or financial discipline, namely, they pay more attention to their fund position. Not only can this be confirmed by the results of statistical estimation, but by means of our theoretical model it can be explained as rational behavior. Moreover, as we shall see in chapter 14, section 3.1 below, the tendency of city banks to be swayed by the demand for funds imposes limits on monetary stabilization policy in Japan.

2. Estimation of Interest Rates

Next we shall estimate variations in interest rates which are closely related to bank behavior.

2.1 The Call Rate

In the general equilibrium theory presented in chapter 5, section 2, the equilibrium level of Bank of Japan loans was given by

$$\bar{C} = C_1([a:\bar{r}], r_c, \bar{i}, [c:\bar{i}_d]).$$

The equilibrium call rate r_c may be found by rearranging this equation as follows:

$$r_c = f(\bar{C}, [a:\bar{r}], \bar{i}, [c:\bar{i}_d]) \tag{15}$$

$$\frac{\partial r_c}{\partial \bar{C}} < 0, \quad \frac{\partial r_c}{\partial [a:\bar{r}]} > 0, \quad \frac{\partial r_c}{\partial \bar{i}} > 0, \quad \frac{\partial r_c}{\partial [c:\bar{i}_d]} < 0.$$

An estimate of the call rate along these lines was made in Suzuki [41], chapter 3, section 5, and in Suzuki [43], where the following results were obtained (the form of the function was the same in both cases, so only the latter is given here).

$$r_c = -20.4489 + 2.4096\bar{r} - 3.7033\bar{C} + 1.1497P_r$$
$$\quad\quad\quad\quad\quad (6.91) \quad\quad (-3.11) \quad\quad (3.78)$$

$$\bar{R} = 0.9426 \quad\quad\quad d = 1.4121$$

(Estimating period: 1961 II–1966 III)

This equation and equation (15) may be interpreted along the following lines. First, the variables $[a:\bar{r}]$ showing the availability and cost of Bank of Japan loans in equation (15) are represented only by $\bar{r}$ in the estimating equation. Second, the amount of credit allocated or rationed as Bank of Japan loans $\bar{C}$ in equation (15) is not actually the outstanding volume of Bank of Japan loans in the estimating equations, but is represented by the ratio of the amount by which deposits with the Bank of Japan exceed required reserves to total deposits of financial institutions with the Bank of Japan. This is based on the idea that the impact on bank behavior is not achieved through Bank of Japan credit allocations themselves, but depends on the extent to which Bank of Japan credit meets the marginal shortage of funds in the money market that remains after adjusting for seasonal fluctuations in the Treasury's account with the public, and the demand for Bank of Japan notes.[4] In the estimating equation, this marginal amount is taken as the amount of deposits with the Bank of Japan in excess of required reserves, and to eliminate the trend it is simply divided by total required reserves. Third, the bank lending rate $\bar{i}$ does not enter into the estimating equation, but the profit rate P_r of corporations, which is an important shift parameter of the net returns from bank lending function $R(L)$ is included in the estimating equation. Fourth, the availability and cost of deposits does not enter the estimating equation at all.

An exactly similar type of regression was estimated for the more recent period 1963 II–1972 II and published by the Bank of Japan Research Department [4]. One equation from that study is the following:

$$r_c = -2.146 + 3.032\,\bar{r} - 9.910\,\bar{C} - 0.088\frac{D_b}{L_b}$$
$$\quad\quad\quad\quad (15.07)\quad (4.97)\quad\quad (1.99)$$

$$\bar{R} = 0.928 \quad\quad d = 1.626$$

In this equation the cost and availability of Bank of Japan credit $[a:\bar{r}]$ is represented only by $\bar{r}$. However, the amount of Bank of Japan credit allocated is represented by the proportion of required reserves accumulated by month-end (i.e. exactly halfway through the measuring period that begins on the 16th of one month and ends on the 15th of the following month). The justification for this measure is that if Bank of Japan credit allocations are too large or too small vis-à-vis the net fund shortage or surplus, this will be automatically reflected in the rate of accumulation of required reserves. Lastly, $\frac{D_b}{L_b}$ is the ratio of deposits held by business enterprises to their borrowings. This indicator shows the extent to which corporate enterprises hold surplus deposits relative to their need for bank loans, and is therefore a substitute variable for $[c:\bar{i}_d]$, the cost and availability of deposits in equation (15). Therefore the difference between this estimating equation and the previous one is in the inclusion or exclusion of the variables $\bar{i}$ and $[c:\bar{i}_d]$.

Turning to the call rate, the estimating equation in the Bank of Japan Statistics Department's financial model was as follows:

---

4. For a more detailed theoretical and practical interpretation of Bank of Japan credit rationing, see below, chapters 10 and 11.

$$RLC = -6.7741 + 1.8233\,RNDIS + 3.8089\,RR + 16.034$$
$$ (8.35) (12.26) (3.06)$$

$$\cdot\,\frac{ZBLD + CURBN}{D'B} - 43.2375\,\frac{LNB + LCNETB}{D'B}$$
$$\phantom{\cdot\,\frac{ZBLD + CURBN}{D'B} -} (6.66)$$

$$+\,0.2530\,RLC_{-1} - 0.2848\,QQ_1 - 0.1044\,QQ_2$$
$$ (5.27) \phantom{RLC_{-1} -} (4.45) (1.61)$$

$$+\,0.2111\,QQ_3$$
$$ (3.29)$$

$$\bar{R}^2 = 0.981 \qquad d = 2.081$$

Key to symbols:
RLC = Call rate
$RNDIS$ = Official discount rate
RR = Reserve requirement rate
$ZBLD$ = Fund surplus ($-$) or deficit of banks
$CURBN$ = Cash held by banks
$D'B$ = Deposits at banks (private and public sector)
LNB = Bank borrowing from Bank of Japan
$LCNETB$ = Liabilities of banks to other financial institutions
$QQ1 \sim 3$ = Seasonal dummies

Apart from the distributed lag RLC_{-1} and the seasonal dummy $QQ1 \sim 3$, this equation is made up of four explanatory variables. The correspondence between these four and those in the theoretical equation (15) is as follows: the official discount rate $RNDIS$ is a substitute variable for $[a:\bar{r}]$, which shows the cost and availability of Bank of Japan credit in the theoretical equation. The required reserve rate RR is an estimate of β, which is a shift parameter for equation (13). The variable $(ZBLD + CURBN)$ shows the trend of movements in bank funds, while $(LNB + LCNETB)$ shows the amount of banks' borrowed funds; both are proxy variables for this cost and availability of deposits $[c:\bar{i}_d]$ and Bank of Japan credit allocations $\bar{C}$ in the theoretical equation. In order to allow for the trend, each is divided by the volume of deposits $D'B$ and shown as a ratio.

Thus interpreted, the estimating equation covers all the variables in theoretical equation (15) with the exception of the bank lending rate $\bar{i}$, and is of the same type as the Bank of Japan Research Department's equation.

2.2 *The Bank Lending Rate*
Chapter 3 demonstrated that the flexibility of quoted bank lending rates in Japan is extremely limited, and that the rates do not adequately perform

the function of equilibrating the supply and demand for loans. Variations in the loan interest rate are, on the whole, determined by periodic revisions in the discretionary lending rates that are instutionally related to the official discount rate. Consequently, in the theoretical model presented above, bank lending rates are treated as exogenous variables, with the bank lending rate $\bar{i}$ being exogenously given. The following discussion is about nominal, published lending rates, unadjusted for the effects of compensatory balances.

For the purposes of building a theoretical model, this necessary simplification is only a first approximation, for actual movements in the lending rates are by no means uninfluenced by the supply and demand for loans or by the arbitrage relationship with other rates of interest, which do move flexibly. This is confirmed by Suzuki [43], where the results of estimation period 1961 II–1966 III (quarterly basis) are published. Here we summarize those results.

First, the simple correlation between bank lending rates (average of all banks' contracted lending rate) and the official discount rate (the standard discount rate) is extremely high at 0.9417. This shows that variations in bank lending rates are largely decided on the basis of an institutional consensus on discretionary lending rates which move in conjunction with the official discount rate. It is interesting to note, for example, that there has been no turning point when lending rates started to turn up before the official discount rate was raised, and there has been no incident when the banks' lending rates started to turn down before the official discount rate was lowered.[5]

Second, table 7.2 shows the results of estimating an equation for the hypothesis that variations in bank lending rate perform the function of balancing the supply and demand for funds using three explanatory variables (partly with a distributed lag). The three variables are: the official discount rate, the call rate—both of which are variables in the supply of loans function—and the corporate profit rate, which is a variable in the demand for loans function. The official discount rate (to which variations in bank lending rates reacted with a distributed lag) was always statistically significant, but the significance of the call rate was low and the sign conditions for the corporate profit rate were contrary to that expected by the hypotheses. From the results, the hypothesis that the bank lending rate performs the pricing function of equilibrating the supply and demand for funds is rejected.

Third, despite the second conclusion, equation (5) in table 7.2 makes

5. After the period covered by the estimating equation (1961 II–1966 III), the average contracted lending rate for all banks turned upward in advance of the official discount rate on two occasions: August 1969 and March 1973. The reason was that, combined with a flattening out in bank lending rates, the proportion of long-term loans (which are at higher rates) increased. Hence, even in these two instances there was no case of an individual contracted rate rising ahead of the rise in the official discount rate.

Table 7.2   Regression Analysis of Bank Lending Rates

Dependent Variable	Explanatory Variables					Constant	$\bar{R}$	d
	$\bar{r}$	r_c	P_{r_1}	P_{r_2}	Lags			
1 i	0.3293 (0.0405)	0.0058 (0.0114)	(−)0.0586 (0.0106)			6.6185	0.9765	1.0200
2 „	0.3764 (0.0550)	0.0015 (0.0168)		(−)0.0687 (0.0272)		6.4625	0.9528	0.6740
3 „	0.1802 (0.0424)	0.0220 (0.0086)	(−)0.0352 (0.0088)		0.3612 (0.0778)	4.2026	0.9891	1.9863
4 „	0.1532 (0.0533)	0.0252 (0.0113)		(−)0.0317 (0.0182)	0.4802 (0.0881)	3.3279	0.9821	1.4381
5 „	0.1331 (0.0549)	0.0204 (0.0115)			0.5374 (0.0863)	2.5982	0.9800	1.2903
1 „	◎	△	×					
2 „	◎	△		×				
3 „	◎	◎	×		◎			
4 „	◎	◎		×	◎			
5 „	◎	○			◎			

Key: ◎ = Significant at 5% level
  ○ = Significant at 32% level
  △ = Consistent with sign conditions of hypothesis but not significant
  × = Inconsistent with sign conditions and not significant
  ( ) = Standard deviation
Symbols: $\bar{r}$ = Quarterly average value of Bank of Japan's basic discount rate
  P_r = Profit rates, derived from corporate survey data (Hojin Kigyō Tōkei Kihō; seasonally adjusted by Census Method X-11 program) as follows (%):
  $$\frac{\text{Operating Profit} \times 4}{\text{Inventory} + \text{Fixed Capital}} = P_{r_1}; \quad \frac{\text{Operating Profit in Past Year}}{\text{Inventory} + \text{Fixed Capital}} = P_{r_2}$$
  r_c = Weighted average (by volume) of central call rate (unconditional) and over-month-end call rate (%)
  i = All banks' average contracted lending rate (%)

it clear that when a distributed lag is used, the call rate is found to have a significant impact on the bank lending rate separate from the official discount rate.

In addition to the official discount rate and the related discretionary lending rates influencing the bank lending rate, the idea that the supply and demand for funds or interest arbitraging may have some influence is also adopted in the Bank of Japan's econometric model. In this model, the bank lending rate is explained by the official discount rate and the long-term preferential lending rate as two exogenous variables, and the ratio between the net excess investment by the corporate sector (investment minus savings) and the banks' lending to the private sector (corrected for trend), as an endogenous variable. The third variable is an ex post ratio of

Chart 7.1 Rates on Regulated Bank Loans and their Relation to Changes in Institutionally Determined Rates

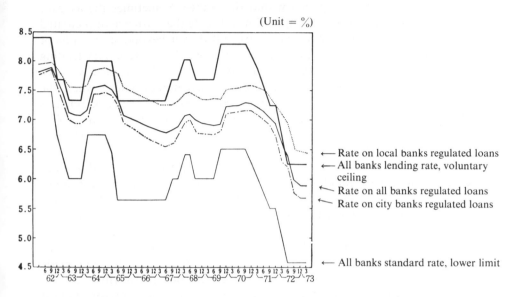

(Unit = %)

← Rate on local banks regulated loans
← All banks lending rate, voluntary ceiling
← Rate on all banks regulated loans
← Rate on city banks regulated loans

← All banks standard rate, lower limit

the external demand for funds for investment in real goods by the corporate sector and the amount of credit allocated to the private sector by the banks, which may also be interpreted as representing the availability of bank loans as seen from the point of view of business enterprises (i.e. variable b in the theoretical model of chapter 5). Following this interpretation, the relative size of the excess demand for bank loans (which underlies their availability) does affect the bank lending rate.

In 1973 the Bank of Japan also published some interesting results of estimating the relation between bank lending rates and the supply and demand for funds and other discretionary interest rates (Bank of Japan Research Department [4]).[6] The study separates the average contracted lending rate of all banks into the rate on regulated loans (less than one year *and* over 1 million yen) and those on nonregulated loans (over one year *or* less than one million yen). The regulated rate is derived from a weighted average of interest rates on the outstanding balance of loans set by the Federation of All Banks Associations. The lower limit for regulated loan rates is generally the "standard" lending rate (the current Bank of Japan discount rate on commercial bills plus 0.25 percent), while the upper limit is the voluntary ceiling (since there are no statistics on overdraft rates, the discussion here is restricted to "discounts on other commercial bills and loans"

6. These estimates were computed by Haruhiko Terada.

which are currently set at the standard rate plus 1.75 percent). Chart 7.1 shows the upper and lower limits for such regulated loan rates, and the average rates actually applying within that range. Sometimes the average level of these rates exceeds the upper limit despite the existence of regulated rates. The reason is that loans which are rolled over beyond six months or high risk loans can in exceptional cases be above the discretionary lending rate ceilings, and for these, loan agreements are reached as if for new loans. The phenomenon occurs either during an easy-money phase when the average rate on regulated loans in the preceding tight-money period remains at or near the ceiling, or when the drop in the ceiling rate is large. This applies particularly to the local banks, whose regulated loan rates are high in relation to city banks.

Chart 7.2 shows the line joining the numerical values of the difference between the proportion of all banks' regulated loans and the proportion of loans granted below the ceiling rates. (This difference is called the proportion of loans at unadjusted rates). If this value is positive, this implies that regulated loans are actually being made at rates higher than ceiling rates on regulated loans; the greater their number, the greater the tendency toward lower rates. Conversely, a negative value implies that loans are being made at rates below the ceiling rate, although these are not necessarily regulated loans; the greater their number, the greater the resistance to lower interest rates or the more likely it is that rates will turn upward.

Turning to the rates on all banks' nonregulated loans, these are the weighted average of rates on all nonregulated long-term loans over one year or on loans less than one million yen. By tradition, such long-term

Chart 7.2   Proportion of Loans at Unadjusted Rates

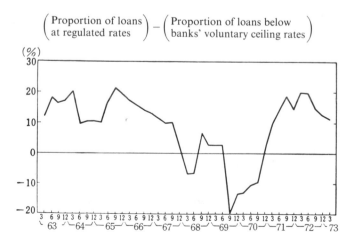

lending rates are based on the most preferential rates granted by the long-term credit banks and the trust banks, such as loans to electric power utility companies, which are normally contracted for ten years but in fact run to fifteen years. However, because these prime rates have always been closely related either to the standard rates available at government financial institutions (the Development Bank of Japan or the Small Business Finance Corporation) or to the issuing conditions in the government and corporate bond markets, they have typically been "political" rates rather than market rates so that, like the rates on regulated loans, the institutional influence is dominant (see chart 7.3). On the other hand, rates on small-sized non-regulated short-term loans are not subject to such institutional factors.

Tables 7.3 and 7.4 give the results of estimating explanatory variables for regulated and nonregulated rates. Following the discussion above, regulated rates are introduced as the first explanatory variable, with the supply and demand for funds and the arbitrage relationship with other interest rates subsequently being introduced as additional explanatory variables.

The first equation in table 7.3 shows that 84.1 percent of the amplitude of fluctuation in the rates on regulated loans can be explained by changes in the official discount rate in the same period. This demonstrates the size and speed of the impact on revisions in the regulated rates of changes in the discount rate. The statistical explanatory power of equation (2), which adds to equation (1) by inclusion of a proxy variable for the supply and demand

Chart 7.3   Relationship between Nonregulated Long-Term Bank Lending Rate, Prime Rate, and Official Discount Rate

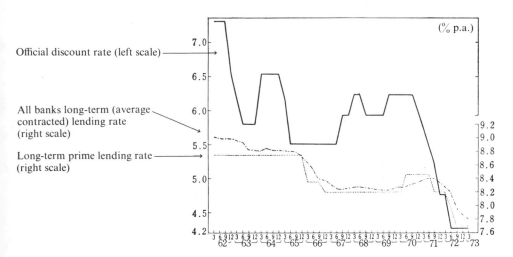

Table 7.3 Estimation of Interest Rate on Regulated Bank Lending

Dependent Variable	Explanatory Variables					Constant	$\bar{R}^2$ (d)
	Impact of Current Quarter Official Discount Rate	Impact of Previous Quarter Official Discount Rate	Impact of Supply and Demand for Funds	Impact of Crude Bank Lending Rate	Impact of Call Rate		
Interest Rate on Regulated Bank Lending							
1	0.466 (10.74)	0.071 (1.61)				0.004 (0.42)	0.841 (1.284)
2	0.466 (11.96)	0.049 (1.20)	(−)0.004 (3.04)			0.086 (3.05)	0.872 (1.702)
3	0.466 (12.79)	0.048 (1.15)	(−)0.019 (2.73)	(−)0.018 (2.23)		0.947 2.78	0.888 (1.781)
4	0.476 (9.99)	0.064 (1.00)	(−)0.019 (2.69)	(−)0.018 (2.21)	(−)0.009 (0.33)	0.976 (2.75)	0.885 (1.766)

Notes: 1. Nonexplanatory variable: amount of rise or fall in all banks' regulated lending rate (end-quarter data).
2. Estimation period: 1963.Q1–1972.Q2.

Table 7.4 Estimation of Interest Rate on Nonregulated Bank Lending

Dependent Variable		Explanatory Variables					
		Impact of Prime Long-Term Lending Rate	Impact of Call Rate	Impact of Supply and Demand for Funds	Impact of Short-Term Lending Rate	Constant	$\bar{R}^2$ (d)
Interest Rate on Nonregulated Lending	1	0.972 (29.00)		(−)0.019 (10.48)		0.531 (1.84)	0.962 (0.760)
	2	0.891 (28.96)	0.044 (6.33)	(−)0.007 (2.68)		0.645 (3.01)	0.980 (0.830)
	3	0.698 (13.12)	0.047 (8.12)	(−)0.003 (1.43)	0.196 (4.10)	0.775 (4.35)	0.987 (1.004)

Notes: 1. Dependent variable is quarterly nonregulated lending rate of all banks.
2. Explanatory variables are: (a) 8-quarterly average of best long-term lending rate of long-term credit and trust banks;
    (b) Ratio of corporate sector deficit to change in borrowings from financial institutions as proxy for supply and demand situation for funds;
    (c) 8-quarter average of all banks' regulated lending rate.
3. *t* values are shown in parentheses.
4. Estimating period: 1963.Q1–1972.Q2.

for funds (the ratio of corporate cash and deposit holdings to borrowings), is somewhat higher, showing that, apart from institutional factors such as the banks' regulated rates, rates on regulated loans are independently influenced by the supply and demand for funds. In equation (3), the proportion of loans at unadjusted rates is added as an explanatory variable, and the explanatory power of the estimating equation is further enhanced, demonstrating the necessity, in judging movements in bank lending rates, of paying due attention to this factor. To test the impact of the call rate, equation (4) includes the call rate as an explanatory variable; but the result is that the sign conditions are perverse and the statistical significance of the equation is lower. The reason is that changes in the call rate are strongly influenced by the official discount rate (i.e. there is multicollinearity), so that the impact of the call rate and the official discount rate on the bank lending rate are statistically indistinguishable. Thus the interpretation of the impact of the official discount rate in equation (3) cannot be restricted to a straightforward institutional effect, but must be extended to include the broader implications of interest determination through the effect of short-term money-market rates on the lending attitude of financial institutions.

In the case of the rate on nonregulated loans, the regression results for all equations tabulated in table 7.4 show the predominant influence of the prime lending rates. Whereas changes in prime lending rates are quite rapidly reflected in new long-term loans, retrospective changes in rates on outstanding loans are rare, so that the overall effect of such changes is spread out over a prolonged period. As a result, the problem shifts to the lag structure between the prime long-term lending rate on new loans and the average long-term lending rate. After much experimenting, it was found that an equally weighted lag structure spread over eight quarters provided the best results. Without appropriate statistics of the time-composition of long-term loans proper treatment is problematical, but the above result suggests that long-term loans are generally turned over once every two years on average.

Equation (1) in table 7.4 adds the supply and demand for funds to the best long-term lending rate as an explanatory variable, and equation (2) incorporates the call rate. Both variables are significant, confirming the independent influence of these two factors on nonregulated loan rates. Equation (3) adds to equation (2) the rate on regulated short-term loans to check the impact on nonregulated loan rates of small-sized loan rates. All variables are significant, demonstrating that banks' prime long-term lending rates, the supply and demand for funds, the call rate, and the rate on short-term regulated loans all have an independent influence on nonregulated loan rates.

8 Corporate and Household Asset Selection Behavior

Chapter 6 presented a theory of bank behavior and chapter 7 showed that estimated results supported the theoretical conclusions. This chapter deals with the corporate and household units of the nonbank private sector and studies their equilibrium in theoretical and empirical terms.

1. *Behavior of the Corporate Sector*

1.1 *Corporate Asset Selection*
The theoretical model in chapter 5 showed that the balance sheet of the corporate sector in Japan can be simplified as follows:

$$D_b + PK_b \equiv L_b \tag{16}$$

Equation (16) shows that the basic asset selection behavior of Japanese corporations may be formalized as a selection between monetary deposits and real capital goods, determined within an internal budget constraint which is decided by the size of bank borrowings.[1]

---

1. Of course, modern Japanese companies have other sources of finance such as capital increases, bond issues, accounts payable, and internal reserves separate from their borrowings. On the assets side, they also hold securities and accounts receivable, which are investments distinct from real physical capital or deposits. However, given the particular characteristics of the financial system and the predominance of overborrowing and indirect finance, capital increases and bond issues are restricted in an overall sense by the lending activities of banks. Moreover, the relative size of investments in securities and the size of internal reserves are small. Finally, intercorporate credit (accounts payable or receivable), together with other forms of lending and borrowing within the corporate sector, are nothing more than the activation of idle balances resulting from deposits supplied by the banking system. Consequently, from a broader perspective, simplification to a model with a choice between real capital and deposits within an asset budget determined by loans as a proxy for bank credit may be considered an

Following the theory presented in chapters 5 and 6 and the statistical analysis of chapter 7, these bank borrowings L_b are not determined by changes in bank lending rates but, given the existence of excess demand, are rationed out by the banking sector. For this reason the choice left to the corporate sector is limited internally by the asset budget permitted by the amount of bank loan allocations. Within the overall budget the relative size of corporate deposits D_b and corporate borrowing L_b is set by the compensatory deposits rate α dealt with in chapters 6 and 7. Therefore the corporate sector does not merely have borrowings L_b allocated by the banking sector: by itself determining the compensatory deposit rate α, it influences bank asset selection behavior and in turn receives the feedback effect on bank lending L_b.

The asset selection behavior of Japanese corporations may be explained by a very general type of expected utility maximization hypothesis.[2] One may postulate that the higher the expected real rate of return on real capital goods, the higher the proportion of borrowings that would be used to invest in such goods, and the less that would be held in the form of deposits. Conversely, the higher the rate of return on deposits, the higher the proportion that would be held in the form of deposits and the less that would be devoted to investment in real capital goods.

In order to confirm this, regression analysis was carried out on (1) the ratio of corporate deposits to borrowed money and (2) the ratio of the value of real capital held by corporations to borrowed funds. The results are presented in table 8.1.[3] Since expectations about the rate of return on real capital are probably influenced by the experience of the preceding year, the expected rate of return on real capital is represented by (a) a weighted average of the rate of return on total capital over the four preceding quarters. As table 8.1 shows, it was found that as (a) rises, (1) decreases and (2) increases (and conversely). For the interest rate on deposits, the difference between the rate payable on borrowed money and the deposit interest rate was divided by the deflator for private-sector plant and equipment investment, and this ratio (b) was added to (1) as an explanatory variable. In this case, if (b) increased, this would mean that the cost of holding deposits with borrowed money, or the cost of holding deposits in place of real capital, had also increased. Alternatively, if (b) were to decrease, that would imply that these kinds of costs had decreased. From the size of the t values and the

---

adequate description of the basic asset selection behavior of Japanese companies. Whenever phenomena treated in this book cannot be explained within this simplified corporate asset selection model, the model has been appropriately expanded.

2. The reader is referred to Suzuki [41], part 2, where there is a detailed theoretical examination of the application of J. Tobin's theory of asset selection to the asset selection behavior of Japanses companies.

3. The estimate was produced by Kuniko Sawamoto, economist at the Research Department of the Bank of Japan.

Table 8.1 Estimation of Corporate Asset Selection Behavior

	a Corporate Profit Rate $\sum_1^4 \omega_1 RK$	b Cost of Holding Deposits $\dfrac{RLB - RDCB}{PIF}\quad\dfrac{RLB}{PIF}$	c $\dfrac{Exports}{Sales}$ $\sum_1^2 \omega_2 \dfrac{EX}{SAL}$	d Net Worth Ratio $\dfrac{NWC}{AS}$	e Distributed Lag $\left(\dfrac{KF}{LBT}\right)_{-1}$	f Constant	Coefficient of Determination Adjusted for Degrees of Freedom Standard Deviation	Durbin-Watson Ratio Degrees of Freedom
1 Deposits $\dfrac{DCB}{Borrowings\ LBC_{-1}}$	(−)1.2953 (3.96)	(−)1.2633 (2.15)	1.3544 (3.24)			56.7698 (8.81)	0.859 0.685	0.559 37
2 Physical capital $\dfrac{KF}{Borrowings\ LBT}$	0.2915 (2.45)	0.5743 (1.21)		0.3694 (2.44)	0.8287 (13.66)	(−)4.3512 (2.36)	0.997 0.407	2.275 36

Notes: 1. Estimating period: 1962.Q1–1972.Q1
2. Values in parentheses are + statistics
3. $\omega_1 = (0.4, 0.3, 0.2, 0.1)$; $\omega_2 = (0.25, 0.75)$

Symbols: DCB = Corporate deposits (at all banks, etc.)

LBC = Loans to corporations (mutual banks and credit associations)

KF = Fixed assets (excl. land) of all corporations

LBT = Borrowings of all corporations from financial institutions

NWC = Net worth of all corporations

AS = Net assets of all corporations

RLB = Average contracted lending rate of all banks, etc.

$RDCB$ = Average interest rate on corporate deposits (weighted average of ordinary and term deposits)

RK = Rate of return on capital of corporations in all industries

PIF = Deflator for plant and equipment investment in private sector

$\dfrac{EX}{SAL} = \dfrac{Exports}{Total\ sales}$; ratio for all industries from BOJ's short-term economic forecast of leading companies

size of the parameters in table 8.1, it was found that increases in (b) were associated with decreases in (1), and decreases in (b) were associated with increases in (1).

In addition to these results, it was also found in the first regression that if (c), the ratio of exports to total sales, rose, then (1) also rose, and if (c) declined, (1) also declined. This implies that with large export receipts flooding into the corporate sector, corporate deposits would increase for a time because there was a lag in the portfolio adjustment process. During 1971–72 these export leads occurred on a huge scale, and a large inflow of short-term, export-related funds into the corporate sector was observed, so this kind of relationship showed up very significantly.

In the second regression analysis, an increase in the ratio of net worth to total assets (d) was associated with an increase in (2), and a distributed lag (e) was also found to exist with a significant statistical relationship. Concerning any cause-and-effect relationship between (d) and (2), there are various possible interpretations, but a fundamental explanation of this relationship would be that when firms carry out large-scale plant and equipment investment projects, whether or not they have to resort to borrowed funds, they frequently increase their capital, thus establishing this kind of relationship. The explanation for (e), the existence of a statistically significant distributed lag, is that it takes a considerable amount of time to make real capital investments (in plant and equipment, etc.) and therefore there is a continuous adjustment process between the actual (2) and the level of (2) desired by the company.[4]

In addition to these observed relationships between real capital and deposits within a budget constraint set by borrowed funds, particular motives for the holding of real capital or deposits (such as deposits for transactions motives) or structural conditions (on account of the real capital coefficient) no doubt have some influence. As seen in table 6.1, the holdings of cash currency and deposits by Japanese corporations can be explained to a statistically significant degree by as many as five variables: namely, the asset motive variables (the expected rate of return on real capital, etc.), a variable reflecting the precautionary motive, a variable reflecting unpredictable or unforeseen changes in the ease or difficulty of obtaining bank loans (the availability of bank credit), and a fixed proportion of borrowed funds.

1.2 *Fluctuations in Corporate Investment*
The same basic analysis applies to fluctuations in holdings of real capital, or corporate investment. As we saw in the previous section, corporate

---

4. If the actual value is continuously converging toward the desired value, the actual value will be a weighted average of the desired value and the actual value in the preceding period. Consequently, the actual value is a function of the factors that influence the desired value and the actual value in the preceding period, with a distributed lag.

investment is heavily influenced by two primary factors: (1) the size of the asset budget (given credit rationing), which is determined by the amount of borrowed funds allocated by the banking sector; and (2) the expected rate of return on real capital, which itself affects the division within the budget constraint between deposits and real capital (the asset motive). Therefore, in Suzuki [41], chapter 10, section 2, the quarterly rates of change in the absolute value of real capital $\hat{K}$ are explained by the quarterly rates of change in total assets $\hat{A}$ and the expected rate of return on real capital r_K. The equation is as follows:

$$\hat{K} = -3.3978 + \underset{(8.73)}{0.6746\,\hat{A}} + \underset{(3.70)}{0.3385\,r_K}$$

$$\bar{R} = 0.8833 \qquad d = 1.9094.$$

The factors affecting corporate plant and equipment investment may be divided into more detailed components. For instance, there is no doubt, first of all, that the asset budget A is determined in an ex post sense by credit allocations from the banks, but from an a priori point of view, the ease or difficulty of bank borrowing (the availability of bank credit, or b in the theoretical model of chap. 5) must clearly be considered. Also, the expected rate of return r_K, (real) demand, supply capacity (and the underlying capital stock), and expectations about the price level are further subdivisions.

In chapter 5, section 2, the corporate investment function given in the general equilibrium structure was a function of the availability and cost of bank credit $[b:\bar{i}]$, the deposit interest rate $\bar{i}_d$, the price level P, and real gross national expenditures y:

$$I = I([b:\bar{i}], \bar{i}_d, P, y) \tag{17}$$

Also, not explicitly included in equation (17) is the hidden shift parameter of the capital stock. The 1971 econometric model of the Bank of Japan estimated (17) directly for secondary and tertiary industries. The two estimating equations took the following form:

$$IF2 = 231.7038 + \underset{(3.92)}{0.1868} \sum_{1}^{4} \left[\frac{5-t}{10} (K\phi R2 \cdot \phi - KF*2_{-1}) \right]_{-t}$$

$$+ \underset{(3.38)}{209.35} \left[\sum_{1}^{2} \left(\frac{3-t}{3} \right) AVAIL_{-t} \right] \cdot \phi_{-1} + \underset{(1.66)}{0.0219\,KF*2_{-1}}$$

$$+ \underset{(3.77)}{11.57} \left[\frac{1}{2} \sum_{0}^{1} \left(\frac{\Delta YC2}{YC2_{-1}} \right)_{-t} \right] \cdot \phi + \underset{(8.16)}{0.7674\,IF2_{-1}}$$

$$\bar{R}^2 = 0.993, \quad s = 107.0, \quad d = 2.14$$

$$IF3 = -77.1463 + 0.8132 \sum_{1}^{4} \left(\frac{5-t}{10}\right)\left(\frac{YC3\phi}{PIF}\right)_{-t}$$
$$ (4.87)$$

$$+ 10.71 \left[\sum_{1}^{2}\left(\frac{3-t}{3}\right) AVAIL_{-t}\right] \cdot \left[\sum_{1}^{4}\left(\frac{5-t}{10}\right)\left(\frac{YC3\phi}{PIF}\right)_{-t}\right]$$
$$(2.40)$$

$$+ 0.0253\, KF*3_{-1} + 0.5358\, IF3_{-1}$$
$$(1.69) \phantom{+ 0.0253\, KF*3_{-1} + } (4.90)$$

$$\cdot\bar{R}^2 = 0.992, \quad s = 104.9, \quad d = 2.27$$

$IF2 =$ Plant and equipment investment by secondary sector (manufacturing) industries

$IF3 =$ Plant and equipment investment by tertiary sector (service) industries

$KF*2 =$ Gross capital stock, secondary sector

$KF*3 =$ Gross capital stock, tertiary sector

$K\phi R2 =$ Equilibrium capital coefficient

$YC2 =$ Secondary sector corporate income

$YC3\phi =$ Tertiary sector, income of nonfinancial corporations

$\phi =$ Index of mining and manufacturing production

$PIF =$ Deflator for private sector plant and equipment investment

$AVAIL =$ Availability

Where the equilibrium, capital coefficient, and "availability" are obtained by the following equations:

$$K\phi R2 = 17.398\left(\frac{1}{4}\sum_{0}^{3} WPIM_{-t}\right)(1 - RC1) \div \left(\frac{1}{4}\sum_{0}^{3} PIF_{-t}\right)$$

$$\left[\left\{0.1925 - RC1 \times \frac{1}{4}\sum_{1}^{4}\left(\frac{KF}{KF*}\right)_{-t}\right\}\frac{1}{4}\sum_{0}^{3}\left(\frac{100 \cdot DF}{PIF \cdot KF_{-1}}\right)_{-t}\right.$$

$$\left. + \left\{1 - 0.521\, RC1 \times \frac{1}{4}\sum_{1}^{4}\left(\frac{KF}{KF*}\right)_{-t}\right\} \times \frac{1}{4}\sum_{0}^{3} RLB1 + 2\right]$$

$KF =$ Net capital stock of private sector (plant and equipment)

$KF* =$ Gross capital stock of private sector (plant and equipment)

$WPIM =$ Wholesale price index of manufactured products

$RC1 =$ Corporate tax rate

$DF =$ Capital consumption allowances of private-sector corporations

$RLB1 =$ Average contracted lending rate of city banks

$RLB2 =$ Average contracted lending rate of local banks

$$AVAIL = -0.0048 + 0.4024 \frac{\Delta LBPSA}{LBPSA_{-1}} - \frac{IF + II - SC - DF}{LBPSA_{-1}},$$

$$LBPSA = \frac{LBP}{SFLBP} \times 100$$

SC = Corporate savings
LBP = Bank loans to private sector (adjusted for underreporting)
$SFLBP$ = Seasonal adjustment factors for bank loans to private sector
IF = Plant and equipment investment of private-sector corporations.
II = Inventory investment of private-sector corporations.

This equation is extremely complex, but it corresponds to theoretical equation (17) in the following ways. First, by estimating a fairly complicated variable, the availability of bank credit b is explicitly introduced.

Second, the bank lending rate $\bar{i}$, through its influence on the equilibrium capital coefficient, affects the level of business enterprises' desired investment in plant and equipment. Interestingly, a nonequilibrium $\bar{i}$ affects investment in a similar way to the availability of credit b.

Third, the effects of prices and real gross national expenditure are each represented by the level of corporate income in each industry sector.

Fourth, the stock of plant and equipment, a shift parameter not treated in the theoretical equation, is explicitly estimated and used for the stock adjustment principle.

Fifth, the deposit interest rate $\bar{i}_d$ is omitted. At some point in the future when the deposit interest rate or the public and corporate bond rates are liberalized, there may be greater amplitude of fluctuation in these rates, which would permit them to be included with slightly more statistical significance. They would then act as the opportunity cost of self-financing.

Table 8.2 shows the estimation of equation (17) in slightly simpler and more easily manageable form. This is a regression of five forms of corporate investment: private-sector inventory investment, plant and equipment investment by large manufacturing corporations, plant and equipment investment by large nonmanufacturing corporations, plant and equipment investment by medium and small manufacturing enterprises, and plant and equipment investment by medium and small nonmanufacturing enterprises. Real income (y) and a proxy variable for bank credit are explanatory variables common to all five functions. For the latter, the absolute increase in cash and deposits (or "money supply" broadly defined) was used, the reason being that when bank credit is readily available, asset portfolio adjustments are delayed and corporate money holdings increase, and conversely (see also chap. 3, table 6.1 above).

Table 8.2 Estimation of Private-Sector Corporate Plant and Equipment Investment Function

1. Inventory Investment Function

| Dependent variable | Explantory Variable | | | | Constant | $\bar{R}^2$ | d |
| | Stock Variable | Demand Variable | Financial Variables | | | | |
	$KIIP_{-1}$	ϕ	$\Delta\left(\dfrac{CD}{WPI}\right)$	$\Delta\left(\dfrac{M}{WPI}\right)$			
Private-sector inventory investment	$(-)0.9044$ $((-)6.4498)$	170.6945 (8.0813)	12.1643 (2.6634)		34.2960 (1.9377)	0.8012	0.9367
	$(-)0.9192$ $((-)5.6243)$	171.1593 (7.2591)		6.7614 (2.2962)	263.6283 (1.5849)	0.7940	0.9221

2. Plant and Equipment Investment Function

Dependent variable	Explanatory Variable						Constant	$\bar{R}^2$	Durbin-Watson Ratio
	Stock Variable $\left(\frac{KF}{WPI}\right)_{-1}$	Demand Variable $\frac{S}{WPI}$	† $\frac{IPML}{WPI}$	Financial Variables $\Delta\left(\frac{CD}{WPI}\right)$	$\Delta\left(\frac{M}{WPI}\right)$	Profit Variable $\left[\Delta\left(\frac{n}{S}\right)\right]_{-1}$			
Plant and equipment investment by large manufacturing corporations	(−)0.1445 ((−)6.8934)	0.2022 (11.3172)		0.4482 (3.0808)			17.9136 (6.2210)	0.9366	0.8631
	(−)0.1498 ((−)5.8224)	0.2050 (10.4048)			0.0668 (1.8548)		18.1775 (5.4551)	0.9287	0.6057
Plant and equipment investment by large nonmanufacturing corporations		0.0394 (21.3575)		0.2654 (4.9635)			4.7597 (4.1601)	0.9678	0.7462
		0.0355 (14.0053)			0.0700 (4.8717)		3.5516 (3.2598)	0.9674	1.0470
Plant and equipment investment by medium and small manufacturing enterprises		0.0334 (10.6692)	0.0772 (4.4525)	(−)0.0224* ((−)0.5762)		69.6501 (3.2108)	(−)3.5664 ((−)3.8973)	0.9836	0.9836
		0.0334 (11.1262)	0.0827 (5.0163)		(−)0.0035 ((−)0.6931)	56.1179 (1.8926)	(−)3.0689 ((−)2.5654)	0.9837	0.9114
Plant and equipment investment by medium and small nonmanufacturing enterprises		0.0282 (21.3030)		0.0055 (0.1265)		296.3235 (3.1857)	(−)7.4585 ((−)4.6680)	0.9731	0.9708
		0.0256 (15.2189)			0.0167* (1.8863)	363.4088 (3.7998)	(−)8.5355 ((−)5.2020)	0.9750	1.1954

Table 8.2—Continued

Notes: 1. Parameters for explanatory variables are shown in the upper section of each row; figures in parentheses below are test statistic + for each variable.

2. All data are seasonally adjusted quarterly (SAQ) statistics.

3. The dependent variable in the inventory investment function is increase in private corporate inventories at 1965 prices (GNP basis, ¥1,000).

4. The dependent variable in the plant and equipment investment function is new additions to fixed assets (*Seasonally Adjusted Statistics of Corporate Enterprises*, ¥100m).

5. Large corporations are those capitalized at over ¥100m; medium and small enterprises are those below this.

6. Estimating period: 1960.Q1–1972.Q1.

Symbols: $KIIP$ = Corporate inventory investment (GNP basis, 1965 prices, ¥ billion)

ϕ = Index of mining and manufacturing production (1970 base)

WPI = Wholesale price index (1965 base)

M = Money supply broadly defined (M_2, end-quarter statistics, quarterly averages of 3-month moving average data, ¥100m)

KF = Corporate fixed asset formation

S = Corporate sales (*Seasonally Adjusted Statistics of Corporate Enterprises*, ¥100m)

CD = Cash currency and deposits held by corporations (—"—)

π = Net profit/loss of corporations (—"—)

$IMPL$ = New investment in manufacturing production facilities by large corporations (—"—)

For the plant and equipment investment function, appropriate sectoral data (by scale of enterprise and manufacturing/nonmanufacturing) has been utilized for the dependent variable.

* = Lagged 1 quarter

† = Proxy variable for parent company investment

In addition, in the equations for private-sector inventory investment and large manufacturing companies, the stock adjustment principle is explicitly introduced through a stock variable. To allow for the impact on component or subsidiary manufacturers of parent company investment, plant and equipment investment by large manufacturers is introduced as an explanatory variable for medium and small manufacturers' investment. Also, a profit variable was added to the explanatory variables for medium and small enterprise investment on the grounds that considerations of profitability (e.g. capital stock or prices) were influential, separate from real demand y.

The results in table 8.2 show that the explanatory variables for inventory investment and large corporations' investment were significant, and that the explanatory power of the equation is considerable.[5] In contrast, the signs for the financial variables in medium and small enterprise investment are perverse, and in nonmanufacturing sectors the significance is low. This is probably because, on average during the estimating period (1960 I–1972 I), banks did not aggressively extend credit to medium and small enterprises and as a result upturns and downturns in their investment did not follow the trend of bank credit extensions. Judging from 1972, when bank credit was more readily available and led to a recovery in both manufacturing and nonmanufacturing investment by medium and small companies, if this episode had been included in the estimating period, the significance of financial variables would probably have been higher.

2. *Behavior of the Household Sector*

The preceding section examined the asset selection behavior of the corporate sector. Given that corporate investment fluctuates in this way, household savings must show corresponding fluctuations. As the theoretical model of chapter 5 showed, a simplified balance sheet of the household sector is as follows:

$$M_h + D_h \equiv W_h \tag{18}$$

Equation (18) shows that the Japanese household sector's budget is composed of the amount of savings taken from income and, within that, households' selection between cash and deposits. The volume of household savings W_h is of course equal to corporate investment PK_b. This savings-investment equilibrium and its financial aspect are, in dynamic terms,

5. This computation was performed by Kagehide Kaku, economist at the Bank of Japan's Research Department.

reconcilable in the following way: Assume that corporate borrowings ΔL_b are allocated among the corporate sector, and as a result there is an increase in deposits ΔD_{b1}. In this case, changes in the corporate balance sheet are as follows:

$$\Delta L_b \equiv \Delta D_{b1}$$

Next, assume that the corporate sector decides to invest an amount $I(=\Delta PK_b)$ on the basis of the expected rate of return on real capital, deposit interest rates, etc., and that it reduces the increase in deposits to ΔD_{b2}, adjusting its assets by holding the difference I. As a result, the change in the corporate balance sheet is:

$$\Delta L_b \equiv \Delta D_{b2} + I$$

As the corporate sector invests the amount I, there is an equivalent flow of funds from the corporate sector to the household sector:

$$\Delta D_{b1} - \Delta D_{b2} = I$$

In the household sector, due to an inflow of funds from the corporate sector, savings S are created, but part of this is held in the form of cash ΔM_h and the remainder is held in the form of deposits ΔD_h. Consequently, changes in the household balance sheet are:

$$S \equiv \Delta M_h + \Delta D_h$$

The outflow of funds from corporate deposits ($\Delta D_{b1} - \Delta D_{b2}$) is equal to the increase in deposits and cash of the household sector:

$$\Delta D_{b1} - \Delta D_{b2} \equiv \Delta M_h + \Delta D_h$$

Looked at from the standpoint of changes in the banks' balance sheets, at first when loans are made to the corporate sector the change in banks' balance sheets is as follows:

$$\Delta L_b \equiv \Delta D_{b1}$$

The corporate asset selection process results in new investment taking place, and, through the multiplier, an increase in income occurs so that an equal amount of savings is generated in the household sector. But equally, the asset selection process of households results in an increase in savings, part of which is in the form of cash balances, so that on the banks' balance sheets there is excess credit creation equivalent to the increase in cash holdings ΔM_h of the household sector:

$$\Delta L_b - (\Delta D_{b2} + \Delta D_h) \equiv \Delta M_h$$

The financial deficit corresponding to the overextension of credit is made up through Bank of Japan borrowings ΔC, and so the final effect on the banks' balance sheet is:[6]

$$\Delta L_b \equiv \Delta D_{b2} + \Delta D_h + \Delta C$$

In the process of these economic events, the determination of the increase in loan volume ΔL_b by the banking sector, the reaction to $\dfrac{\Delta D_{b2}}{\Delta L_b} = \alpha$ by the banking sector, and $\Delta D_h (= \Delta D^*)$ and ΔC, have already been examined in chapters 6 and 7. Section 1 above dealt with the selection of ΔD_{b2} and ΔPK_b by the corporate sector (the internal division of the budget). Therefore the remaining economic behavior to be analyzed concerns the choice between cash currency M_h and deposits D_h in the household sector.

Since the deposit interest rate in Japan has been extremely rigid, however, there is hardly any change in holdings of cash currency M_h and deposits D_h on the basis of asset motivations. In reality, cash currency is held almost entirely for transactions motives, and the residual savings are held as deposits. From the point of view of monetary policy, too, the asset selection behavior of households among cash currency M_h and deposits D_h is simply one of the factors taken as given in the determination of bank behavior. One of the problems for the future will be that, if direct financing becomes more widespread and the proportion of securities held directly by households increases, then a deeper analysis of household asset selection behavior will be required.

Another factor omitted from the theoretical model in this book is the fact that in recent years the dependence on borrowed funds for private-sector housing investment has been rising, and therefore the impact of monetary policy (through bank behavior) on housing investment is gradually becoming very important.[7] It will therefore be extremely interesting in the

6. For a detailed explanation of the financial aspects of the relation between the dynamic processes of investment, savings, and income based on the balance sheets of firms, households, and banks, the reader is referred to Suzuki [40], chapter 6.

7. For a study of the development of loan finance for housing by the banks between 1965 and 1975 and its relation with private housing investment, the reader is referred to a study by the Bank of Japan Research Department [5]. In this paper, new private-sector construction starts (by area) are taken as the unexplained variable, and new housing loans by the banks as one of the explanatory variables for the following regression equation. The results give a quantitative estimate of the impact of bank behavior on housing investment.

future to analyze the household sector as operating under an asset budget constraint determined by borrowing and saving, with cash, deposits, negotiable securities, and housing as the four assets for portfolio selection.[8]

3. *Liquidity of the Nonbank Sector and Money Supply*

The preceding section considered the asset portfolio selection behavior of business enterprises and households. Turning to the effects on the real economy, a frequently discussed topic concerns the size of money balances, or amount of money supply, held by the nonbank private sector (i.e. business enterprises and households together or, more broadly, the liquidity of the nonbank private sector), and its impact on the real economy. Here we shall examine the liquidity of the nonbank private sector, taking the money supply as the centerpiece of the analysis.

3.1. *The Concept of Liquidity*
The word *liquidity* is used in two senses: it is used in discussing the liquidity (i.e. marketability) of such assets as securities, and it is also used in reference to the liquidity (i.e. holdings of money balances) of economic units such as business enterprises.

In the first sense, we mean the ease or difficulty of converting the asset into money. In this case, cash currency itself has 100 percent liquidity, and the same applies to demand deposits, whereas time deposits cannot be converted into money until a specified time interval has passed.[9] For securities, the degree of difficulty or ease of switching into cash depends on their marketability or the time until redemption. Consequently, the liquidity of these financial assets is lower than cash. Further, since for physical assets such as land and commercial or industrial goods time and

$$I_h = -2.287 + 1.9189\, y_{-1} + 0.3137\, L_{-1} - 1.136\, P_{-1}$$
$$(2.87) \quad (6.55) \qquad (3.36) \qquad (4.18)$$

$$\bar{R}^2 = 0.945 \qquad d = 1.904$$

Where I_h is new private construction starts (by area); y_{-1} is real GNP in the preceding period (a proxy for expected income); L_{-1} is new housing loans of all banks and mutual banks plus increase in loans of the Government Housing Loan Corporation in the preceding period; and P_{-1} is the price index of urban land (residential) in the preceding period.

8. The first pioneering analysis of the Japanese personal sector's asset selection behavior in this form was performed by Kazumasa Katō [18].

9. According to J. Tobin's definition, the liquidity of an asset is measured by the time taken for that asset to attain its "full value," and according to this definition money therefore possesses 100 percent liquidity. Tobin places the ratio of selling value (value in exchange) to full value on the vertical axis in a graph, and time along the horizontal axis, so that the curve drawn (the functional relation) defines liquidity. See Suzuki [41], p. 152.

effort are required to find an appropriate price before they can be converted into cash, they are far less liquid than time deposits or securities. Also, regardless of whether an asset is a financial or physical asset, when it is used as collateral its liquidity is far lower.

In contrast, when liquidity is discussed with reference to the liquidity of economic units such as business enterprises or financial institutions, the first consideration is the relative liquidity of the total spectrum of assets held by that economic unit. But in considering the ease or difficulty of obtaining usable cash for any one economic unit, we are concerned not only with the liquidity of the range of assets that it holds, but also with future trends in its return on capital and its capacity to obtain credit from other units. The liquidity of economic units is therefore not only a matter of the amount and type of assets currently held by the economic unit, but, for example, a corporation is affected by the future earnings forecast or its ability to obtain bank credit (the availability of bank credit *b*).

Specifically, the liquidity components for nonbank private-sector corporations and individuals are:

1. volume of money held;
2. liquidity and quantity of other nonmoney financial assets held;
3. trend of net worth;
4. the availability of bank credit.

The volume of money balances (1) can be found from the month-end and monthly average value of money supply statistics, that is, the volume of money held by nonbank private-sector businesses and individuals as a whole. However, the division of cash currency between these two groups cannot necessarily be ascertained, because in Japan there is no statistical breakdown of the holdings of cash currency by economic unit. However, it is possible to estimate at quarterly intervals month-end values for deposit money from statistics of deposits by holder (from all banks, mutual banks, and credit corporations—half-yearly for the latter).

Next, for (2), the volume and liquidity of all nonmoney financial assets, the same data as the above may be used for fixed-term time deposits. Money supply statistics for the private sector outside financial institutions provide the total volume of holdings, and in addition a rough estimate can be made of the composition of the ownership by business enterprises and individuals from statistics of depositors.

For holdings of financial assets other than fixed-term deposits, business enterprises are importantly affected by the liquidity structure of negotiable securities held and intercorporate finance. For individuals, negotiable securities, savings deposits other than fixed-term deposits (e.g. money in trust, loan trusts, insurance premiums, and post-office savings deposits) are also important.

Although there is some problem in the prompt reporting of the assets held by corporations, the Bank of Japan Statistics Department's *Short-Term Economic Forecast for Enterprises*, *Analysis of Business Operations*, and the *Corporate Enterprise Statistics* of the Ministry of Finance provide quarterly (and if not, semiannual) data. The liquidity of negotiable securities varies with their type and maturity, and the liquidity of intercompany credit also varies with the type and schedule of installments payable; thus, even after detailed analysis one can do no more than make an overall judgment.

For individuals' holdings of these assets, especially in the case of securities, the only method available is to estimate the various economic units' holdings from statistics showing the underwriting and absorption of the securities. For trusts, leaving aside the question of whether bearer bonds are held by individuals or not, some statistics are available. If one regards life insurance statistics, post-office life insurance, and post-office savings as entirely taken up by individuals, then these statistics are also available. However, there is again some delay in the collection of such statistics; and also, since such statistics would include a wide variety of other components, even if the volume of holdings of each type were known, it would be difficult to judge the degree of overall liquidity.

For corporations, since the trend value of net worth (3) depends fundamentally on the outlook for corporate profits, the Bank of Japan's *Short-Term Economic Forecast for Business Enterprises* is a useful reference as an assessment of business conditions, although there are limitations in the degree to which its figures are capable of quantitative analysis.

Finally, for the availability of business credit as perceived by business enterprises and individuals (4), the chapter in *Short-Term Economic Forecast for Business Enterprises* entitled "Lending Attitudes of Financial Institutions" is again useful, and it is also possible to make estimates to a certain extent from trends in the average contracted lending rates for all banks. However, again there is the difficulty that there are limitations to the quantitative application of these surveys.

Among the elements which comprise the liquidity of corporations and individuals, currency and fixed deposits may be relatively well monitored from money-supply statistics and statistics of deposits, both in aggregate and classified by holders. For other components of liquidity there are limits to quantitative analysis due to problems of accuracy and delays in collection and publication.[10] A point not to be overlooked is that negotiable

10. A quantitative analysis of liquidity is to be found in the Bank of Japan Research Department's *Short-Term Economic Forecast for Main Industries*, in the section entitled "Judgment of Fund Situation." Here a diffusion index is taken as an indicator of liquidity, which itself derives from a regression analysis of the diffusion index for "Judgment of Cash Currency Level," the diffusion index for "Judgment of Business Conditions" (as an indicator of net worth), and the diffusion index for "Financial Institutions' Lending Attitude" (an

securities and intercorporate credit as components of corporate and individual liquidity are to a great extent determined by money-supply volume and the availability of loan credit. This is because when corporations or individuals convert negotiable securities or accounts receivable into cash, they must either exchange them for cash held by other corporations or individuals, or they must obtain credit from banks (by placing securities or commercial bills with the banks and borrowing against them as collateral). Thus the difficulty or ease of switching into cash from negotiable securities or intercorporate credit ultimately depends on the quantity of money or the availability of bank credit.[11]

Since trends in (3), the value of net worth, must be the same as trends in corporate savings, from the standpoint of the economy as a whole the direction of movement over time must be largely determined by the volume of money supply and the availability of credit which, like individuals' savings, are the sources of finance for investment activity. In contrast, the liquidity of fixed-time deposits has some independent determinants separate from the volume of money supply. This is because these deposits may be converted into cash at the option of the holder and are not, therefore, already constrained by the volume of money or by the availability of credit.[12]

---

indicator of bank credit availability b). The equation below for 1967 II–1973 III was estimated by Haruhiko Terada of the Bank of Japan Research Department.

$$L = -0.26 + 0.92\,M + 0.47\,b + 0.39\,P_r$$
$$\phantom{L = -0.26 + {}} (5.0) \qquad (5.7) \qquad (4.2)$$

$$\bar{R}^2 = 0.95 \qquad d = 1.5$$

The statistical significance of each of the explanatory variables M, P_r, and b in the equation is exceptionally high, supporting the underlying thesis of this book, namely, that the primary elements in the concept of corporate liquidity are cash currency holdings, expectations regarding net worth, and the availability of bank credit.

11. The liquidity of negotiable securities and intercorporate credit is not solely decided by these two elements. When an economic unit holds securities or accounts receivable (short-term claims resulting from sales of commodities), depending on how readily it judges that it can convert these into cash when it is required to economize somewhat on the use of cash balances, such holdings may raise its liquidity independently from the total quantity of money and the availability of credit. However, there are limits to this process of economizing on money balances.

12. Note that even for deposit money and fixed-term deposits, if cash is withdrawn from these accounts the position of financial institutions deteriorates, the availability of credit declines, and therefore these accounts are indirectly dependent upon the availability of credit. As set out in part II, table 6.1, a fixed proportion of corporate borrowings is always held in the form of deposits, and since these deposits cannot normally be drawn upon, their liquidity must be considered to be quite low. However, at the same time that these deposits cannot be withdrawn, they nevertheless are utilized as working balances, and cannot be written off as having no value for liquidity.

Looked at in this way, the essence of liquidity for corporations and individuals as a whole depends on money, fixed time deposits, and the availability of credit. Of these three, the availability of credit is of slightly different character and is, in an ex post sense, reflected in the first two. Leaving it aside for the moment, let us take the first two as representative of corporate and individual liquidity, both because of their convenience from the technical point of view of available statistics, and from the point of view of theory.

By international convention, money (inclusive of demand deposits) is known as M_1, or the money stock, and if time deposits are added this becomes M_2, or money supply broadly defined. Also, though there is some variation according to country, if personal savings deposits are added the sum is known as M_3. Although there is no problem of M_1 being 100 percent liquid, there are some problems in regarding time deposits as having the same liquidity as the remainder of the money stock. Also, individuals' fixed-term and savings deposits are essentially savings that have been set aside and must consequently be judged to have a rather low degree of liquidity.

Since it is statistically difficult to exclude individuals' deposits from fixed-term deposits, and since the deposits held by individuals as savings may at any time, at the option of the holder, in fact be used as a means of payment by conversion into cash, the use of M_1 alone would imply the omission of an important component of liquidity. It therefore seems appropriate to use M_2 as a primary indicator of liquidity in conjunction with M_1. However, since personal savings deposits other than fixed time deposits have a quite distinct characteristic as savings set aside, there are considerable problems in adopting M_3 as an indicator of liquidity. Furthermore, on an international basis the range of M_3 statistics is not consistent.

3.2 *Components and Fluctuations of the Money Supply*
The analysis presented here of the components of M_2 (money supply broadly defined) and the fluctuations of each of those components is based on the view of liquidity given above. Table 8.3 shows a breakdown of M_2 and its holders. The proportions of M_1 and fixed time deposits are in the ratio 4:6, and their breakdown is such that approximately half of M_1 is accounted for by corporate holders, while the majority of fixed time deposits are accounted for by individuals. The breakdown by holders of cash currency is not known, but it is believed that most of the notes and coin are held by individuals. Table 8.4 gives estimates of the lagged correlation coefficients for the timing of fluctuations in each of these components. Leaving aside problems of the size of the correlation coefficients, the results of these findings may be summarized as follows:

Table 8.3 Composition of Money Supply by Components and by Holders

(Unit = ¥ billion, %)

	Cash Currency	Demand Deposits	Money Supply M_1	Time & Savings Deposits	Money Supply M_2
Total	4,453 (23.0) [8.9]	14,929 (77.0) [29.8]	19,381 (100.0) [38.7]	30,652 [61.3]	50,033 [100.0]
Nonfinancial corporations	n.a.	9,576 (49.4) [19.1]	n.a.	12,397 [24.8]	n.a.
Individuals	n.a.	4,748 (24.5) [9.5]	n.a.	17,523 [35.0]	n.a.
Local governments and other public-sector corporations	n.a.	605 (3.1) [1.2]	n.a.	733 [1.5]	n.a.

Notes: 1. Upper row represents average yen values for FY1970; ( ) = component % of M_1; [ ] = component % of M_2.
2. Statistics differ from published figures due to the exclusion of Nōrin Chūkin and Shōkō Chūkin banks, which use different classifications for sectoral analysis of holders.

Table 8.4   Timing of Fluctuations in Components of Money Supply

X	Y	Lag Relationship between X and $Y (X_{t} \rightarrow Y_{t+n})$		
1. Demand deposits of corporations	Demand deposits of individuals	-1 $+0.677$	0 $+0.749$	$+1$ $+0.646$
2. Demand deposits of corporations	Time + savings deposits of corporations	0 $+0.714$	$+1$ $+0.757$	$+2$ $+0.686$
3. Demand deposits of corporations	Real GNP	$+2$ $+0.206$	$+3$ $+0.245$	$+4$ $+0.185$
4. Real GNP	Demand deposits of corporations	$+1$ -0.586	$+2$ -0.703	$+3$ -0.618
5. Demand deposits of corporations	Time + savings deposits of individuals	$+1$ $+0.026$	$+2$ $+0.153$	$+3$ $+0.103$

Notes: 1. Figures in upper section of each row indicate length of lag (n) between variables
(e.g. $+1$ implies that Y lags X by 1 quarter, -1 implies that Y leads X by 1 quarter).
2. Data are 3-quarter moving averages of seasonally adjusted quarterly changes.
3. Estimation period: 1961.Q3–1972.Q1.

1. At the start of an easy-money period, both the demand deposits of corporations and individuals (deposit money) recover. The reason why individuals' demand deposits fluctuate almost simultaneously with corporate deposits is that the working balances of individual business owners represent a high proportion of individual demand deposits, and these deposits reveal the same pattern of fluctuation as that of corporate business deposits. Another way of putting this is to say that the level of corporate deposits D_b, having experienced an unanticipated decline owing to the restraints on the availability of bank credit b, returns to the desired level.

2. About one quarter after the recovery of demand deposits, corporate time deposits begin to increase. This is because the expected returns from real capital are still low, because uncertainty remains about the timing of the recovery of the business cycle, and because deposits held for asset motives and precautionary motives increase in the form of fixed-term deposits. At this stage also, fixed time deposits of individual business owners increase for the same reason, while households' fixed-term deposits have not yet reached the stage of full-scale recovery, and therefore their rate of increase is still low. Consequently, individuals' fixed time and savings deposits as a whole are probably not unduly high.

3. Real economic activity, such as corporate investment in plant and equipment, lags about three-quarters behind upturns in the ratio of corporate enterprise deposits to sales or the recovery in corporate demand deposits.

Chart 8.1   Actual Marshall _k_ and Desired Marshall _k_

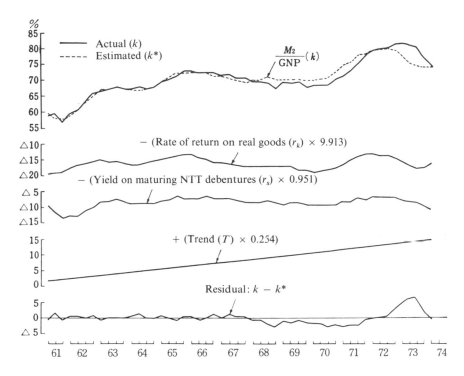

This is because initially unintended declines in corporate deposits tend to be replenished. When sufficient funds have been accumulated for asset and pecuniary motives, and in addition when bank credit allocations increase, the corporate asset budget increases sharply.

4. After a further two to three quarters, there is a full-scale upswing in the business cycle and corporate deposits are run down as business enterprises engage in investment. Also, as personal income rises and the level of consumption expenditure increases, the rate of growth of cash currency similarly rises. As uncertainty about the outlook for the business cycle dissipates, the expected rate of return on physical capital rises and there is a shift within the corporate asset budget of deposits held for precautionary or asset motives to investment in physical capital goods.

5. The pattern traced by individuals' savings and fixed-term deposits during these phases is a gentle one, with a reduction in the rate of growth during tight-money periods and an increase during easy-money periods. Although it is difficult to be precise about their timing, these deposits generally lag about two quarters behind corporate demand deposits. However, it is difficult to discern any statistical correlation between the

two. The pattern of fluctuation in individuals' savings and fixed-term deposits is somewhat vague, because at the same time that the rise in individual income is producing a build-up of individuals' time deposits, individual business-owners are simultaneously running down their deposits for investment purposes and these two effects are superimposed upon one another.

Having studied the components of the broadly defined money supply and their fluctuations, we can turn now to examine trends in the behavior of total money supply. In the upper section of chart 8.1, the solid line shows the ratio of M_2/GNP (nominal), or Marshallian k on a quarterly basis. During the period Marshallian k in Japan exhibited a rising trend, within which there were four main components. Partly because of the low level from which they started following the severe postwar inflation (which had caused massive depreciation of monetary assets), the rate of growth of individuals' savings was in excess of the rate of growth of nominal GNP, and therefore the rate of growth of individuals' savings deposits also exceeded the rate of growth of nominal GNP.

Second, since the asset turnover ratio of corporations is in a long-term, downward trend owing to the rise in the capital coefficient, the total volume of corporate assets grows in excess of nominal GNP. To match this, corporate borrowings and corporate compensatory deposits also show a higher trend growth than nominal GNP.

Third, since money is a luxury good, there is a tendency as income rises for a greater proportion of income to be held in the form of money balances (i.e. the elasticity of money balances with respect to income is greater than unity).

Fourth, money is used in current transactions (represented by the nominal GNP) and, in addition, in Japan for the purchase and sale of existing assets such as shares and land, and for financial transactions. But as assets are accumulated and financial markets develop, these latter kind of transactions increase at a more rapid rate than the current transactions, so that the quantity of money held for transactions purposes has increased at a more rapid rate than nominal GNP.

These factors account for the rising trend in Marshallian k, but since k exhibits cyclical fluctuations, it is appropriate to measure it in terms of deviation from the trend. In other words, it is correct to judge whether there is excess liquidity or a shortage of liquidity in the nonbank private sector with the ratio of M_2 to nominal GNP and to adjust for trend.

We now turn to an analysis of the cyclical fluctuations in detrended k. In the financial model of chapter 5, the private nonbank sector in Japan was summarized in just two variables: broadly defined money supply $(M_h + D_h + D_b)$ and real capital PK_b. Here we shall relax the simplification a little to include bonds. When the nonbank private-sector preference for bonds or real goods increases, intended k declines, and when these preferences weaken, k rises. The preference for bonds depends on their yield; the preference for real goods depends on the expected rate of return, and the preference for holdings of money balances depends on the deposit interest rate. However, as we saw in part I, until 1972 virtually no fluctuation in deposit interest rates occurred. Therefore, omitting deposit interest rates, desired $k*$ may be said to depend on its own trend T, the bond yield r_s, and the expected rate of return on real capital goods r_k.

Estimating Marshallian k with these three variables for the period 1960 I–1973 III, using the yield on maturing NTT bonds for r_s, and the ratio of operating profits to total capital for r_k as in section 1.2 above, we have:

$$k* = -9.913r_k - 0.951r_s + 0.254T + 87.319$$
$$(-6.745) \quad (-4.443) \quad (13.312) \quad (32.403)$$

$$\bar{R}^2 = 0.925 \qquad d = 0.313$$

It is clear from the t values shown in parentheses that the statistical significance of the three independent variables is exceptionally high.[13] The regression coefficient 0.925 is also at a sufficiently high value. The dashed line in the upper section of chart 8.1 shows the estimated value of Marshallian k, $k*$. In the second section of the chart the contribution rates of the variables are shown. Since the parameter for the variable T is 0.254, this means that in Japan Marshallian k tends to rise on average about 1 percentage point ($= 0.254 \times 4$) per annum. Also, as chart 8.1 shows, after allowing for the trend in k, its fluctuations mainly reflect the cyclical variations in the yield on securities and the expected rate of return on capital.

In this regression equation there is one problem. The Durbin-Watson statistic is very low, at 0.313. The reason for this may be observed in the residual $(k - k*)$, which does indeed exhibit serial correlation. The existence of the residual implies that there is a difference between intended and actual Marshallian k (i.e. $k*$ ex ante and ex post), due to the actual supply of money. Consequently, when $(k - k*)$ is positive (for example, in 1972–73), money supply was growing in excess of the desired rate and an "excess liquidity" situation was created. Conversely, when $(k - k*)$ is negative, (for example, in 1970), the money supply was being squeezed below the desired level and a situation of "liquidity shortage" was created. In a period of excess liquidity, the nonbank private sector will adjust to the excessive

13. This computation was performed by Shigehisa Hattori and Masaru Nakano of the Research Department of the Bank of Japan.

quantity of money (M_2) by increasing its holdings of real capital and securities, so that the price of land and other existing assets will rise, share prices will rise, and interest rates will be lowered, while in periods of liquidity shortage the converse will hold.

3.3 *Determinants of Money Supply*

Having considered the components and fluctuations in broadly defined money supply from the standpoint of the asset selection behavior of corporations and households, we now turn to consider the determinants of overall fluctuations in the broadly defined money supply.

Given that the total quantity of money is composed of cash currency held by businesses and individuals in the nonbank private sector, plus demand deposits and fixed-term deposits, the factors determining its overall movements may be described by consolidating the balance sheets of the government, the Bank of Japan, the city banks, and the foreign sector, netting out the flow of funds between these four sectors and considering the flow of funds between the four consolidated sectors and the corporate and individual nonbank private sector. Such an analysis reveals that corporate and individual nonbank private-sector holdings of cash, demand deposits, and fixed-term deposits rise and fall for the following reasons:[14]

1. Expansions and contractions in the volume of credit granted to corporations and individuals outside the banking system and to local government bodies by the banks;

14. Changes in the balance sheets of the government, Bank of Japan, the banking system, and the foreign sector with a simplification of capital accounts are as follows. By comparison with the theoretical model of the balance sheets of the Bank of Japan and the banking system in part II, table 5.2, this represents an extension necessary to incorporate the determinants of money supply. It also incorporates the government and foreign sectors excluded from table 5.2.

1. *Government:* Excess investment + increase in foreign exchange + increase in government deposits = new issues of government bonds;

2. *Bank of Japan:* Increase in loans + net purchase of securities + increase in foreign exchange reserves = increase in cash held by banking system (including deposits at Bank of Japan) + increase in cash currency held by corporations and individuals + increase in government deposits;

3. *Banking System:* New credits to the private sector + increase in holdings of government bonds + increase (net purchases) of foreign exchange + increase in cash currency holdings (including deposits at Bank of Japan) $\equiv$ increase in demand deposits + increase in time and savings deposits + increase in borrowings from Bank of Japan;

4. *Foreign Sector:* Overall surplus on international balance of payments $-$ increase in foreign exchange held by banks $\equiv$ increase in foreign exchange held by government and Bank of Japan.

If the balance sheets of the above four sectors are consolidated and the flow of funds between the four sectors eliminated, we are left with the flow of funds among corporations and individuals in the nonbank private sector, that is:

2. Expansions or contractions in the volume of credit advanced by the banks to the government through the underwriting or redemption of government debt. In these instances, the government is effectively making disbursements of funds or withdrawing funds from corporations and individuals in the nonbank private sector.

3. When corporations or individuals export goods and import capital, receipts of foreign exchange from overseas are recorded. Similarly, the import of goods and export of capital implies remittances of foreign exchange. When this foreign exchange is bought from or sold to banks, there is an effect on the money supply.

Table 8.5 shows the different contribution ratios of assets corresponding to the money supply for 1965–72. In the table, the government sector has been further divided into two elements—central government and other government agencies (local government bodies, public-sector corporations, etc.)—so that there are four groups of assets whose expansion or contraction together correspond to fluctuations in M_2. It is important to note that there is no necessary relationship between fluctuations in the component elements of bank assets and those of the money supply (cash currency, demand deposits, and time deposits), except in the case of corporate deposits, which are held as compensating balances against bank loans. Whereas the composition of bank assets is determined by the behavior of the banks, the composition of bank liabilities is determined by the choices of the individuals and corporations that hold those claims.

Increase in cash currency held by corporations and individuals
+ increase in demand deposits + increase in time and savings deposits
≡ increase in government securities held by the Bank of Japan and by the banking system
+ (net excess of government investment − new issues of government bonds)
+ increase in credit from the banking system to private sector
+ overall surplus on international balance of payments.

In the above equations the left-hand side represents the increase in the quantity of cash currency, deposit currency, and savings deposits held by the private nonbank sector, that is, the increase in broadly defined money supply. The right-hand side shows the components of the changes. The sum of the first two items represents (2) in the main text, the third item represents (1), and the fourth represents (3).

Table 8.5 Increase in Money Supply and Constituent Factors

	Annual Increase		Year-on-year Increase (%)			Contribution Ratios for Assets Corresponding to M_2 (%)			
	M_1	Quasi Money	M_1	M_2	Of Which Quasi Money	Foreign Assets	Credit to Central Govt.	Credit to Local Govt. + Other Public Sector	Credit to Private Sector
CY 1965	15,830	22,889	18.2	18.0	17.9	3.5	9.4	2.8	84.3
1966	14,288	26,995	13.9	16.3	17.9	2.2	15.2	1.8	80.8
1967	16,526	29,224	14.1	15.5	16.4	-3.7	15.1	1.3	87.3
1968	17,862	32,699	13.4	14.8	15.8	6.4	12.1	3.0	78.5
1969	31,275	41,185	20.6	18.5	17.2	9.3	5.8	1.8	83.1
1970	30,770	47,605	16.8	16.9	16.9	5.9	1.9	2.1	90.1
1971	63,336	68,273	29.7	24.3	20.8	18.1	-2.6	2.2	82.3
1972	68,330	98,093	24.7	24.7	24.7	7.5	3.6	2.5	86.4

Note: M_1 = Cash currency + demand-type deposits; quasi money = Time + savings deposits; $M_2 = M_1$ + quasi money. These are year-end statistics.

PART III
Japan's Monetary Instruments

In part III, consideration is given to Japan's monetary instruments. Given the structural conditions examined in part I and the monetary mechanism studied in part II, my objective in part III is to ask how the instruments of Japanese monetary policy operate, and what effect the instruments have on the banking system.[1] The impact of each instrument upon the behavior of banks is examined individually here, while the overall impact of monetary policy on the Japanese economy is considered separately in part IV.

1. This book is concerned mainly with an analysis of the functioning of monetary policy and the mechanism whereby it has its effects. Readers interested in the institutional aspects of monetary policy should refer to Bank of Japan Economic Research Department [1] and [2].

9 The Supply and Demand for Funds and Monetary Stabilization

1. *The Financial Surplus/Deficit of the Private Sector*

1.1 *Component Elements of the Financial Surplus or Deficit*

Chapters 6–8 explored the asset selection behavior of the banking sector, the corporate sector, and the household sector, which together comprise the private sector. The net effect of the interaction of the asset selection behavior of these three groups, confirmed in chapter 8, section 2, was a growing financial deficit for the private sector as a whole.

The banks extend loans to the corporate business sector, which is thereby enabled to acquire more (i.e. invest in) real capital within its asset budget; this leads to an increase in national income and the accumulation of savings in the household sector corresponding to the size of the corporate sector's investment. Part of this increment will be held as cash currency for transactions purposes in proportion to the increase in national income. The funds that have flowed out of derivative corporate deposits through the process of implementing investment projects flow back to the banking sector as (primary) deposits of the household sector equivalent in size to the sector's accumulation of capital, but the part required for cash currency purposes does not flow back. The banking sector therefore finds that its overall lending to the private sector exceeds its deposits from the private sector by the amount of the net cash currency demand, and consequently experiences a financial deficit. Since the deficit cannot be made up from within the private sector, it must be made up outside the private sector, that is, by reliance on central bank credit.

The core of monetary policy lies in providing the credit necessary to offset the financial deficit of the private sector, and in devising the methods for supplying that credit; monetary policy has also developed as a means of influencing bank lending, which is the starting point in the process of creation of the financial deficit. In accomplishing these immediate tasks,

151

the wider role of monetary policy is to control the level of aggregate expenditures in the economy and thereby to achieve stable prices.

Since the financial surplus or deficit of the private sector varies from day to day, monetary policy must operate through daily stabilization operations to supply or absorb credit on a day-to-day basis. A proper understanding of monetary policy in practice therefore requires knowledge, both of the fluctuations in the component elements of the daily financial surplus or deficit of the private sector, and the appropriate instruments for daily stabilization operations. The widespread lack of understanding of monetary policy among the general public stems mainly from ignorance about these details.

The financial surplus or deficit of the private sector is derived from the change in the demand for cash currency, on the one hand, and as a result of transactions on current and capital account between the private sector and the government and foreign sectors, on the other. Current transactions with the government sector involve tax payments, which are a deficit item in the private sector's flow of funds, and payments by the government to firms and households in the private sector for services relating to public-sector investment and other government expenditures and transfers that are surplus items for the private sector. Transactions on capital account include the underwriting of government bonds or government-guaranteed bonds, deposits with the post-office savings system, payment of premiums into the postal life assurance system, and repayments of borrowings from government-owned financial institutions—all of which are deficit items for the private sector. Conversely, the redemption of government or government-guaranteed debt, withdrawals of deposits from the post-office savings system, or payments to the private sector by the postal insurance scheme, and new financing by government financial institutions for the private sector all constitute surplus items for the private sector. The net balance of current and capital transactions is reported as the "Net Balance of Receipts (Δ) or Payments to Private Sector on the Treasury's General Account (incl. Bond Issues)." (See table 9.1 below.)

Turning to transactions between the private sector and the foreign sector on current and capital account, any net balance reflected in purchases and sales of foreign exchange by the Foreign Exchange Special Account must equal the financial surplus or deficit of the private sector. If the private sector sells foreign exchange obtained as a result of a surplus with the foreign sector, the private sector will experience a financial surplus, and conversely, if it is in deficit with the foreign sector and buys foreign exchange from the Foreign Exchange Special Account, the private sector will experience a financial deficit. The financial surplus or deficit resulting from current and capital transactions with the foreign sector is reported as the "Net Balance of Receipts (Δ) or Payments to Private Sector by Foreign Exchange

Table 9.1   Factors for the Supply and Demand for Funds

(Units = ¥100 million)

	Net Banknote Issue	Increase or Decrease (△) in Reserve Requirements	Net Balance of Receipts (△) or Payments to Private Sector on the Treasury's General Account (incl. Bond Issues)	Net Balance of Receipts (△) or Payments to Private Sector by Foreign Exchange Special Account	Net Other Receipts (△) and Payments	Bank of Japan Credit Increase or Decrease (△)	Loans	Net Purchases (△) or Sales (△) of Bills and Bonds
1962	3,115	682	1,099	731	905	2,872	△ 1,295	4,167
1963	2,415	51	5,758	△318	2,010	△ 959	△ 453	△ 506
1964	2,649	△263	2,342	230	721	535	5,173	△4,638
1965	3,496	21	△ 710	△367	996	5,590	1,133	4,457
1966	4,981	445	△ 613	△421	1,548	8,008	△ 2,261	10,269
1967	6,304	245	△ 794	3,008	792	5,127	481	4,646
1968	7,694	586	△ 4,064	3,494	4	8,854	3,785	5,069
1969	7,447	812	△ 9,331	4,466	228	13,352	4,116	9,236
1970	8,517	△ 35	△20,066	43,998	△ 3,746	△19,196	△16,725	△2,471
1971	19,030	782	△18,498	17,397	1,310	22,223	14,413	7,810
Cumulative total	65,648	3,326	△44,882	72,218	4,768	46,406	8,367	38,039

Note: Net Banknote Issue + Increase or Decrease (△) in Reserve Requirements − Net Balance of Receipts (△) or Payments to Private Sector on Treasury's General Account (incl. Bond Issues) − Net Balance of Receipts (△) or Payments to Private Sector by Foreign Exchange Special Account + Net Other Receipts (△) and Payments = Increase or Decrease (△) in Bank of Japan Credits.

Special Account" (see table 9.1 above). To summarize, the financial surplus or deficit of the private sector can be expressed in the following identity:

> Private Sector Financial Surplus/Deficit $\equiv$ Net change in private sector holding of cash currency + net balance of Treasury's General Account (incl. issues of government bonds) with the private sector + net balance of the Foreign Exchange Special Account with the private sector   (19)

1.2 *Seasonal Fluctuations in the Private Sector's Financial Surplus/Deficit and Irregular Disturbances*

The private-sector financial surplus/deficit shown in (19) reflects both seasonal and irregular fluctuations in each of its three components, and itself exhibits seasonal and irregular fluctuations. The seasonal variations largely result from the seasonality of the net balance of the Treasury's General Account and the net change in private-sector holdings of cash currency. The annual seasonal pattern of the Treasury's account is as follows:

April	Large disbursements (payments in settlement of accounts for preceding fiscal year, subventions to local governments, etc.)
May–July	Net receipts (corporate tax payments, personal income taxes, etc.)
August	Large receipts (from personal income-tax payments, combined with relatively low expenditures)
September	Net disbursements (subventions to local government)
Oct.–Dec.	Large disbursements (payments for rice harvest, subventions to local government, year-end bonuses to government employees)
Jan.–Feb.	Large receipts (income-tax payments, etc.)
March	Approximate balance between receipts and disbursements

This seasonal pattern is to a great extent determined by institutional factors, as well as by nature. For example, subventions to local governments are institutionally arranged to occur in April, June, September, and November, while payments for public works tend to be concentrated in March and April when the fiscal year ends and settlements are made, and at year-end in December. On the receipts side, corporate tax payments follow the closing of accounts in June and December, the income tax on bonus payments is deducted at source in July and January, while income-tax statements are filed in August, December, and March. Receipts on the Treasury's Food Account are quite stable throughout the fiscal year, but on the payments side, disbursements are concentrated in the fall harvest, peaking in October.

Table 9.2   Seasonal Adjustment Factors for Component Elements of the Private-Sector Financial Surplus or Deficit

	Jan.	*Feb.*	*Mar.*	*Apr.*	*May*	*June*
Government receipts from private sector	96.27	81.41	171.72	90.08	81.75	109.24
Government payments to private sector	43.09	67.63	178.56	121.81	79.88	93.78
Month-end banknote issue outstanding	99.18	100.24	100.98	100.09	95.66	101.52

	July	*Aug.*	*Sept.*	*Oct.*	*Nov.*	*Dec.*
Government receipts from private sector	91.35	96.96	106.52	79.13	73.88	121.89
Government payments to private sector	77.22	70.77	116.74	104.19	106.26	140.51
Month-end banknote issue outstanding	100.52	97.35	96.06	95.32	96.38	116.80

The overall seasonal pattern of the Treasury's General Account on both the receipts and payments sides can be confirmed by reference to the seasonal adjustment factors shown in table 9.2.

Seasonal variations in the banknote issue (i.e. private-sector holdings of cash currency) are also shown by the seasonal adjustment factors in the same table. The banknote issue tends to expand in February–April, reflecting the spring upturn in consumer spending and settlements at the fiscal year-end; in May there is a contraction following the reflux of funds used by consumers in the Golden Week period; and in June and July there is another tendency to expansion due to the midsummer gift-giving season and the resumption of consumer expenditures with the summer season. Subsequently, in August–November these funds flow back and there is a contraction, until a huge expansion occurs in December due to bonuses, year-end gifts, year-end consumer spending, and the year-end settlement of corporate accounts, most of which flows back in January, when there is again a contraction.

Reflecting the seasonal elements in the net balance on the Treasury's General Account and the change in the private sector's holdings of cash currency, the overall financial position of the private sector exhibits a deficit in December, January, and February, a surplus in March, April, and May, deficits again in June, July, and August, and a surplus once more in September, October, and November. The largest single variation is the financial deficit in December due to the big increase in demand for cash currency at that time.

In the past, the largest irregular cause of variation in the private sector's financial surplus or deficit was the fluctuation in the Special Food Account within the Treasury's General Account depending on whether there had been a good or bad rice harvest. After 1965, harvest conditions stablized and an independent distribution system was set up so that the relative importance of the Special Food Account within the public sector's overall financing requirements was diminished, and its disruptive influence on the private sector was also reduced. In its place, however, the net balance of the Foreign Exchange Special Account emerged as the major unpredictable element, with net transfers of yen funds resulting from short-term capital flows reaching the enormous sum of ¥489,500 million at the time of the Deutsche Mark crisis in May 1971, and ¥1,643,300 million at the time of the Nixon shock in August 1971.

Between 1955 and the early 1970s there were two occasions when the private sector experienced massive financial surpluses due to irregular factors. The first was in the fourth quarter of 1955, when the Special Food Account made enormous disbursements following an excellent harvest, and a simultaneous balance of payments surplus meant that the Foreign Exchange Special Account had made large disbursements. The second occasion was in 1971, particularly in the May and August episodes just mentioned, when fears of an upward revaluation of the yen during international monetary crises produced huge inflows of funds from abroad and the Foreign Exchange Special Account made massive yen disbursements to absorb the inflow. Since in both cases the Bank of Japan attempted to offset the private sector's financial surplus by winding down its loans to the banking system, overloan was temporarily eliminated.

In practice, seasonal and irregular variations in the private sector's financial surplus or deficit also occur on a minute, day-to-day scale. The Business Department of the Bank of Japan therefore forecasts the three component changes in the private sector's financial surplus or deficit in equation (19), estimates the daily movements in the total, and decides on the combination of instruments it will utilize and the policy stance to be adopted in conducting stablization operations.

1.3 *Trends and Cycles in the Private Sector's Financial Surplus or Deficit*
Having adjusted for seasonal or irregular variations as described in the preceding section, the private sector as a whole exhibits a widening secular deficit corresponding to the annual increase in the demand for cash currency. This is because, of the three factors accounting for the private-sector financial surplus or deficit in equation (19), the balances of the Treasury's General Account and the Foreign Exchange Special Account with the private sector will, over the long run, be in equilibrium. In the case of the Treasury's General Account, so long as the Treasury is unable to receive credit directly

from the Bank of Japan—for example, by the Bank of Japan underwriting government bonds—it is impossible for it to run a long-term secular deficit: it must, from a funding point of view, balance its books. Equally, so long as the government does not resort to obviously inefficient behavior, such as not utilizing tax revenue for financing government expenditures or redeeming government debt, but uses it simply for accumulating cash reserves, the Treasury's General Account cannot exhibit a secular surplus.[1] Similarly, the Foreign Exchange Special Account and the international balance of payments are unable to sustain either secular deficits or surpluses because of the international financial constraints that would come into force.[2]

Thus, under "normal conditions," the net balances with the private sector of the Treasury's General Account and the Foreign Exchange Special Account are in equilibrium, so that in terms of the trend in the private sector's financial position, the sector shows a deficit equal in size to what is known in Japan as "growth currency," or the increase in the private sector's cash currency holdings parallel with the growth of the economy.

However, the secular trend toward an increasing financial deficit is also subject, over the medium term, to fluctuations in the business cycle. The reason is that, during a cyclical expansion in economic activity, all three components of the total private-sector surplus or deficit tend to move into deficit, and conversely move into surplus during a downturn in economic activity, and these forces tend to have a dominant effect in aggregate. During economic expansions cash currency tends to increase relative to trend, reflecting higher consumption expenditures and higher levels of cash settlement between companies; and during economic recessions these forces moderate so that it declines relative to trend.[3] Similarly, during economic expansions, the Treasury's General Account experiences a natural increase in tax receipts, post-office savings deposits, postal insurance premiums, and contributions to the post-office pension scheme, so that on the revenue

1. Unfortunately, recent fiscal policy has exhibited this kind of inefficient behavior. From about 1970 onward, the Treasury's General Account with the private sector showed huge net absorptions or net withdrawals on account of the steep rise in surplus funds from the Trust Fund Bureau due to the delay in implementation of budgeted expenditure programs. From the viewpoint of efficient appropriation of fiscal revenues, this constitutes a major problem. (For actual statistics of the General Account's net withdrawals from the private sector, see table 9.1.) An increase in such net withdrawals during periods of overheating in the business cycle, balanced by net disbursements of such funds during recessions, is rational behavior; but from 1970 onward there was a growing tendency toward surplus irrespective of the state of the business cycle, which must call into question the wisdom of the policy.

2. The Foreign Exchange Special Account recorded huge net withdrawals when the country's foreign exchange reserves were increasing rapidly in 1971 and 1972, but after the floating of the yen in February 1973, this situation reversed itself.

3. For details of cyclical fluctuations in the demand for cash currency, see Yoshio Suzuki [40], chapter 3.

side it tends to absorb funds from the private sector. On the expenditure side, too, because there is a tendency to underestimate tax revenues (or alternatively, there is a time-lag between the increase in revenues and an increase in expenditures), and because there is an attempt to hold back expenditures for policy reasons, the overall trend is toward a surplus. In economic recessions not only do these factors go into reverse, but expenditures outpace revenues, so that combined with policy pressures to step up expenditure, the balance of the Treasury's General Account with the private sector tends to exhibit a deficit (= private-sector surplus). Finally, the balance of the Foreign Exchange Special Account tends to show net receipts during economic upswings as the balance of payments moves toward a deficit, and net disbursements during economic recessions as the balance of payments moves toward a surplus.

An accurate summation would be that the consolidated financial surplus or deficit of the private sector therefore normally exhibits a secular financial deficit corresponding over the long term to the increase in private-sector holdings of cash currency, but that it also shows cyclical fluctuations parallel to fluctuations in the economy.

2. *Stabilization Operations in the Money Market*

The private-sector financial surpluses or deficits examined in the preceding section appear, in concrete terms, in the form of excess demand for the available supply of funds on a day-to-day basis in the short-term money markets.

First, let us assume that there will be a prospective financial deficit as a result of an increase in cash currency requirements of the private sector. As we saw in chapter 8, section 2, such an increase leads to an exactly similar increase in loans relative to deposits for the banking sector as a whole (because loans made from the banks' derivative deposits flow back as primary deposits to the banking system except for an amount corresponding to the increase in cash currency). Therefore, adding up the demand and supply in the short-term money market where individual banks are attempting to accommodate among themselves for the net financial surplus or deficit, there will always be excess demand equal to the increase in demand for cash currency holdings by the private sector.

A deficit in the Treasury's General Account with the private sector is the amount by which private-sector receipts from the government exceed private payments to the government. Therefore, assuming these transactions to be by firms and households, since the total deposits of firms and households with the banks must have decreased by the difference between receipts and payments, deposits with the banking system will have fallen below bank lending by the same amount, producing a financial deficit in the banking sector. The result is an excess of demand over supply in the short-term money market.

The same argument applies to the Foreign Exchange Special Account. When firms and households buy foreign exchange from the account for payment to the foreign sector, their yen funds held on deposit will decline by the amount required to purchase the foreign currency. The banking sector therefore experiences a deficit equal to that amount, and this shows up again as an excess of demand over supply in the interbank market.

Where the other party in the transactions with the General Account or the Foreign Exchange Special Account is neither firms nor households but is the banking system itself, the case is even more straightforward. So long as the government and the foreign sector do not hold deposits with the banks, such payments by the banks add nothing to deposits in the banking system; therefore, this is a straightforward case of a deficit to the banking sector and produces an excess of demand over supply in the short-term money market.

In these instances, we have traced the consequences of a private-sector financial deficit, but in the converse case of a private-sector financial surplus, either deposits or the cash held by banks increases and this produces an excess of supply over demand in the money markets. Since the financial surplus or deficit of the private sector is thus reflected every day in the supply-demand situation in the money market, this supply-demand situation also exhibits the same four elements of seasonal variation, irregular disturbances, and secular and cyclical trends.

Daily stabilization operations of the Bank of Japan are therefore concerned with two issues: (1) neutralizing changes in the financial surplus or deficit due to seasonal or irregular elements and counteracting any disruptive effects on the money market and on bank behavior of temporary disturbances; and (2) devising an appropriate policy stance and response to the remaining cyclical or secular elements in the financial surplus or deficit after other factors have been neutralized, in order to produce the desired policy impact on the money market and on bank behavior.

As will be explained in chapters 10 and 11, until the start of the "New Scheme for Monetary Control" in 1962, most of the burden of (1) and (2) was shouldered by loan policy. However, it was difficult for such changes in Bank of Japan credit to convey the distinction between (1) technical adjustments intended to neutralize seasonal or irregular variations, and (2) policy adjustments to cyclical or secular fluctuations, either in terms of their subjective acceptance by the city banks or in terms of their objective effect on monetary policy. After the introduction of the New Scheme for Monetary Control, however, the Bank of Japan tried to adjust for the technical factors in (1) and (2) within the framework of the secular trend in the financial deficit (i.e. corresponding to the long-term growth in cash currency requirements). The New Scheme was implemented through operations in the bond and bill markets, and changes in loan policy were utilized as the primary method of achieving broader policy adjustment effects. (In practice, since the maneuverability afforded by loan policy was much greater, it was frequently also used to adjust for (1); on this point see chapter 10.)

Neutralizing the seasonal or irregular changes in the private sector's financial balance requires a supply of Bank of Japan credit (in the case of a deficit) or its absorption (in the case of surplus) in an amount exactly corresponding to the size of the predicted deficit or surplus. Given such a supply (or absorption), there will be no net impact on the short-term money market or on bank behavior. For these purposes the most suitable instrument is the purchase or sale of short-term government securities and commercial bills at the call rate or bills discount rate prevailing in the money market—in short, open-market operations.

However, in correcting for cyclical or trend variations in the financial deficit (after having adjusted for seasonal and irregular disturbances) and in exerting a deliberate policy impact, Bank of Japan loan allocations are the most appropriate instrument. This is because Bank of Japan credit also causes changes in money-market interest rates and has a direct effect on commercial bank lending attitudes.

Naturally, this division is only one of principle, so that technical adjustments (1) are sometimes accomplished by loan policy, and policy adjustments (2) are sometimes achieved by operations in bills and bonds. The reason why loan policy is sometimes used for technical stabilization purposes is that, like operations in commercial bills, adjustments to the volume of outstanding loans can be made with ease, and therefore it is often the best antidote to unforeseen disturbances. Equally, the reason why operations in bonds or commercial bills are sometimes used for stabilization policy is that when these transactions do not take place in the market, but occur outside the market directly between the Bank of Japan and a city bank (or with a designated bank via a money-market broker), the effect is identical to the allocation of the same amount of Bank of Japan loans. Moreover, if operations in the market in response to the private-sector financial deficit are either too large or too small, the difference can ultimately be adjusted for by variations in loan allocations and an identical policy effect can be achieved.

The reserve requirement system is not an instrument for daily stabilization purposes because it requires banks to maintain required levels of deposits with the Bank of Japan averaged over one month. Taking a slightly longer perspective, use of reserve requirements to offset the cyclical or trend fluctuations in the private-sector financial deficit is not without meaning, but since as a matter of operational practice the financial deficit is allowed to expand in a tight-money policy phase, and to contract in an easy-money phase, it is difficult to manipulate reserve requirements as an instrument for stabilizing the supply-demand situation in the short-term money market.

Finally, statistics for the private sector's financial deficit and its counterpart in the form of Bank of Japan credit are shown in table 9.1. Over the period 1963–72, the private-sector financial deficit reached a total of ¥4,640,600 million, mostly accounted for by an increase of ¥6,564,800 million in private-sector holdings of cash currency, the net absorption of ¥4,574,700 million by the Treasury's General Account, and a net disbursement of ¥7,222,100 million from the Foreign Exchange Special Account. The reason for the bias toward surpluses and deficits in these two accounts respectively, is that from 1970 onward the Trust Fund Bureau experienced a huge accumulation of surplus funds in the General Account, and in 1970–71 the rapid increase in foreign exchange reserves put the Foreign Exchange Special Account into deficit in yen terms. From the viewpoint of resource allocation, both were highly inefficient and ought not to continue over an extended period.

To meet the private-sector financial deficit of ¥4,640,600 million, the Bank of Japan supplied loans of ¥836,700 million and purchased ¥3,803,900 in bonds and commercial bills, thus equilibrating the supply and demand for funds in the money market. Since, over the long term, Bank of Japan loans are limited on the upper side by the system of loan ceilings applied to commercial bank loans, these loans cannot increase indefinitely. Therefore, within this limit, credit allocations have a meaningful policy impact on short-term money-market interest rates and on bank behavior, but the ex post absolute amount of the increase over a long period is not very meaningful in itself. On the other hand, one may say that purchases of bonds and commercial bills to some extent reflect the amount of the secular expansion of the private-sector financial deficit deliberately allowed for by the Bank of Japan.

10　Loan Policy

The day-to-day objectives of monetary stabilization are: (1) to neutralize seasonal and irregular fluctuations in the financial surpluses and deficits of the private sector, and thereby to eliminate disruptive effects on the short-term money markets and on bank behavior; and (2) at the same time, to devise methods and attitudes suitable for supplying an amount of credit that will have a deliberate policy impact on the short-term money markets and on bank behavior sufficient to offset the remaining cyclical and secular elements in the private sector's financial surpluses and deficits.

This chapter and chapters 11 and 12 examine how the impact of policy upon financial institutions is achieved through the supply of credit and through the various instruments of monetary policy. From the preceding chapters it will already be clear that the primary instrument of monetary policy is loan policy, namely, the allocation by the Bank of Japan of credit to individual city banks and the conditions (discount rate) on which these loans are made.

1. *Revision of the Penal Rate System and the Change in Loan Policy*

Throughout the prewar and postwar eras, the primary instrument of monetary policy in Japan was loan policy, but from the standpoint of economics, the effects of policy were different in each era. As explained earlier, loan policy after 1955 was implemented through a special system of credit allocation by the Bank of Japan. In order to understand the characteristics of loan policy in this period, it is necessary to return to the revision of the discount rate system that was implemented from August 1955 onwards, and to the changes in the penal lending rate system.

1.1 *Penal Lending Rate System, 1945–1954*
Under the structure of interest rates that prevailed in July 1955 prior to

the revision of the penal lending rate system, the official discount rate (the rate at which Bank of Japan discounts commercial bills) stood at 1.6 sen per diem (or 5.84 percent p.a.),[1] whereas the cost of deposits was just below 2.0 sen p.d. (or 7.30 percent p.a.), and the maximum lending rate stood at 2.4 sen p.d. (or 8.76 percent p.a.). The call rate (unconditional) stood at 2 sen p.d. (or 7.3 percent p.a.). Consequently, rather than raising funds in the call money market, it was cheaper for the banks to acquire funds by borrowing from the Bank of Japan at the official discount rate. Moreover, if these funds were utilized to make loans, a broad interest spread could be obtained.

However, the official discount rate in fact only applied to each bank within a specified range, and if loans were made to any bank in excess of that range, a higher rate was applied for a given range until another rate became applicable. In July 1955 this second tier of interest charges stood 3.65 percent above the official discount rate at 9.49 percent. This second tier of rates was higher than the deposit interest rate, the bank lending rate, or the call rate, and in this sense, relative to market rates, it could be called a penal rate.

Before July 1955 the official discount rate was not changed very often within the framework of overall loan policy, and in a policy sense, changes in the official discount rate were relatively insignificant. Instead, policy achieved its effects through variations in the amounts of, and changes in, the rates at which these additional discounts were made. For example, during a tight-money period, rates were raised at the upper end of the scale and the amount of loans available at the lowest tier was restricted, so that the second tier of interest rates became applicable on Bank of Japan loans at an earlier stage. As a result, the city banks found that it was more advantageous to restrict their loan behavior until they could repay loans from the Bank of Japan borrowed at the second tier, or penal rate. In effect, the policy altered the area of profitability within which the banks operated. Chart 10.1 illustrates how, when the range *bc* is reduced or there is an upward shift in the range *de* (the range to which penal rates on Bank of Japan loans apply), actual loans L are shifted from the profit-maximizing level L^* considerably to the left. This makes it clear that Bank of Japan loan policy at that time had its effects on bank behavior through the "cost effect" by significantly raising the discount rate for the higher loan tiers.

The computation of individual loan limits for the application of higher rates was quite complicated and subject to frequent alteration. Basically, more restrictive limits were imposed upon those banks which were more

1. In Japan it was customary to compute interest on a per diem basis rather than per annum, using sen (= 0.01 yen) as the unit of account. In announcing the discount rate, the Bank of Japan followed this custom until August 1969. Here all sen per diem rates have been converted to a percent per annum basis.

Chart 10.1   Contrast between Ceiling on Bank Lending and Penal Rate System

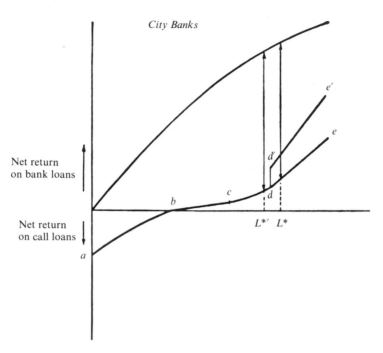

aggressive in expanding loans, and to that extent it cannot be denied that a certain degree of arbitrariness entered into the allocation of loan limits for individual banks.[2] However, the important thing to note is that Bank of Japan credit was not rationed as the straightforward result of a situation of excess demand due to subequilibrium interest rates. For as long as banks were willing to pay penal rates of interest, the Bank of Japan supplied them with credit, at least in principle. Moreover, for those banks that were not in an overlent position, loans were available if they so desired. This fact may be appreciated from table 1.4 in chapter 1, in the statistics of Bank of Japan loans granted to local banks, trust banks, and the long-term credit bank. In this sense the loan policy of the Bank of Japan until July 1955 contained only minor discriminatory elements, and was, in an economic

2. An example of the formula used from March 1954 to August 1955 is given in Toshihiko Yoshino [62], to which the reader is referred. Valuable material on the significance of the revision of the Higher Rate System and the interest-rate structure associated with the official discount rate in August 1955 is also given in [62].

sense, distinct from the credit-rationing system that became the main vehicle of lending policy thereafter.

1.2 *The Start of Credit Rationing*

The reform of August 1955 meant that the function previously performed by the second tier of interest rates was henceforth taken over by the single official discount rate. In practice this meant that the official discount rate which had been held at 5.84 percent throughout both tight-money periods and easy-money periods since October 1951, was raised by 1.46 percent to a level of 7.3 percent, and at the same time the higher tier of interest rates was henceforth only applied in exceptional circumstances. At its new level the official discount rate either only fractionally exceeded the prevailing deposit interest rates and call rates of July 1955, or indeed equalled them. Because the international balance of payments was in surplus at that time and there had been a good rice harvest, the Foreign Exchange Special Account and the Special Food Account had recorded large disbursements, so that commercial bank borrowings from the Bank of Japan were at an unusually low level. Consequently, since at year-end the overloan positions of the banks were temporarily eliminated, the official discount rate was in conformity with similar rates in Europe and North America at the upper end of the money market.

Although the thinking behind the alteration in Bank of Japan loans from a system based on the irregular application of higher rates toward one centered on variations in the official discount rate was entirely appropriate, nevertheless, when the new system was first put into effect during the tight-money policy of 1957, it was unfortunate that a different problem emerged. For when the policy was initiated in March 1957, the official discount rate was raised by one rin per day (= 0.1 sen = 0.365 percent p.a.) and at the same time the amounts to which the higher rates applied increased. But whereas there had been two levels applying previously, henceforth there was only one, and the incremental official discount rate applied to this amount was 3 rin p.d. (= 1.095 percent p.a.). Again, in May of the same year the official discount rate was again raised by 0.73 percent to a level of 8.395 percent. However, despite the fact that this was a tight-money period, the level of 8.395 percent was still considerably lower than the 9.49 percent which had applied previously at the second tier. Of course, a base rate of 9.49 percent could have been imposed, but since the coverage at this higher second-tier rate had already been broadened at the start of the tight-money policy, such a measure would have been quite exceptional at the time. Thus, as a result of shifting from a loan policy that was centered on higher rates at different tiers to the operation of a single discount rate, the interest rate that would have had to be applied on incremental Bank of Japan loans was not set high enough. This did not mean the revised system was in itself unworkable; it simply meant that the basic problem at that time was in the policy environment which effectively prevented increases in the official discount rate in excess of 3 rin p.d. (1.095 percent p.a.).

Thus, the level of the official discount rate relative to the second tier of interest rates was low and provoked an excess demand for Bank of Japan loans so long as the level remained below that required to equilibrate supply and demand. It was under these conditions that the "daily fund guidance" administered through "credit rationing" to city banks began. Similarly, it was against this background that the control of city banks' loan volume was initiated after 1955.

2. Effects of the Credit-Rationing Mechanism

2.1 Daily Fund Position Guidance—Credit Rationing

The Bank of Japan frequently directs the disposition of funds of the city banks that are its clients, and attempts in general terms to exercise moral suasion over the amounts loaned to customers of the city banks. This system is widely known as "window guidance," but originally there was nothing systematic about it. It evolved as a result of the excess demand for Bank of Japan loans described in earlier chapters and through daily contact with the clients who were making these loan contracts.[3] The situation is that the Bank of Japan and the client banks to which it makes loans are in frequent daily contact and are constantly seeking to ensure a mutual understanding. As a creditor seeking to ensure the security of its loans, the Bank of Japan pays close and continuing attention to the inflow and outflow of funds at each bank. Ultimately, all daily movements in each bank's settlement of commercial bills, foreign exchange settlements, receipts of cash at tellers' counters, or payments to the government through direct debiting of their accounts at the Bank of Japan or tax withholdings on such accounts, are all reflected in the changes in the cash currency holdings of that bank, in its call money borrowings from the call market, and in borrowings from the Bank of Japan.

The Bank of Japan therefore monitors these daily fluctuations in fund flows among its client banks, it notes the impact these flows are having upon call money and borrowings from the Bank of Japan, and how much will be used for additions to deposits at the Bank (mainly reserve deposits under the reserve requirement system), and on this basis it decides the volume of Bank of Japan loans. Also, it seeks to control the amount of money borrowed in the call market (call money) and additions to reserve deposits. Within the Bank of Japan's window guidance these operations

---

3. For a description of the evolution of window guidance and its early workings, see Kazuya Ikura [12].

are known as "daily fund guidance," or, in the terminology of economics, these are the realities of credit rationing.[4]

It is appropriate to divide the Bank of Japan's daily fund guidance into two kinds of effect: those corresponding to the changes in *conditions* attached to Bank of Japan loans, and the changes resulting from the fluctuations in the *volume* of Bank of Japan loans. Effects corresponding to the former are the hardening of the Bank of Japan's attitude toward the banks, which in reality means the raising of the cost of Bank of Japan loans. For example, this may happen during a tight-money period when the Bank of Japan may demand some repayment of its loans. An example of an occasion when the pressure to accelerate repayments increases may be seen in the "dance" of the daily interest rate. Like the interest charged on loans by city banks, interest rates on Bank of Japan loans are charged for both the day on which the loan is made and for the day of repayment. If a loan is made on the first day of the month and repaid on the twentieth, the net number of days for which the loan is outstanding is nineteen days, but the normal practice is to charge interest for twenty days. Therefore, during a tight-money period when pressure to repay is more severe, the frequency of borrowing

4. Using a format similar to that shown below, the commercial banks build up a forecast of their own fund situation which they use to manage their operations. (For purposes of simplification, foreign exchange transactions have been omitted.)

Bank Fund Flow Table
(Head Office Fund Division)

Receipts	*Items*	*Payments*
Fund Movements		
Balance from previous day	Balance at Bank of Japan	
	(1) Cash currency	
	(2) BOJ interoffice remittances	
	(3) BOJ checks	
Deposits	(4) BOJ agents accounts	Withdrawals
Credit exchange	(5) Clearing of checks	Debit exchange
Inflow of funds	(6) Domestic transfer settlements	Outflow of funds
Funding	(a) BOJ borrowings	
	(b) Call money borrowing	
	(c) Call loans	
	Net Balance at Bank of Japan	Amount forecast for day
	Total	

It is clear from the table that the items that make for financial surpluses or deficits are: (1) cash receipts to be placed on deposit at the Bank of Japan, less the distribution of cash to bank branches from deposits at the Bank of Japan; (2) telegraphic transfers between other branches of the Bank of Japan; (3) settlements by means of Bank of Japan checks for funds owed to or from other banks; (4) receipts of tax payments, etc., at own bank branches as agent for the Bank of Japan or withdrawals of Treasury funds from deposits at the Bank of Japan; (5) net settlements of check clearings; and (6) settlement of domestic transfers.

and repayment increases, and the average period of each borrowing becomes shorter, so that, for example, banks are paying four days of interest for a net loan period of three days, or, in an extreme case, when a bank borrows in the evening and repays the next morning it is paying two days' interest. In practice, the Bank of Japan normally permits credits obtained on commercial bills to be extended so that interest is not levied twice on a single day. However, given greater pressure to repay during tighter-money periods, and because of the shortening of the average period for commercial bills,

---

Adding these six items to the balance carried forward from the previous day, these fund movements will be estimated to yield either a surplus or a shortfall, and each bank's own fund division will decide either to supplement the shortfall (or utilize the surplus) in the light of reserve requirement needs and the next morning's fund movements by (a) calling on (or repaying) Bank of Japan borrowings, (b) borrowing more (or repaying) call money, or (c) calling in call loans (or making call loans). In this way a suitable balance will be left as the end-of-day balance with the Bank of Japan. This is the daily work of the fund division, but viewed from the standpoint of the financial industry as a whole, so long as transaction (1) consists of the withdrawal or deposit of banknotes and subsidiary coin for different branches, it does not influence the volume of cash held by banks (high-powered money held by banks inclusive of deposits at the Bank of Japan), because it is only a transfer between vault-cash and banks' deposits with the Bank of Japan. However, if net cash receipts or payments were to occur between banks and the private nonbank sector at the tellers' counters, there would be a change in cash currency held by banks.

Viewed from the banking system as a whole, this change is of course identical with that in cash held by the private nonbank sector. BOJ interoffice remittances (2) and BOJ checks (3) are cash transfers between various offices of the same bank, or between several banks, and therefore they do not imply any change in cash held by the banking system as a whole. BOJ agents accounts (4) cause direct changes in cash held by banks. So long as transactions are limited to ordinary checks and bills, the clearing of checks (5) may cause changes among the holders of these high-powered money balances but no change in their total amount. But sometimes check clearances involve such transactions as governmental revenue or expenditure, or collection of bills rediscounted by BOJ at maturity. In this case they would cause changes in the amount of high-powered money held by banks. Lastly, domestic transfer settlements (6) are funds transferred within the banking system, causing no changes in high-powered money held by banks.

To sum up, from the viewpoint of the banking system as a whole, transactions that cause changes in high-powered money held by banks are: cash receipts and payments at tellers' windows (part of [1]), transactions with the Treasury in which banks act as agents for BOJ (4), and transactions with the Treasury as a result of check clearances (part of [5]). The last two categories reflect the net surplus or deficit of the government.

In addition, the collection of bills rediscounted by Bank of Japan at maturity (part of [5]) may be included in changes in BOJ loans (a). Therefore, changes in high-powered money held by banks are counterbalanced by (a) Bank of Japan loans, (b) call money, and (c) call loans. As (b) and (c) are simply transfers of cash within the banking system, they cannot be utilized to counterbalance changes in high-powered money held by the total banking system. From the viewpoint of the banking system as a whole, changes in high-powered money held by banks are counterbalanced only by changes in Bank of Japan loans. Net receipts from the private nonbank sector at the tellers' counters clearly affect the high-powered money held by banks and are equal to the movement of funds from the nonbank private sector to the banks.

effective interest rates may potentially be higher, and the city banks are continuously kept aware of this by the fact that their loans from the Bank of Japan could become very expensive at any moment.

This kind of effect of credit rationing is parallel to the "cost effect" of changes in the official discount rate. However, because the official discount rate is at a subequilibrium level, the effect is not necessarily very large.

The more important effect of the Bank of Japan's daily fund guidance or credit rationing is that which derives from restriction of the *volume* of loans. We have already examined the "liquidity effect" of changes in the Bank of Japan's loans in chapter 6, section 2.3, where chart 6.4 showed how a reduction in Bank of Japan loans $\bar{C}$ had the effect of shifting curve R_{c1}^* to the left in the range to the right of point c. In this case, the curve shifted from the solid line to the dashed line to the right of c'. Conversely, when Bank of Japan loans $\bar{C}$ increase, in the range to the right of c' the curve shifts from the dashed line to the solid line. The horizontal shift in R_{c1}^* is the "liquidity effect" described in chapter 6, section 3, and produces a decrease (or increase) in the profit-maximizing loan level L_1^*.

An increase of Bank of Japan loans $\bar{C}$ produces an expansion in city bank loans L_1 through the "liquidity effect," and decreases tend to reduce L_1. However, since Bank of Japan loans are restricted by an upper ceiling, there is no cumulative multiplication of these Bank of Japan loans. Therefore, what matters most about changes in the volume of Bank of Japan loans is the effect of relatively minor variation in credit rationing, which affects city banks' awareness of the change in the availability of Bank of Japan credit a, thus transferring the impact to the call rate r_c and city bank loans L_1. After the imposition of the loan ceiling system, central bank purchases of securities were extended in order to ensure that the liquidity effects of expansion of Bank of Japan purchasing operations gradually became more important.

It is worth considering the effects of small fluctuations in the volume of Bank of Japan's credit rationing. The first point to establish is that, in its day-to-day monetary management, the Bank of Japan does not have a very wide degree of freedom in deciding daily loan volume. The amount of loans the bank can alter for policy purposes on a day-to-day basis is actually extremely limited. To show this, it is necessary to return to the question of the composition of the private sector's financial deficit or surplus.

Financial deficits and surpluses of the private sector were summarized in the following identity:

Net private-sector financial surplus/deficit ≡
 Net change in private-sector cash balances
 + Net receipts from Treasury by private sector (including government bond issues)

+ Net receipts by private sector from Foreign Exchange Special
Account   (19)

In this identity, private-sector cash balances can be further subdivided
into cash currency held by the nonbank public and cash (including deposits
at the Bank of Japan) held by the banks as vault cash or reserves to meet
demands for payment and interbank settlements and also to meet reserve
requirements.

Thus we may write:

Net private-sector financial surplus/deficit $\equiv$
    Net change in cash held by banks
+ Net change in cash currency held by the nonbank public
+ Net receipts from Treasury by private sector (including government
   bond issues)
+ Net receipts by private sector from Foreign Exchange Special
   Account   (20)

The last three items in equation (20) are, for the purposes of day-to-day
monetary management, given conditions. The question of how much of its
savings the nonbank private sector—business enterprises and households—
chooses to hold in the form of cash is decided by asset portfolio preferences,
and the Bank of Japan is unable to affect it at this stage. Movements in the
Treasury's accounts and the Foreign Exchange Special Account are also
ultimately determined by the action of those concerned, and the Bank of
Japan can have no direct influence in the short term, though it can indirectly
in the medium term. With respect to the last three items in the equation, the
Bank of Japan must passively supply credit in the event of a financial
deficit, and is obliged passively to absorb funds in the event of a financial
surplus. In a word, when cash withdrawals by the nonbank private sector
out of deposits (item 2), tax payments (item 3), or yen payments to the
Foreign Exchange Special Account that are the counterparts of foreign
exchange purchases (item 4) produce a financial deficit, failure by the Bank
of Japan to supply credit implies the possibility that somewhere in the
banking sector a bank will be unable to meet demands for payment and
orderly financial conditions will be disrupted.

The question remains, how can Bank of Japan loans $\bar{C}$ be actively
varied? The only cushion for Bank of Japan loans $\bar{C}$ to move independently
from the private-sector financial surplus/deficit is item 1 on the right-hand
side: the increase or decrease in the volume of cash held by banks. We first
consider how Bank of Japan loans $\bar{C}$ can be increased. Since the official
discount rate is typically set at a subequilibrium level, there is usually excess
demand for Bank of Japan loans, and therefore it is relatively easy to allow

$\bar{C}$ to increase. Given a financial deficit originating in the last three items in equation (20) and passive adjustment by the Bank of Japan, implying that it is willing to permit an increase in city bank loans, these institutions will tend to respond by increasing their borrowings of cheaper Bank of Japan loans and repaying their borrowings of more expensive call money. Thus, lending banks in the call market will find they have more funds on hand, and since these will be added to their reserve requirements or vault-cash, item 1 in equation (20) will increase, restoring equation (20) to equilibrium. Conversely, the mechanism whereby $\bar{C}$ is deliberately reduced calls for the opposite action through item 1.

In Japan, bank holdings of cash (including deposits at the central bank) are only 2 to 3 percent of total deposits, compared with approximately 10 percent in the United States and 8 percent in Britain. This difference arises either explicitly through the low level of required reserves, or because cash held as prudential reserves against demands for payment to depositors has customarily been extremely low in Japan.

However, no matter how low the official reserve requirements rate, so long as the banks continue to add any surplus cash to their required reserves, from their daily settlement or payment requirements, Bank of Japan loans can be reduced independently from the financial surplus/deficit position of the private sector. The reason is that even if deposits at the Bank of Japan vary from their intended daily base, no disruption of financial conditions will occur and no bank will be unable to meet its payment obligations. In effect, therefore, the method by which Bank of Japan loans are reduced by deliberate policy is through adjusting its advances to the city banks via daily guidance exercised on their fund position.

It will be clear from the above that the Bank of Japan has limited options in dealing with supply and demand in the short-term money market as reflected in the private sector's financial surplus/deficit: complete nullification of any financial deficit with Bank of Japan credit, or the partial offsetting of any deficit which develops by allowing some rundown of deposits at the Bank. But since in Japan required reserves are only about 1 percent on average of total deposits, the margin for expansion or contraction of deposits at the Bank of Japan is extremely limited.[5]

Despite the fact that this margin of maneuverability is small, if pressure is continually applied every day to the rate of build-up of required reserves for the whole month, it will have a considerable impact. Since the Japanese reserve requirement system requires the average level of deposits at the

5. For a statistical analysis of the facts that Bank of Japan credit moves almost in parallel with the private-sector financial surplus/deficit, that movements in Bank of Japan credit do nevertheless reflect deliberate policy, and that as a result banks' idle cash balances are activated, leading to sizable fluctuations in the call rate (i.e. the interest elasticity of cash held by banks is low), see Suzuki [41], part 1, chapter 3.

Bank of Japan to be maintained at a particular level from the sixteenth of one month to the fifteenth of the next, if payment reserves temporarily fall below the required level, the bank in question could, in an extreme case, withdraw all its deposits at the Bank of Japan. However, from that day onward until the fifteenth its average level of required deposits would be higher and its need for cash or deposits in the succeeding days would be correspondingly greater.

Herein lies the purpose of the Bank of Japan's vigilant day-to-day policy actions. Having forecast the banking system's daily fund needs and their components, the Bank attempts to ensure smooth functioning of the totality of credit institutions, supplying credit passively if need be, so that deposits at the end of the business day are adjusted (to a desired level) by varying the level of loans plus bills bought and sold through short-term money-market dealers, and thus adjusting the progressive additions to official reserve requirements. As a result, if, for example, additions to reserve requirements lag behind, the banks will be urged either to borrow more money in the call market (where it is more expensive) in order to avoid incurring some loss of prestige, or be charged higher penal rates for failing to satisfy their reserve requirements. (Under the reserve requirement system there is provision for a charge of 3.75 percent p.a. above the official discount rate on any shortfall.) Conversely, if the rate of addition to reserve requirements is in excess of what is required, the demand for call market money will weaken.

The cost and availability of Bank of Japan credit $[a : \bar{r}]$ as affected by and affecting the call rate r_c through the Bank of Japan's credit rationing $\bar{C}$ (described in the theoretical call money demand function in part II) work in practice through this kind of mechanism. Therefore, a decline in $\bar{C}$ implies a reduction small enough to induce a slowdown in the build-up of required reserves at the Bank of Japan, and increases in $\bar{C}$ imply an increase small enough to induce a slight acceleration in the rundown of required reserves. The latitude of freedom available to vary $\bar{C}$ as implied by the expression "credit rationing" does not in practice exist. On the whole, therefore, it would not be unrealistic to say that Bank of Japan credit moves approximately in parallel with the financial surplus/deficit of the private sector because the proportion available for deliberate policy-manipulation is so small.

However, small movements in this policy component do have a sizable impact on the call rate, since bank holdings of cash have such a low elasticity to interest rates. This was demonstrated in part II, chapter 7, section 2.1, in the regression analysis of the call rate. Since Bank of Japan credit fluctuations are reflected in the rate of accumulation of required reserve deposits, this explains why the quantity of reserves in excess of reserve requirements, summarized in the variable a, is such a good explanatory variable for the call rate and why it has such high statistical significance. Similarly good results are obtained by use of a variable that shows what percentage of required reserves has been attained during the first half of the month (i.e. 16th to end-month) as a proxy variable for the severity or ease of credit rationing.

2.2 Loan Ceilings and Moral Suasion

In the preceding section we examined the mechanism by which short-term money-market interest rates such as the call rate and the bills discount rate were influenced by variations in the volume of Bank of Japan loans $\bar{C}$. The rationing of $\bar{C}$, as described in part II, chapters 5 and 6, affects the cost and availability of Bank of Japan loans $[a : \bar{r}]$ as experienced by city banks, and affects bank behavior by two distinct routes. First, as described in the preceding section, through influencing the call rate r_c, i.e. $\bar{C} \rightarrow [a : \bar{r}] \rightarrow r_c$. Second, the route we shall examine in this chapter is through directly determining city bank loans L_1, i.e. $\bar{C} \rightarrow [a : \bar{r}] \rightarrow L_1$.

When Bank of Japan loans are deliberately varied so that the process of reserve accumulation is accelerated or retarded, on the one hand the demand for call money weakens or strengthens, but on the other hand either banks will desire to increase profits by expanding loans using any surplus after meeting reserve requirements (subject to some cash drain), or they will restrict their loans in order to avoid losses due to a cash drain. This is the "liquidity effect" examined in part II.

The strength and speed with which variations in Bank of Japan credit $\bar{C}$ directly affect city bank loans depends on the size of the variation in availability a and the length of the time-lag required for city banks to adjust their loan portfolio. As the computation in table 7.1 in chapter 7, section 1.2 shows, the city bank profit-maximization point on curve R_{c1}^* is not fixed because of its relation to the slope of the curve (under the condition that there is no corner solution), and therefore city bank reaction to changes in fund volume (and hence the "liquidity effect" of monetary policy on city banks) is smaller than that for other banks. A change in the rate of accumulation of deposits to meet reserve requirements does not induce banks immediately to adjust their loans. In order to make them react rapidly and adjust their loans, the Bank of Japan has used a form of moral suasion to affect city bank loan plans known as *Zōkagaku Kisei* or "loan increase ceilings." Below I examine the origin and effects of moral suasion.

The credit rationing which occurs through daily fund guidance is conducted day-to-day on the balance of funds held at the Bank of Japan by each city bank. At any one point in time, this position is determined by the balance of settlements due to and from the bank, but in a wider perspective, the balance is a result of the particular bank's loan behavior and deposit collecting activities. To demonstrate this we may rewrite the money flow

Table 10.1　Reserve Requirement Rates

Effective Date	All Banks — Deposits of More than ¥20 Billion — Time Deposits %	All Banks — Deposits of More than ¥20 Billion — Other Deposits %	All Banks — Deposits of More than ¥100 Billion — Time Deposits %	All Banks — Deposits of More than ¥100 Billion — Other Deposits %	All Banks — Deposits of ¥100 Billion or Less but More than ¥20 Billion — Time Deposits %	All Banks — Deposits of ¥100 Billion or Less but More than ¥20 Billion — Other Deposits %	All Banks — Deposits of ¥20 Billion or Less — Time Deposits %	All Banks — Deposits of ¥20 Billion or Less — Other Deposits %	Mutual Loan and Savings Banks & Credit Associations (Deposits of More than ¥20 Billion) — Deposits of More than ¥100 Billion — Time Deposits %	— Other Deposits %	Deposits of ¥100 Billion or Less but More than ¥20 Billion — Time Deposits %	— Other Deposits %	The Central Cooperative Bank for Agriculture and Forestry — Time Deposits %	— Other Deposits %
Sept. 11, 1959	0.50	1.50					0.25	0.75						
Oct. 1, 1961			1.00	3.00	0.75	2.25	0.25	0.75						
Nov. 1, 1962			0.50	1.50	0.50	1.50	0.25	0.75						
Apr. 1, 1963			0.50	1.50	0.50	1.50	0.25	0.75						
Dec. 16, 1963			0.50	3.00	0.50	3.00	0.25	1.50	0.25	0.75	0.25	0.75		
Dec. 16, 1964			0.50	1.50	0.50	1.50	0.25	0.75	0.25	1.50	0.25	1.50		
July 16, 1965			0.50	1.00	0.25	0.50	0.25	0.50	0.25	0.75	0.25	0.75		
Sept. 5, 1969			0.50	1.50	0.25	0.75	0.25	0.75	0.25	0.75	0.25	0.75		
Sept. 16, 1969			0.50	1.50	0.25	0.75	0.25	0.75	0.25	0.75	0.25	0.75	0.25	(a) 0.75

Reserve rates on balances of deposits, excluding foreign currency deposits, deposits of which amount is equivalent to the import guarantee money deposited with the Bank of Japan and nonresident free yen deposits, but including savings and installment savings

| | All Banks | | | | | | Mutual Loan and Savings Banks & Credit Associations (Deposits of More than ¥20 Billion) | | | | The Central Cooperative Bank for Agriculture and Forestry | |
| | Deposits of More than ¥100 Billion | | Deposits of ¥100 Billion or Less but More than ¥20 Billion | | Deposits of ¥20 Billion or Less | | Deposits of More than ¥100 Billion | | Deposits of ¥100 Billion or Less but More than ¥20 Billion | | | |
	Time Deposits	Other Deposits	Time Deposits	Other Deposits	Time Deposits	Other Deposits	Time Deposits	Other Deposits	Time Deposits	Other Deposits	Time Deposits	Other Deposits
	%	%	%	%	%	%	%	%	%	%	%	%
May 1, 1972	0.50	1.50	0.25	0.75	0.25	0.75	0.25	0.75	0.25	0.75	0.25	0.75
June 1	0.50	1.50	0.25	0.75	0.25	0.75	0.25	0.75	0.25	0.75	0.25	0.75
July 1	0.50	1.50	0.25	0.75	0.25	0.75	0.25	0.75	0.25	0.75	0.25	0.75

Reserve rates on balances of nonresident free yen deposits

| | All Banks | | | | | |
| | Deposits of More than ¥100 Billion | | Deposits of ¥100 Billion or Less but More than ¥20 Billion | | Deposits of ¥20 Billion or Less | |
	Time Deposits	Other Deposits	Time Deposits	Other Deposits	Time Deposits	Other Deposits
	%	%	%	%	%	%
May 1, 1972	0.50	1.50	0.25	0.75	0.25	0.75

Reserve rates on increased amount of liabilities on nonresident free yen accounts

June 1	25.00% (Basic term: from April 21, 1972 to May 20, 1972)
July 1	50.00 (Basic term: from May 21, 1972 to June 20, 1972)

Reserve Rates on Balances of Deposits, Excluding Foreign Currency Deposits and Nonresident Free Yen Deposits, but Including Savings and Installment Savings

	All Banks						Mutual Loan and Savings Banks & Credit Associations (Deposits of More than ¥ 20 Billion)				The Nōrinchūkin Bank		Long-Term Credit Banks & Authorized Foreign Exchange Banks	Reserve Rates on Principal of Money in Trust (Including Loan Trust) Outstanding	Reserve Rates on Debentures Outstanding / Increased Amount of Liabilities on Nonresident Free yen accounts
	Deposits of More than ¥ 1,000 Billion		Deposits of ¥1,000 Billion or Less but More than ¥ 100 Billion		Deposits of ¥ 100 Billion or Less		Deposits of More than ¥ 100 Billion		Deposits of ¥ 100 Billion or Less but More than ¥ 20 Billion						
	Time Deposits	Other Deposits	Time Deposits	Other Deposits	Time Deposits	Other Deposits	Time Deposits	Other Deposits	Time Deposits	Other Deposits	Time Deposits	Other Deposits			
	%	%	%	%	%	%	%	%	%	%	%	%	%	%	%
Jan. 16, 1973	1.00	2.00	0.75	1.75	0.25	1.00	0.25	1.00	0.25	1.00	0.25	1.00	0.25	0.25	(b) 50.00
Mar. 16	1.50	3.00	1.00	2.00	0.25	1.00	0.25	1.00	0.25	1.00	0.25	1.00	0.50	0.50	(b) 50.00
June 16	1.75	3.25	1.00	2.25	0.25	1.25	0.25	1.25	0.25	1.25	0.25	1.25	0.75	0.75	(b) 50.00
Sept. 1	2.00	3.75	1.00	2.50	0.25	1.50	0.25	1.50	0.25	1.50	0.25	1.50	1.00	1.00	(b) 50.00
Dec. 10	2.00	3.75	1.00	2.50	0.25	1.50	0.25	1.50	0.25	1.50	0.25	1.50	1.00	1.00	(b) 10.00
Jan. 1, 1974	2.25	4.25	1.25	2.75	0.25	1.50	0.25	1.50	0.25	1.50	0.25	1.50	1.00	1.00	(b) 10.00
Sept. 12	2.25	4.25	1.25	2.75	0.25	1.50	0.25	1.50	0.25	1.50	0.25	1.50	1.00	1.00	(Abolished)

	Deposits of More than ¥ 1,500 Billion		Deposits of ¥ 1,500 Billion or Less but More than ¥ 300 Billion		Deposits of ¥ 300 Billion or Less		Deposits of More than ¥ 300 Billion		Deposits of ¥ 300 Billion or Less but More than ¥ 50 Billion		The Nōrinchūkin Bank		Long-Term Credit Banks & Authorized Foreign Exchange Banks	Reserve Rates on Principal of Money in Trust Outstanding
	Time Deposits	Other Deposits	Time Deposits	Other Deposits	Time Deposits	Other Deposits	Time Deposits	Other Deposits	Time Deposits	Other Deposits	Time Deposits	Other Deposits		
	%	%	%	%	%	%	%	%	%	%	%	%	%	%
Nov. 16, 1975	2.00	3.75	1.00	2.25	0.25	1.00	0.25	1.00	0.25	1.00	0.25	1.00	0.50	0.50

Source: The Bank of Japan

Notes: 1. Through March 31, 1970, reserve rate of 0.5% was applied as a transitional measure.

2. Basic term: from May 21, 1972 to June 20, 1972.

equation of table 5.2 in chapter 5 from the city banks' balance sheet as follows:

$$M_1 - C_1 - C_{l1} \equiv D_1 - L_1$$

On the left we have cash currency holdings M_1, borrowings from the Bank of Japan C_1, and call money borrowings C_{l1}, namely, (*a*) to (*c*) in table 9.3. On the right we have the net result of deposit collecting activity D_1, and loans, L_1. In addition to its daily monitoring of each bank's balances at the Bank, the Bank of Japan also receives reports on a longer-term basis concerning loans L_1 and deposits D_1 which form the background to the day-to-day fund positions. These reports are not only ex post, but also give a forecast of future fund-raising activity (call money borrowings, borrowings from the Bank of Japan, settlements etc.) and the outlook for deposits and loans either on a monthly or a quarterly basis. This information is a vital element of the Bank of Japan's policy-making, and particular attention is paid to what banks themselves think about the future credit lines, and particularly loan levels, and their background. For example, since the tight-money policy of 1953–54, whenever banks' loan plans have appeared overaggressive, a more appropriate level has been indicated, and banks have been required to cooperate, thus being made acutely aware of the authorities' intentions. This process is known as "window guidance" in a narrow sense or, in more general terminology, "loan controls."

Sometimes the whole process is completely abandoned during easy-money periods, but even in these cases the Bank of Japan continues to monitor future loan plans and the prospective fund positions of banks. In the tight-money policy of 1964, restrictions were again introduced, this time on the increase in loans rather than on the absolute amount. (From 1965 the tight-money policy was ended and the loan increase ceilings were once again abandoned.) The major difference between the pre-1964 system and loan increase ceilings was that the monthly basis of loan assessment was shifted to a quarterly basis and each bank was allowed, in the light of special factors or seasonal variations, to formulate its own monthly plan, thus allowing some flexibility.

Loan ceilings of this kind were enforced from the third quarter of 1967 to the third quarter of 1968 during the period of tight-money policy, and from October 1968 the fund position (the volume of second-line reserves) was also taken into account, so that banks with better fund positions were permitted slightly greater loan increases, and hence the expression "position guidance." When the tight-money policy was ended in the fourth quarter of 1970, position guidance was also dropped. However, the supervision of city bank loans was in effect restored from the third quarter of 1972 and imposed with increasing force from the first quarter of 1973. It has continued even in the easy-money period beginning in 1975.

Turning to the effect of loan controls, as this involves control by the Bank of Japan (who is the creditor) over the debtor in order to ensure the safety of loans, the issue is a complicated one. Since the choice of loans levels is determined by the Bank of Japan's judgment of what is an appropriate policy and not by the profit-maximization point of city banks, there is not necessarily any guarantee that the banks will abide by the Bank of Japan's moral suasion. In fact, in the tight-money policies of 1957, 1961–62, 1967–68, 1969–70, and 1973–74 the banks appeared to be observing the Bank of Japan's "loan assessments," but at the same time were making *fukumi-kashidashi* ("hidden" or off-balance sheet loans). Of course, there is a limit to the extent of these loans, and their accumulation soon becomes a burden, so that in the end the banks are forced to restrict them. However, it is difficult in these cases to prevent the lag in effect of policy from being extended. For moral suasion to be fully effective, therefore, it is essential that the banks have some incentive to conform to the authorities' suasion. Ultimately, the main reason why banks adhere to the moral suasion of the Bank of Japan is that, as debtors, the banks judge it to be in their best interests to abide by the creditor's (Bank of Japan's) wishes.

For example, if any bank does not adhere to guidance, the Bank of Japan may withdraw its loans (and lend that amount to other banks), or it may compel the bank to borrow more expensive call money or to sell commercial bills. In that event, the marginal net return on call loans (the opportunity cost of loans) $-\dfrac{\partial}{\partial C_{l1}} R_c^*(L_1)$ will increase for that bank, and the amount of loans which that bank must make to achieve the profit-maximization point decreases. This is clearly disadvantageous from the point of view of its ranking with other banks, and induces the bank to accede to the Bank of Japan's suasion. Also, if a bank does not follow the Bank of Japan's assessments, the Bank may reduce the average term of its loans, effectively raising their interest rate as described previously. This also raises the value of $-\dfrac{\partial}{\partial C_{l1}} R_c^*(L_1)$ for the bank relative to other banks, shifts its profit-maximization point, puts it at a disadvantage in its ranking with other banks, and induces it to accept Bank of Japan suasion as preferable. Finally, the Bank of Japan can reduce the amount of the permitted loan ceiling for any bank that does not observe this guidance. (Formerly this would have been done through the higher rate application system.) This again has the clear effect of shifting the profit-maximization point to the left (i.e. requiring less loans), is disadvantageous for the bank's rank vis-à-vis its competitors, and induces the bank to adhere to Bank of Japan suasion. Looked at in this way, the Bank of Japan's loan controls amount to a supplement to daily fund guidance (which refers to the way in which Bank of Japan loans are "rationed"). Thus Bank of Japan window guidance can be divided into daily fund guidance and loan controls, the two together comprising the credit-rationing mechanism and making it effective.

In the tight-money policy of 1973, loan controls were extended to the long-term credit banks, the trust banks, local banks, and mutual banks, as well as to the leading credit corporations. The form of these controls was looser than those applied to city banks, and the margin of flexibility granted to each was quite extensive, but it provided an extremely interesting test case by which to judge how far these other banks adhered to the Bank of Japan's moral suasion. These banks effectively became recipients of Bank of Japan credit when the bank engaged in the purchase of securities ("operations"), and in order not to be discriminated against in the allocation of such credit, they adopted an attitude of cooperation similar to city banks. However, to the extent that tight loan controls are hard to impose and distortions tend to occur if imposed for any length of time, the normal method of loan restriction for these financial institutions is through their access to funds (the liquidity effect) and their profitability as affected by the call rate (the cost effect). Conversely, it is probably fair to say that by deliberately creating a financial environment which compels banks to restrict their loans because of lack of funds or because of profitability considerations, moral suasion over these institutions operates by speeding up the rate of loan adjustment.[6]

2.3 *The Loan Limit System*

The preceding section examined the realities of adjustments in Bank of Japan loan volume $\bar{C}$ and their effects. In addition, the Bank of Japan imposes individual loan ceilings on each of the ten city banks whose dependence on Bank of Japan borrowings is especially high. This is called the Loan Limit System, and was first introduced after the abolition of the Higher Rate System in November 1962. (The latter had actually lost operational significance following the reforms of August 1955; see above.)

The Loan Limit System, in common with the Higher Rate System, sets a specific volume of Bank of Japan loans for each bank and imposes penal rates of interest on borrowings in excess of that level. However, there are important differences in the essential character of the two systems.

In the Higher Rate System, it was expected that the higher rate would apply to a certain portion of loans during a tight-money period, and that

---

6. When monetary policy became much tighter in the fourth quarter of 1973 through mid-1974, some trust banks, local banks, mutual banks, or credit corporations were spared from the Bank of Japan loan assessment framework and began to propose loan plans somewhat below Bank of Japan loan assessments. This meant that those banks' behavior was fundamentally determined by a "liquidity effect" accompanying the deterioration in fund position and a "cost effect" accompanying a rise in the bills discount rate, and was evidently not very closely connected with any direct effects of window guidance.

the "cost effect" accompanying such higher rates would come into effect. In contrast, under the new Loan Limit System, it is expected that banks voluntarily refrain from exceeding the loan limits even in tight-money periods, so that the effect of the squeeze and the penal rates is not to be found in a "cost effect," but, because the banks are attempting to remain within the loan limits, in a "liquidity effect." Thus, under the loan limit policy there is no general acceptance of the idea that loans in excess of the loan limit are merely subject to a higher penal interest rate, but rather that such excess loans are out of the question, and there is an obligation to repay them immediately. This characteristic is reflected in the high level of penal rates which are set at 4 percent above the official discount rate.

The character of the Loan Limit System can be better appreciated with the help of chart 10.1, which shows the profit-maximization point for a city bank subject to loan limits or to the Higher Rate System. The net return on call loans function $abcde$ is the net return on call loans function for city banks under the Higher Rate System, bc being the range in which it receives low-interest loans at the official discount rate, cd being the range where it borrows call money, and the point d where the Bank of Japan's higher rates come into force. Beyond point d the slope of the curve is steeper than for bc or cd. As a result, the profit-maximization point is just to the right of d, where the bank's loans are L^*. On the other hand, the curve $abcdd'e'$ is the net return on call loans function for city banks under the Loan Limit System, and the point d is where Bank of Japan loans exceed the loan limit. Under this system, since loans in excess of the limit are in principle forbidden, banks exceeding the limit lose face, are put under strong pressure to repay, and become subject to more vigilant fund guidance so that this is a kind of fixed cost they must bear, shown in chart 10.1 by the line dd'. Also, since loans beyond d' attract a 4 percent penalty over and above the official discount rate, the slope of $d'e'$ is steeper than that of de. Because it has this shape, the profit-maximization point occurs just before the point d, denominated by $L^{*'}$. In fact, since the start of the Loan Limit System there has not been a single bank which has exceeded the limits imposed, even during tight-money periods.

The ultimate aim of the Loan Limit System is to cause fixed costs to occur for other banks when their call loans turn negative, just as for city banks those fixed costs are designed to occur when their negative fund position exceeds a certain point. To the extent that a negative fund position can mean loss of status (just as in the British case a bank with less than 8 percent of deposits held in the form of cash loses face), the Loan Limit System is an attempt to impose a kind of monetary discipline on city banks based on making them conform to a certain negative fund position as a criterion of that monetary discipline.

In terms of economics, the existence of this discipline suggests a stable equilibrium point. Since the profit-maximization point of the net return on call loans function is almost a corner maximum at the point where higher fixed costs come in, there is a good chance that there will be stability just before that point. However, if there were no such point with fixed costs entering in, the number of unknowns—corporate profit rate, discount rate, call rate, etc.—would multiply so that the slopes of the net return on bank loans function and the net return on call loans function would become uncertain and the profit-maximization point would be subject to a wide distribution with unstable equilibrium. Consequently, the effects of a monetary policy that caused the profit-maximization point to shift would also be more unpredictable.

The Loan Limit System thus attempts to stabilize the otherwise unstable city bank profit-maximization point. If the profit-maximization point is immediately below the loan limit level, the "liquidity effects" of purchases and sales of securities by the Bank of Japan and changes in the reserve requirement rates may also be expected to be more predictable. This is because, even though changes in reserve requirements and Bank of Japan operations in securities shift the net return on call loans function (i.e. they have a "liquidity effect"), in order definitely to shift the profit-maximization point and to have a definite impact upon the volume of loans, such measures would in fact be relying upon the existence of the fixed costs shown by *dd'* in chart 10.1.

It is not easy to judge the extent to which this kind of supplement to the expected liquidity effect actually occurs because some banks that have an available margin within the limits may not be able to borrow freely up to that limit. Despite the fact that there may be some available margin within the loan ceilings, the Bank is regulating and rationing its loan volume on a daily fund guidance basis. The reason city banks restrict their borrowings within the loan limits may be either deliberately to avoid the costs associated with the 4 percent penal rate, or it may be because the Bank of Japan does not supply more credit than this and therefore the banks are externally constrained; but there can be no definite answer. What is known, however, is that the estimating results of table 7.2 (in chap. 7, sec. 1.2) reject the hypothesis that city banks' profit-maximization point is near a corner solution under the Loan Limit System. The standpoint adopted in this text is therefore skeptical both toward the view that the Loan Limit System functions in an elementary way (i.e. by imposing a straightforward external constraint on loan volume), and toward the view that the city bank profit-maximization point, like that of other banks, is a near-corner solution.

3. *Official Discount Rate Policy*

Having considered variations in the *volume* of Bank of Japan loans in the preceding sections, we are now in a position to study variations in the

Table 10.2 Basic Money Rates of The Bank of Japan (Unit = % p.a.)

Effective Date	Discounts		Secured Loans				Overdraft
	Commercial Bills	Export Trade Bills	Export Trade Bills	Import Trade Bills	C	Others	
1960 Aug. 24	6.94	5.11	5.48	6.94	7.30	7.67	8.03
1961 Jan. 26	6.57	4.75	5.11	6.57	6.94	7.30	7.67
July 22	6.94	4.38	4.75	6.94	7.30	7.67	8.03
Sept. 29	7.30	4.38	4.75	7.30	7.67	8.03	8.40
1962 Oct. 27	6.94	4.38	4.75	6.94	7.30	7.67	8.03
Nov. 27	6.57	4.38	4.75	6.57	6.94	7.30	7.67
1963 Mar. 20	6.21	4.02	4.38	6.21	6.57	6.94	7.30
Apr. 20	5.84	4.02	4.38	5.84	6.21	6.57	6.94
1964 Mar. 18	6.57	4.02	4.38	6.57	6.94	7.30	7.67
1965 Jan. 9	6.21	4.02	4.38	6.21	6.57	6.94	7.30
Apr. 3	5.84	4.02	4.38	5.84	6.21	6.57	6.94
June 26	5.48	4.02	4.38	5.84	5.84	6.21	6.57
1967 Sept. 1	5.84	4.02	4.38		6.21	6.57	
1968 Jan. 6	6.21	4.02	4.38		6.57	6.94	
Aug. 7	5.84	4.02	4.38		6.21	6.57	

	A	Discount of Export Trade Bills	Loans Secured by Export Trade Bills	Loans Secured by Other Instruments
1969 Sept. 1	6.25	4.25	4.50	6.75

		Discounts of Export Usance Bills in Yen	Discounts of Export Advance Bills	Loans Secured by Export Advance Bills	
1970 May 15	6.25	5.00	5.25	5.50	6.75
Oct. 28	6.00	5.00	5.25	5.50	6.50
1971 Jan. 20	5.75	5.00	5.25	5.50	6.00
May 8	5.50	5.00	5.25	5.50	5.75
July 28	5.25	5.00	5.25	5.25	5.50

Table 10.2—*Continued.*

Effective Date	A	Discounts of Export Usance Bills in Yen	Loans Secured by Export Advance Bills	Loans Secured by Other Instruments
Aug. 10	5.25	5.25	5.25	5.50

	B			
Dec. 29	4.75	4.75	4.75	5.00
1972 June 24	4.25	4.25	4.25	4.50

	B	Loans Secured by Other Instruments
Oct. 2	4.25	4.50
1973 Apr. 2	5.00	5.25
May 30	5.50	5.75
July 2	6.00	6.25
Aug. 29	7.00	7.25
Dec. 22	9.00	9.25
1975 Apr. 16	8.50	8.75
June 7	8.00	8.25
Aug. 13	7.50	7.75
Oct. 24	6.50	6.75

Note: 1. A = Discount rate on commercial bills and interest rate on loans secured by government securities or specially designated debentures.

2. B = Discount rate of commercial bills and interest rates on loans secured by government securities, specially designated debentures, and bills corresponding to commercial bills.

3. C = "Government securities, designated local government securities, designated corporate bonds, designated other debentures, and agricultural bills," excludes agricultural bills since Feb. 1, 1959.

conditions attached to Bank of Japan loans, namely, official discount rate policy.

In the past the Bank of Japan's discount rate was composed of a variety of rates according to the type of paper being discounted or the type of collateral being offered (see table 10.2). For a long time after the reform of the Higher Rate System in August 1955, there was a complicated system with no less than seven rates. In 1967 these were reduced to five, and after further simplification in June 1972, when the discount rate was lowered, the system was reduced to four rates, including one applying to export financing. Subsequently, the export financing system was abolished in September 1972, and since October 1972 there have been just two rates:

1. Rate for discounting commercial bills and for loans against such collateral as government bonds or other designated securities and bills equivalent to commercial bills;
2. Rate for loans against other paper submitted as collateral.

Movements of these two rates until December 1973 are presented in table 9.4. Commercial bank lending rates moving in line with the discount rates are governed by the Temporary Interest Rate Adjustment Law (December 1947) and are subject to ceilings; but since 1958 banks have decided to set their lending rates below this ceiling within a self-imposed range, so that changes in the lending rate have tended to follow the official discount rate. Also, since March 1959 a standard rate system similar to the prime rate in the United States has been introduced. This standard rate applies to discounts on bills of particularly high quality or to high-quality loans, and when the official discount rate is altered, these rates are altered by the same amount. Also, in September 1969, with the switch to annual interest rates, commercial bank loan rates were also switched to the annual rate, and when the official discount rate was lowered in October 1970, the two-tier standard rates were reduced to a single rate.

As of December 1973, maximum bank lending rates as enforced by city banks were as follows:

1. Standard rate on high-quality commercial bills or loans 0.25 percent above official discount rate (on commercial bills);
2. Other bills and loans 2 percent above official discount rate;
3. Temporary overdraft rate 3 percent above official discount rate.

After the lowering of the official discount rate in April 1975, the commercial banks ceased to collaborate in setting maximum lending rates with the view that such actions constituted a cartel in violation of the Anti-Monopoly Law. Instead it became customary for the bank of the chairman of the Association of All Banks to alter its standard lending rate, while all the other banks followed independently. However, the change in the lending rate implemented by the lead bank was still of the same magnitude as the change in the official discount rate, and other banks still followed in exactly the same way as before, so that there was no change in the overall structure of rates.

The maximum deposit rate payable by private financial institutions is also governed by the Temporary Interest Rate Adjustment Law, but in fact the Bank of Japan sets guidelines within this, and published deposit interest rates are enforced for different categories of deposit. Again, although the Temporary Interest Rate Adjustment Law applies a maximum to each category, in fact there has been an attempt at simplification since April 1970 and rates are now set in accordance with the revised guidelines.

However, deposit interest rates do not exactly follow the official discount rates, but during the easy-money period of 1971–72 and the tight-money period after 1973, it was typically observed that deposit interest rates were revised once for every two or three revisions in the official discount rate, and always in the same direction. When changes are proposed to the Interest Rate Adjustment Investigation Committee by the Bank of Japan, after the committee's approval, the Bank of Japan decides on rates for different deposit categories and publishes these as guidelines.

Given these institutional conditions and the Bank of Japan's credit-rationing system already described, what kind of effects does a change in the official discount rate produce?

Effects of a change in the discount rate can be broadly divided into four. First, there is the "cost effect," which refers to the change the discount rate itself produces on the bank behavior. However, since this is a sub-equilibrium rate and is below the short-term money-market rates such as the bills discount rate and the call rate, it has no effect on the determination of banks' profit-maximizing loan level (see chap. 6, sec. 3). Chart 6.6 (chap. 6, sec. 2) shows in the upper section how a change in the discount rate changes the slope of the curve in the range b_1c_1, but it is clear from the graph that there is no effect on the profit-maximization point $L_1{}^*$ which is to the right of c_1. Hence, so long as the official discount rate is not at the same level as the call rate, the "cost effect" of changes in the discount rate itself may be thought to have no impact on banks' loan levels.

Changes in the official discount rate do nevertheless produce a change of a similar magnitude in the call rate and the bills discount rate, usually on the next day. The second effect of changes in the official discount rate is therefore this indirect "cost effect" through changes in the call and bills discount rates. The effect on loans of the indirect cost effect depends partly on the level of the rates but is quite considerable. In chapter 6, charts 6.5 and 6.6, the effect of these rates on the profit-maximizing loans was described and will not be repeated here. Also, the effect on the call and bills discount rates was confirmed in the regression analysis in chapter 7, section 2.1. One point to be noted here is that, in operating its loan policy, when the discount rate is changed, the Bank of Japan's attitude in daily fund guidance tends to shift in the same direction (tighter or easier), so that among statistically measured parameters, not only is there the influence of the official discount rate $\bar{r}$, but also the effect of changes in Bank of Japan loan volume $\bar{C}$. Consequently, it is very hard to separate the two effects statistically. For city banks the subjective cost and availability of Bank of Japan loans $[a : \bar{r}]$ is therefore a unified variable, implying that the thinking behind the theoretical model in chapters 5 and 6, whereby the city banks' attitudes toward call money borrowings and bill sales are affected, is probably quite consistent with reality.

The third effect of changes in the discount rate through changes in institutionally related lending rates is the effect on corporate enterprise investment. However, in this case also, since the nominal lending rates are not equilibrium rates and because their range of movement is very narrow, corporate investment does not necessarily follow the cost effect of changes in nominal lending rates. Because changes in lending rates occur simultaneously with changes in the banks' lending attitudes, and because firms also subjectively experience changes in the cost and availability of bank credit $[b : \bar{i}]$, the discount rate may be said to affect corporate behavior in this way. Also, if one considers the relatively high effective interest rate rather than the nominal rate, the cost effect on corporate investment might be slightly greater. But the effective rate may not be an equilibrium rate either, and since its range of fluctuation is as small as that of the nominal rate, the cost effect cannot be considered very great. However, in the case of long-term interest rates, it is empirically possible to recognize some effects due to the attempt to avoid the cyclical peak in the long-term borrowing rates as the construction of welfare facilities, and other plans with relatively low priority are postponed. In an ex post sense, too, there is a discernible acceleration in investment project starts when long-term borrowing rates are at their bottom.

The fourth effect of changes in the official discount is through the so-called announcement effect. Ever since the tight-money policy of 1957, the discount rate has played a central role in monetary policy, and since both banks and business corporations are affected by changes in the discount rate, they have been able to anticipate the effects of changes in monetary conditions. Banks anticipate that a rise in the discount rate will lead to (1) a reduction in the availability of bank credit, (2) a foreseeable increase in the call rate or bill discount rate, and (3) a possible deterioration in future lending opportunities. In terms of chart 6.6 in chapter 6, this implies (1) a reduction in the range $b_1 c_1$, (2) a steepening of the slope of the loan curve $R_c^*(L)$ in the future, and (3) a weakening of the slope of the present loan curve $R(L)$—all of which have the effect of shifting the future profit-maximizing loan level L^* to the left; and after a time-lag, the bank will in fact have to cut down on its loans. Another announcement effect of the change in the discount rate is, perhaps, to reduce the length of this lag. Also, anticipating a reduction in the availability of bank credit, firms will be on their guard against a reduction in the expected rate of return on real capital due to a slowdown in business activity. Hence, the size of the future asset budget will be reduced slightly and the amount allocated for real physical capital within the asset portfolio will be limited so that a restrictive influence is exerted on overall corporate investment. Corresponding effects on bank behavior and business firms occur in the opposite direction when the discount rate is lowered.

Among these four effects, the second and third have an indirect cost effect, which is intertwined with the fourth announcement effect. The reason is that the second and third indirect cost effects imply that there will be a future impact on the expected profit-maximization point accompanying the change in expected loan interest rate and future call rate. Thus the psychological announcement effect, including expected changes in the call rate and loan interest rate, can be called the basic, most important effect of a change in the discount rate. Since the size of the announcement effect depends on many given psychological conditions, its impact is difficult to gauge in advance. In this sense, movements in the discount rate intended to have such an announcement effect have only a limited degree of precision.

Discount rate policy should be aimed primarily at achieving cost effects. By flexible use of the discount rate which is at the center of the interest-rate structure, the bank lending rate, deposit rates, and short-term money-market rates, yields in the securities market can all be affected, and banks, business firms, and households can be affected in their asset portfolio selection through the cost effect. This is the proper role of discount rate policy, and for that reason it is here proposed that the artificially low interest-rate policy examined in part I be abandoned in favor of a policy that would be consistent with equilibrium interest rates in all the various markets.

11   Bank of Japan Operations in the Bill and Bond Markets

In two respects the lending policy of the Bank of Japan examined in the preceding chapter was highly effective: in its flexibility for purposes of quantitative adjustment, and in the strength of its policy impact. On the one hand, the bank must rely on its ability to adjust flexibly for seasonal shortages or surpluses of funds and irregular fluctuations as its central instrument for daily financial intervention, and on the other, lending policy must be utilized as the instrument for ensuring that current policy has an impact on the short-term money markets and bank behavior while at the same time allowing for fluctuations and the trend in the available funds. As explained in chapter 9, the purpose of monetary stabilization in response to financial surpluses and deficits due to seasonal and irregular fluctuations was to neutralize disruptive influences on the short-term money market and bank behavior.

Moreover, during a sustained period of private-sector financial deficit, the bank still had to provide sufficient funds to meet the increase in the demand for cash currency appropriate to economic growth, and therefore a part was deliberate policy. These actions all involved the supply of Bank of Japan credit in a neutral fashion in such a way that undesirable secondary effects had no impact on policy. On account of its flexibility, loan policy was also used at times for adjustment to seasonal fluctuations or irregular variations and to the secular expansion of the private sector's financial deficit, and therefore frequently appeared to be exerting no policy impact.

It is fair to say that operations in the bill and bond markets in postwar Japan were first initiated and developed in response to the pressures arising from loan policy. This chapter describes the evolution of Bank of Japan operations in bills and bonds, and considers their effect on policy.

1. *Development of Bank of Japan Operations in the Bill and Bond Markets*

1.1 *The New Scheme for Monetary Control and the Activation of Operations in Bonds*

In November 1962 the Bank of Japan initiated the system, described in the previous chapter, of loan limits. Simultaneously, it began to conduct purchases and sales of securities with financial institutions—in particular the purchase of securities—much more actively than before. From this time on, operations in securities could be considered one of Japan's main instruments of monetary policy.

The loan control system imposed a limit on the amount of borrowings from the Bank of Japan by each of the ten city banks that were particularly dependent on Bank of Japan loans. However, in the process of economic growth the private business sector showed a persistent and growing financial deficit. Consequently, if monetary policy was to be conducted almost entirely through loan policy, Bank of Japan loans would have to expand cumulatively in line with this financial deficit. In the process, it would be inevitable that city banks would exceed the loan ceiling imposed on them and, as a result, incur a 4 percent p.a. penalty over the official discount rate (initially, 1 sen per diem) thus counteracting and restricting the city banks' lending. To avoid this situation and in order to permit the use of loan controls as a fairly precise instrument of monetary stabilization while adjusting appropriately to the growing financial deficit, it was necessary to supply sufficient Bank of Japan credit consistent with the stance of policy. The instrument introduced at this time was the purchase of bonds.

Since the secondary market in bonds was closed, the bank's operations in securities between November 1962 and January 1966 were not conducted in the open market but on the basis of repurchase agreements between the Bank of Japan and its client banks, which fixed mutual purchase and resale arrangements. The dealing price was calculated by reference to the yield to initial subscribers and was therefore a theoretical price. Securities involved in these operations included government-guaranteed bonds, financial debentures, electric utility bonds, and certain types of local government bonds, while financial institutions dealing in these transactions included banks, the long-term credit banks, authorized foreign exchange banks, the National Federation of Credit Associations, and the Nōrinchūkin Bank.

From January 1966, when long-term government bonds began to be issued, and from February of the same year when the secondary bond market was reopened, the Bank of Japan was able to employ a new bond purchase and sale technique. This new technique dropped the repurchase conditions, abandoned the theoretical pricing system (adopting instead the prevailing market price as a basic criterion), and introduced the brokerage houses as intermediaries. In these three ways, the new system may be said to have moved closer to genuine open-market operations in comparison with the old techniques. In addition, whereas the old system covered government-guaranteed bonds, financial debentures, electric utility bonds, and certain types of local government bonds, the new system was at first only extended to government-guaranteed bonds, though from January 1967 long-term government bonds issued at least one year earlier also became eligible.

These operations in securities are transactions between the Bank of Japan and ordinary commercial financial institutions, conducted by prior announcement of a purchase price by the Bank of Japan, a poll of intending sellers, and allocation of the amount to be purchased among them. Until January 1966 securities could be sold back at the Bank of Japan's option. In other words, the policy of conducting operations in bonds, like the loan policy, amounted to Bank of Japan credit rationing.

Also, since operations in securities were conducted by prior announcement of the terms and conditions for the purchase of a given amount on a given day, the method was conspicuously lacking in flexibility as a monetary instrument. In practice the method adopted was to purchase securities on days when there was an increase in the financial deficit (during months when there was a seasonal deficit) up to the amount indicated by the longer-term trend and as allowed within the framework of policy. If there was a major shortage or surplus of funds for a short period of time, securities would be purchased on the day of maximum shortage or sold on the day of maximum surplus. However, if seasonal demands differed from those forecast, or if irregular and unforeseen fluctuations occurred—due to sudden changes in government expenditure plans, for example—they could not be counteracted by sales or purchases of bonds. Indeed, on a daily basis, bond operations were completely powerless to deal with seasonal fluctuations or irregular variations, and therefore most of the burden of day-to-day monetary adjustment continued to fall on loan policy. But, as shown in chapter 10, section 2, adjustment of the loan volume $\bar{C}$ has a very sensitive impact on the cost and availability of Bank of Japan credit $[a : \bar{r}]$ as felt by the city banks, and therefore its policy impact is overwhelming. Thus it would be desirable to discriminate among banks in the allocation of loans with the intention of neutralizing seasonality or irregularities; but in practice this is no easy matter.

1.2 *The Move Toward Open Market Operations*
Gradual accumulation of experience enabled the Bank of Japan to move toward a flexible policy for operations in securities suitable for neutralizing seasonal or irregular disturbances. Its first attempt after January 1966 was with short-term government bonds through the short-term money-market brokers in the call market. As explained in part I, chapter 3, the yield on short-term government securities is fixed below the short-term money-

market rates such as the call rate, and therefore almost the whole amount of the issue is underwritten by the Bank of Japan and cannot be used for purchasing or selling operations. However, during the easy-money policy after 1965, the yield on short-term governments and the call rate began to converge and the Bank of Japan seized the opportunity to use the securities as an instrument for stabilization operations. The dealing rate among the short-term money brokers is superficially at a discount to that allowed by the Bank of Japan on short-term governments, but in fact, by utilizing double interest payments per diem on days when loans are renewed, it can be raised to the same level as the call rate. Thus, short-term money brokers extended call loans which they had received from lenders to the Bank of Japan instead of to the city banks that would have been their normal clients.

For the most part, the Bank of Japan undertook these operations in bonds with the purpose of ironing out seasonal shortages and surpluses of funds—that is, by sales of short-term governments to (or absorption of call loans from) money-market brokers on days of sizable fund surplus during seasonally liquid months. Conversely, the bank bought back short-term government securities from (or supplied funds to) the money brokers on days of fund shortage during seasonally illiquid months.

Until July 1969 the Bank of Japan set out to engage in short-term purchases of national bonds, government-guaranteed bonds, and financial debentures. After the technique was introduced, however, the amplitude of seasonal surpluses and shortages gradually increased year by year, with the result that these operations became insufficient to neutralize the seasonal ebb and flow of money either through purchases and sales of short-term government securities to money-market brokers alone, or through regulating the volume of loans. Under the system, bonds were bought on days of fund shortage during seasonally tight-money months and resold on days of fund surplus during seasonally easy-money months. Purchases and sales (1) were conditional upon resale or repurchase within one month (except where the Bank of Japan recognized the necessity for another month's extension), and (2) resale prices were fixed at the same level as the purchase price, with interest for the period during which the instrument was held by the Bank of Japan and charged separately based on the criterion of the central rate in the call market (overmonth-end or money brokers' unconditional lending rate). Thus, despite the fact that bond operations utilized long-term bonds, in their essential features they were equivalent to a monetary stabilization program based on short-term money-market interest rates that neutralized monetary fluctuations through operations in short-term instruments. In this respect they were identical to transactions in short-term government bonds with the money-market brokers.

There were, however, two points in which these operations differed from those in short-term government securities. First, whereas short-term governments were generally sold by the Bank of Japan, these short-term transactions usually involved the Bank of Japan as buyer. Second, whereas operations in short-term government paper were conducted through call market brokers, short-term operations in government bonds were conducted directly with ordinary banks, the long-term credit banks, foreign exchange banks, and those banks with accounts at the Bank of Japan: the mutual banks, the National Federation of Credit Associations, and the Nōrinchūkin Bank.

In 1971 there was a conspicuous surplus of funds in the short-term money market as a result of disbursements from the Foreign Exchange Special Account, which accompanied the massive surplus on the international balance of payments, a slackening of private-sector demand for cash currency due to the business recession, and a slowdown in the growth of tax payments. In particular, in May and August 1971 there were huge inflows of short-term funds due to international currency crises—or, to use the previous terminology, a sudden irregularity produced a vast surplus of funds. In reaction to this, the Bank of Japan withdrew loans and absorbed funds through sales of short-term government securities, but it was clearly foreseen that with these instruments alone the surplus of funds could not be absorbed. In August, therefore, the Bank of Japan created a system for sale of central bank bills with the purpose of supplementing its traditional sales of short-term government securities to money-market brokers. Under this system, the Bank of Japan sold foreign exchange bills (of less than three months' maturity) which it had issued itself to the short-term money brokers and to financial institutions. Interest rates were decided by reference to the call rate, and—where necessary—repurchase conditions were also added. By this means the problem of the shortage of suitable instruments for purchasing operations was solved and the absorption of excess funds from the money market was accomplished much more smoothly.

1.3 *Formation of a Bills Discount Market and the Start of Operations in the Bills Discount Market*

Nineteen seventy-one was an eventful year for Japan's bill and bond markets. The year saw the start of a bill discount market in which, from 1972 onward, open-market purchases and sales formed the centerpiece of Bank of Japan bill and bond operations. Until this time, the only short-term market was for the lending and borrowing of overnight, unconditional, and over-month-end funds in the call market, and therefore call loans formed the main type of secondary reserves for financial institutions with surplus funds. In contrast, in the developed financial markets of Europe and North America, interbank (or call) money is supplemented by the existence of markets in short-term government paper, the commercial paper (= bills discount) market, or by markets for the purchase and sale of longer-term bonds approaching maturity. Since all of these markets comprise the short-term money market, financial institutions in these countries can count as secondary reserves not only call loans but also readily realizable commercial bills in the discount market or the bond market, as well as short-term government bonds and bonds nearing maturity.

In early 1971, market participants moved to create a two to three-month market in commercial bills, and as a result, in late May an attempt was made to initiate such a market for surplus funds until the seasonally tighter period of June to August. At first the bills discount rate was set at 0.25 percentage points above the overmonth-end call loan rate with the intention that the rate should be quoted within a band 25 basis points above and below this level. It was decided that money brokers would decide the quotations based on prevailing market conditions, leaving a brokerage spread of 0.125 percent between selling and buying rates. Eligible bills and notes were prime commercial and industrial bills, foreign trade bills, prime single-name bills, and foreign exchange bills equivalent to these but drawn on financial institutions. Also, since the maturity of these bills was one or two months longer than for those being discounted in the market, an additional discounting term of between two and three months was agreed upon (known as "crossing two mountains" because the term of the bill spans two month-end periods).

In 1972 the easy-money policy persisted, and in anticipation of a decline in the call rate with the easing of supply-demand conditions, demand for longer-term overmonth-end call loans slackened. When the outstanding loan volume fell precipitously, there was a movement among market participants to restrict the short-term markets of less than one month to one dealing primarily in overnight and unconditional money. As a result, from June 1 overmonth-end transactions in the call market were suspended, and simultaneously, eligible bills that had served as collateral for call loans shifted over to the bills discount market, greatly enlarging the scale of the market. Thus Japan's short-term money markets now consist of the call market and the bills discount market. The secondary reserves of financial institutions are now divided between highly liquid, very short-term call loans that serve as payment reserves, and bills bought which have maturities between two and three months, both of which have distinct characteristics and different interest-rate structures. With this change in the market, the Bank of Japan's monetary stabilization program in the short-term money markets was enhanced through the addition of purchase and sale operations in commercial bills.

However, in the June–August 1971 period, enormous inflows of short-term money due to the international monetary crisis produced an unexpected surplus of funds, so that Bank of Japan purchasing operations in the bill market could not take place. On the contrary, the bank was compelled by the need to absorb surplus funds to implement sales of bills drawn on itself from August onward, as described above. The bank absorbed such funds either through sales of bills on the market to short-term money brokers, or from sources that would otherwise have placed such funds in the call market. Thus central bank bills sold in the market were utilized by the brokers as collateral for call funds from lenders. Also, in the seasonally liquid October–December period of 1971, the Bank of Japan sold bills directly to the agricultural and forestry credit associations and to the mutual credit associations, which were highly liquid.

Subsequently, in May 1972, central bank bills were again sold in the market through the money brokers, not on the call market but to the bills discount market at rates set in accordance, not with the call rate but in the light of the going rates on commercial bills. This time the brokers did not use the bills that had been sold as collateral for call loans but resold the bills to buyers in the market. The Bank of Japan's open-market operations date, in reality, from this point in time.

Formal operations by the Bank of Japan in commercial bills began in June 1972. With the seasonal fund shortage due to occur in May–August, the Bank of Japan began its first purchasing operations through the money brokers buying commercial bills in the secondary market, and since then it has actively bought such bills every month. The next step was to conduct these operations directly with financial institutions, a move first made in August 1973.

The development of bills drawn on itself and the purchase and sale of commercial bills added powerful weapons to the Bank of Japan's armory. First, as an instrument of monetary stabilization, the bank can now modify the extent of its adjustment in the market day by day or hour by hour in the same way as with loan policy. In terms of its flexibility it is almost identical to loan policy. Second, the Bank of Japan can now operate its monetary stabilization instruments, supplying or withdrawing Bank of Japan credit at short-term money-market interest rates through the money-market brokers. In this way, the bank can avoid the arbitrariness implicit in credit rationing and its impact on the money market and bank behavior. Third, the implementation of the system of bills drawn on the Bank of Japan has greatly enlarged the scope of operations which had hitherto been restricted by the size of the short-term government bond issue, while the implementation of bill-purchasing operations has greatly expanded the type of bills available, as the volume had hitherto been restricted to the amount of eligible securities held in the market. Fourth, the interest rate applied to short-term purchases and sales of bonds or short-term government securities used to be the call rate, which itself was different from those quoted on short-term governments or bonds. Therefore, for such transactions a secondary market in short-term government securities had no role to play, and trends in the secondary bond market also had no direct relevance. Operations in ordinary bills and central bank bills meant for the first time that central bank purchases and sales were at the rates actually prevailing in the bill market and were specifically conducted using bills that were either circulating in the market or were at least eligible to circulate there, with the result that monetary stabilization actions were consistent with and fostered the discipline of the market.

With the completion of this survey of operating instruments, the functional division among the central bank's stabilization instruments can be summarized as follows. First, in response to seasonal or irregular fund surpluses and shortages, the Bank of Japan uses the system of central bank bills or purchases and sales of commercial bills, to which loan policy is supplementary. In addition, in periods when a fund shortage builds up within the framework allowed by overall policy, the bank conducts purchasing operations in long-term national government bonds and government-guaranteed securities, buying additional bills as necessary. Loan policy is retained to exert an impact on cyclical or trend fluctuations in the ebb and flow of funds. In practice, seasonal, irregular, cyclical, and trend fluctuations form a single whole, and it is difficult to differentiate clearly among them. Indeed, given the shortage of tools with which to operate, such outright distinctions are not feasible, but as a method of analysis the functional divisions adopted here are reasonably accurate.

12 The Reserve Requirement System

1. *Evolution of the Reserve Requirement System*

The history of the reserve requirement system in Japan is comparatively short. The system was established by the enactment in May 1957 of the "Law Relating to the Deposit Reserve System" and actually introduced with the setting of reserve requirement ratios for the first time in September 1959. Initially the ratios were applied to ordinary banks, long-term credit banks, foreign exchange specialist banks, trust banks' banking accounts, and foreign banks in Japan, but after April 1963 the system was extended to mutual banks and credit corporations with deposits in excess of ¥20 billion, and from September 1959 reserve requirements were also applied to the Nōrinchūkin Bank, whose funds had been growing particularly rapidly in the period up to 1969.

In 1971, when modifications to the instruments of monetary policy were widely called for in order to cope with changes due to the internationalization of the economy and changes within the monetary structure, the finance minister's advisory body, the Monetary System Research Council (MSRC) considered the question of reserve requirements as part of its plan for improvement of the instruments of monetary policy necessary to achieve simultaneous internal and external equilibrium. Following about six months of deliberations, the MSRC submitted a proposal to the Minister of Finance at the end of the year entitled "Report on Implementation of the Reserve Requirement System." The report found—

1. that the objectives of policy were becoming more numerous;
2. that it was necessary to consider international equilibrium in managing interest rates;
3. that the illiquidity of the commercial banks had undergone a considerable change;

4. that it was necessary to bring in some instrument for the control of inflows and outflows of short-term capital from abroad.

It therefore made concrete proposals intended to achieve the completion of the reserve requirement system and to press for its implementation. The reforms were put into effect from May 1, 1972, and were based on the recommendation of the MSRC. The key points of the reform were:

1. Life insurance companies were again brought within the range of institutions subject to the system.
2. Accounts subject to reserve requirements included yen deposits, financial debentures, trust monies, foreign currency deposits of residents, liabilities due to nonresidents, and other similar liabilities.
3. The maximum reserve requirement ratio was raised from 10 percent to 20 percent, while the maximum rates applicable to residents' foreign currency deposits or liabilities due to nonresidents was raised to 100 percent.
4. The method of computing reserve ratios was extended from a formula applicable to the outstanding absolute balance of deposits to enable the rates to be applicable to changes in deposits, or to permit both systems to apply simultaneously.

Following these revisions, the Bank of Japan enforced a new reserve requirement scheme from May 1, 1972, which distinguished between non-residents' free yen deposits and other deposits; but the new ratios, the institutions covered by the system, and the range of liabilities included in the scheme were the same as before (see table 9.3).

Subsequently, the Bank of Japan imposed a 25 percent reserve requirement from June 1, 1972, on nonresidents' free yen accounts in excess of the average amount in these accounts between April 21 and May 20 of the same year. In addition, to counteract conditions arising after the flotation of the pound on June 23 and to restrict more tightly the inflow of foreign short-term capital, this ratio was raised to 50 percent on amounts in excess of the average between May 21 and June 20 as from July 1. Thus the reforms of May 1972 were almost immediately implemented as part of the measures designed to restrict inflows of short-term capital from abroad.

By contrast, over the period preceding the tight-money policy of 1973, movements in the reserve requirement ratios were not used at all actively as an instrument of domestic stabilization. It is clear from table 9.3, which shows the changes in reserve requirement ratios from the start of the system to November 1975, that reserve requirements were raised only twice with the imposition of each of two phases of tight-money policy, in 1959 and 1961, and subsequently lowered with the lifting of the policy. In these cases the degree of change was small, and on each occasion the rate was only raised once and lowered either once or twice. But when there was a policy shift in 1967, there was no change made in reserve requirement ratios. However, when there was a shift of policy in 1969, despite the fact that reserve requirements had been raised at the start of the tight-money period, there was no lowering of reserve requirements when the policy was relaxed, and the higher rates remained in force.

The reason why changes in reserve requirements were not used very actively for domestic stabilization purposes is that they lack flexibility as a tool to deal with seasonal fluctuations or irregular changes, and are therefore unsuitable. Moreover, as an instrument designed to impact bank behavior, their effects cannot be expected to be of any great significance, for reasons to be explained in the next section.

Nevertheless, with the imposition of a tight-money policy in 1973, reserve requirements were raised five times, and this requires some special explanation. First, despite the revaluation of the yen in 1971, the balance of payments surplus continued to increase after 1972, so that until the yen was revalued again or floated, a full-scale tight-money policy with a higher official discount rate could not be enforced. Therefore, despite its lack of conviction in the announcement effects of the policy, the Bank of Japan raised the reserve requirement ratios at the earliest opportunity in January 1973. Second, the philosophy behind the second to fifth upward changes in reserve requirement ratios after the floating of the yen in February 1973 was that this would mop up the additional liquidity in the banking sector which had accrued in 1971–72 due to the inflow of short-term capital. These changes in reserve requirements were implemented between late 1973 and early 1974 and had most of their impact on other banks (noncity banks) through the "liquidity effect."

2. *Effects of Changes in Reserve Requirements*

Why can changes in reserve requirements not be expected to have significant effects in Japan? In general one may distinguish three types of predictable effects: "liquidity effects," "cost effects," and "announcement effects."

As explained in chapter 6, section 2.3 and chart 6.5, changes in reserve requirements β shift the profit-maximizing level of loans L^* through the "liquidity effect" and the "cost effect." Raising reserve requirements increases the slope of the curve R_c^* (cost effect) and at the same time shifts R_c^* to the left (liquidity effect), so that in chart 6.5 the solid curve R_c^* shifts to the dashed line III III'. This reduces the profit-maximizing level of L^* (shifts L^* to the left in chart 6.6), causing banks to restrain their lending. Lowering reserve requirements causes the curve R_c^* to shift from the dashed line III III' back to the solid line. Similarly, this increases the profit-maximizing level of L^*, encouraging banks to expand their loans.

These are the "liquidity effects" and "cost effects" of changes in reserve requirements. Concerning the impact of any "announcement effect," this depends on whether or not changes in reserve requirements are interpreted as a major shift in monetary policy. Hence, the size of its impact depends on historical and institutional factors as well as the results achieved by the enforcement of other policy measures, so no conceptual evaluation is possible. If such a change were regarded as a fundamental shift in monetary policy, the effects would probably be similar to those described in chapter 10, section 3 in relation to the "announcement effect" of changes in the official discount rate.

So much for the situation in general terms; in fact, in Japan the impact of these three effects is small. The "announcement effect" is small because reserve requirements have not been utilized extensively as an instrument of stabilization, so that there is no widespread familiarity with them and they are not consciously associated with signaling a shift in monetary policy. This tendency is especially true of private-sector business organizations outside the financial institutions. Apart from its infrequent implementation, this is because changes in reserve requirements, unlike changes in the official discount rate that have a direct impact on bank lending rates, do not have the same immediate consequences. Therefore, hardly any of the "announcement effects" of a change in the official discount rate enumerated in chapter 10, section 3—and particularly the effect on business enterprises—can be attributed to changes in reserve requirements.

The reason why the liquidity effect is small is the same as that given in chapter 11, section 2.1 in connection with the liquidity effects of central bank purchasing or selling operations—namely that, since the liquidity effect concerns movements in the profit-maximizing volume of loans L^* through shifts to the left or right in R_c^*, the effect only occurs when, due to the existence of fixed costs $b_2 c_2$ (as in the case of other banks), the system is close to a corner solution. Since the profit-maximizing level of loans L^* for city banks is unstable, the liquidity effect itself must be unstable, a result confirmed statistically in table 7.2 of chapter 7, section 1.2.

Hence, when reserve requirements are increased so as to absorb funds into the accounts of financial institutions at the Bank of Japan, for any given level of loans the liquidity position of banks deteriorates. Those other banks that have a fund position as shown by the existence of fixed costs $b_2 c_2$ will be motivated to restrain their loans in order to prevent this deterioration in liquidity: this is the liquidity effect. But in the case of city banks which have no similar concern for their fund position, there is no motive to restrain their lending and therefore no liquidity effect.

In Japan discussions about the relative insignificance of the reserve requirement system usually relate to the lack of any liquidity effect on city banks. Even if reserve requirements are raised, it is said, banks will compensate for their shortage of liquidity by resorting to Bank of Japan loans, and therefore the measure is meaningless. Alternatively, the effects of reserve requirement changes depend on the effects on loan policy. Such statements imply that the liquidity of city banks is reduced by higher reserve requirements, but because borrowings from the Bank of Japan increase to compensate for this, the reduction in liquidity does not of itself provide any motive to restrain bank lending, because in these circumstances the cost and availability of Bank of Japan loans $[a : \bar{r}]$ determine the level of bank loans.

PART IV

The Effectiveness of Japan's Monetary Policy

In part IV I consider the effectiveness of Japan's monetary policy within the framework of the financial structure set out in part I, the monetary mechanism of part II, and the impact of the various instruments of monetary policy described in part III.

First, I consider what Japan's monetary policy objectives were in the past, and second, what operating targets or intermediate targets the Bank of Japan was using as monetary variables for the attainment of ultimate policy objectives. Finally, I discuss the transmission mechanism linking the ultimate policy objectives with the operating targets, the conditions contributing to the effectiveness of that mechanism, and the limits to the effectiveness of the policy.

13 The Objectives of Monetary Policy

1. *Ultimate Economic Policy Objectives: Prices, International Balance of Payments, and Effective Demand*

1.1 *The Public Statements of the Bank of Japan*

Since there exists a variety of economic policy instruments and objectives, it is the responsibility of the authorities on economic policy to decide on an optimum combination of policy objectives based on the national social utility function, to decide on the optimum combination of instruments for the realization of those policy objectives, and to expedite them. This process is known as the policy assignment problem.[1]

Among the combination of policy instruments, monetary policy is generally considered most appropriate for stabilization or countercyclical policy consisting of (1) stabilization of the domestic price level, (2) equilibrium in the international balance of payments, and (3) the maintenance of full employment. However, monetary policy inevitably affects other objectives besides (1)–(3), among the most important being (4) the promotion of economic growth, and (5) the efficient allocation of resources.

What has been the ultimate policy objective of Japan's monetary policy since the 1950s? In the eighteen years 1955–72 there have been six phases of tight-money policy and seven phases of ease. As judged by movements in the official discount rate, the tight-money phases were: March 1957–June 1958, December 1959–August 1960, July 1961–October 1962, March 1964–January 1965, September 1967–August 1968, and September 1969–October 1970. Between these periods of tightness and ease there were intervals that were neither tight-money periods nor easy-money periods but periods of neutrality.

---

1. For basic contributions on the problems of policy assignment and policy mix, see J. Tinbergen [57] and R. A. Mundell [27].

Table 13.1 Reasons for Change in Official Discount Rates as Given in Statements of the Chairman of the Bank of Japan Policy Committee

Year/Month	Percentage of Change	Balance of Payments	Wholesale Prices	Effective Demand	Monetary Stabilization Measures Adopted	Other Measures Adopted
1955 8	1.46				Restructuring of official discount rates	Shift from penal rate system to official discount rate operations
1957 3	0.37	◎				
5	0.73	◎		○	Adjustment of short-term money-market rates	
1958 6	Δ0.73	◎				
9	Δ0.37					
1959 2	Δ0.36				Adjustment of interest-rate structure	
12	0.36				Flexible use of interest rates	
1960 8	Δ0.36		◎	○		
1961 1	Δ0.37		◎	○		
7	0.37	◎			More flexible use of official discount rate	
9	0.36	◎		○		
1962 10	Δ0.36	◎		○		
11	Δ0.37	◎		○		
1963 3	Δ0.36					
4	Δ0.37				Further adjustment of interest-rate policy	
1964 3	0.73	◎			Restructuring of official discount rates	
1965 1	Δ0.36	◎		○	Further monetary stabilization	
4	Δ0.37	◎		○		
6	Δ0.36			◎		
1967 9	0.36	◎		○		
1968 1	0.37	◎		○		
8	Δ0.37	◎				

1969	9	0.41		◎		(Shift to percent per annum system)
1970	10	Δ0.25		◎		⎱ Objective of policy shifted from
1971	1	Δ0.25	○	○		⎰ elimination of balance of payment
	5	Δ0.25	○	◎		deficit to elimination of surplus
	7	Δ0.25	○	◎		
	12	Δ0.50	○	◎		Additional impetus to lower interest rates
1972	6	Δ0.50	◎	○		General relaxation of interest rates

Symbols: ◎ = primary target; ○ = subsidiary target

To determine the objectives of policy during the seven easy-money periods and six tight-money periods, one may examine the statements of the chairman of the Bank of Japan Policy Board (see table 13.1). With the exception of two occasions (the tight-money policy switch in December 1959, with the reverse switch to easy money in August 1960, and the tight-money switch in September 1969 with its relaxation in October 1970), the remaining five cases of policy relaxation and four cases of monetary tightening were all initiated by the attempt to correct the balance of payments— a tight-money policy to solve a deficit, and its relaxation owing to improvement in balance of payments conditions. In the two exceptional cases, despite the fact that there was a balance of payments surplus, the policy was primarily initiated in order to curb the rise in domestic prices— particularly wholesale prices—and when the price rise had been calmed, the policy was relaxed.

Also, in cases where correction of a balance of payments deficit was intended, curbing the level of business activity was frequently mentioned, along with the restraint of corporate investment activity. In addition to correction of a balance of payments deficit, the dullness of economic activity was frequently mentioned as a reason for switching to an easy-money policy. On two exceptional occasions, the intention was to curb domestic price increases. Also, in one case, excess corporate investment was mentioned as a reason for imposing a monetary squeeze, while in another, the cautious attitudes toward industrial production, and weak corporate investment intentions, were given as reasons for the relaxation of policy.

The above case histories provide as much as can be derived from the statements of the chairman of the Bank of Japan's Policy Board and indicate the general trend of policy. Finally, however, the case of the five successive reductions in the discount rate in January, May, July, and December 1971 and June 1972 by a total of 1.75 percent must be mentioned, as it represented a major change. On each of these five reductions the elimination of the balance of payments surplus was simultaneously put forward as a specific policy objective along with the promotion of domestic business recovery.

1.2 *A Subjective View of Policy Aims and Their Relation to the Developmental Stages of the Japanese Economy*

In addition to the known facts from the statements of the chairman of the Bank of Japan's Policy Board, it is possible to collate my own experience as an employee of the Bank of Japan itself to give a subjective account of the views of the bank on monetary policy.

The Bank of Japan has had three policy objectives: (1) the stabilization of domestic prices, (2) equilibrium in the international balance of payments, and (3) a level of effective demand appropriate for a viable operating rate for capital plant and equipment. Compared with the general stabilization policy outlined above, the only difference lies in the change in (3), with an effective demand level suitable for a viable operating rate for capital plant and equipment in place of the maintenance of full employment.

That full employment was not acknowledged as an objective reflects Japan's characteristics as an economy. The lifetime employment system in Japan means that alterations in the aggregate supply-demand gap are not accompanied by as much change in the volume of employment as in Europe or North America. These changes are reflected more in the variation in bonuses or overtime payments. Thus, compared with Europe and North America, unemployment has not figured prominently among the stabilization objectives, and indeed, appropriate statistics for judging the existence of unemployment do not in fact exist.[2] For this reason the Bank of Japan has made its judgments, not on the basis of the relation between effective demand and the labor force, but on the relation between effective demand and the level of business activity, especially capital equipment investment and utilization levels.

Concerning the long-term objectives which monetary policy affects derivatively—that is, (4) the promotion of economic growth, and (5) the efficient allocation of resources—there is nothing explicit in the bank's policy statements. However, whenever the discount rate has been lowered (August 1955, January 1961, March 1963, and April and June 1972), either interest-rate policy, the normalization of the structure of interest rates, or greater flexibility of interest rates has been put forward as a policy objective. Thus, to a degree, the efficient allocation of financial resources, and therefore physical resources, has been implicit in the objectives. However, as with the reduction of the discount rate in January 1961, "normalization of interest rates, or the liberalization of interest rate policy" can be read as "the policy of promoting artificially low interest rates."

This subjective judgment of the Bank of Japan on objectives is closely associated with the developmental stage in the Japanese economy. In the postwar era, after the end of American aid and special demand created by the Korean War, and particularly after the immediate postwar recovery was completed, it is fair to say that the regular business cycle began from around 1952–53. 1955 saw the first bottom in the cycle as, with the completion of capital stock adjustment, an intermediate bottom was passed.

Thus, in Japan after 1955, while private plant and equipment entered an intermediate upward expansion phase and the country was fortunate enough to have advantageous opportunities for the introduction of new technology, the economy exhibited vigorous growth; and these two forces

2. Due to the imprecise definition of unemployment as measured in the "Manpower Survey" conducted by the Statistical Department of the the Office of the Prime Minister, these statistics are not often utilized.

together provided the driving force for rapid growth. Rapid growth was the basic condition for improving the national welfare at this stage in its history.

One may define national welfare in a country as consisting of efficiency in the allocation of resources combined with a fair distribution of income.[3]

---

3. The word *welfare* is generally used in two senses—one a strict definition and the other more general. When used in the narrow sense (e.g. in referring to social security or social projects), it implies the activity of redistributing income to lower-income groups. The so-called Six Welfare Laws (Livelihood Protection Act, the Child Welfare Act, the Welfare of the Aged Act, the Mother and Child Welfare Act, Welfare for the Physically Disabled Act, and Welfare of the Mentally Disabled Act) were aimed at these groups, and until comparatively recently the building of a welfare state was considered to mean improvements in this type of welfare, narrowly defined. For example, in the Income Doubling Plan of 1960, the improvement of social security in order to reduce social tensions for those sectors bypassed by economic growth was dealt with in a chapter entitled "Towards a Modern Welfare State."

However, when an improvement in national "welfare" is stated to be necessary as a general objective of economic policy, the word refers to the level of human satisfaction in a broad sense, and to the same concept as social welfare or utility used in modern economics. The objective of economic policy in modern economics is the maximization of social welfare or utility through efficient production and a more equal distribution of income. The pioneer of this philosophy was Pigou, who postulated the conditions necessary for an improvement in the economic welfare of society as (1) an increase in per capita income (which he called the pro rata distribution of national income), (2) a relative increase in the national income among the poorer classes, and (3) a reduction in the range of fluctuation between national income and the income of the poorer classes. If economic welfare in these senses increased, he considered social welfare also to have increased. These three criteria correspond to efficient production (resource allocation), a more equal distribution, and economic stabilization, though today the third is widely considered a necessary precondition for the second, so that in the last analysis the objectives are reduced to the first two.

From this standpoint, the general objectives of economic policy—stable prices, equilibrium in the balance of payments, economic growth, full employment, and an improved distribution of income and wealth—are significant to the extent that they contribute to more efficient production and a more equal distribution of income. The three objectives of monetary policy cited in this book conform to this statement.

In modern economics it was first thought that reliance on market principles was the necessary and sufficient condition for the most efficient production, while the main topic for analysis was the optimal allocation of resources through the price mechanism (the achievement of the Pareto optimum). Therefore, in order to raise the level of national welfare it was considered necessary and sufficient to preserve competitive conditions in the domestic economy. However, in recent years economists have appreciated that: (1) even if competitive conditions were achieved, production was not necessarily of optimal efficiency (a situation known as market failure); and (2) even if production was temporarily optimal, such a Pareto optimum would be contradictory to more equal income distribution, so welfare could not be maximized solely by reliance on market principles.

The reasons for "market failure" are (1) the existence of external effects which distort the market mechanism, (2) the existence of noncompetitiveness in consumption and nonexcludability in public goods, and (3) the existence of industries (e.g. railroads and dams) with declining average cost curves up to the point where those industries become extremely large. Another reason why the Pareto optimum does not ensure a more equal distribution of income is that

The constraints on resources in Japan at this particular stage were, in effect, foreign exchange (to pay for imports of raw materials) and capital plant and equipment. Also, there was some maldistribution of income insofar as there was hidden unemployment among the lower urban classes and the farmers, victims of the dual wage structure. Consequently, investment was promoted to make up the capital deficiency, and exports and foreign capital importation were promoted in order to obtain foreign exchange. Further, in order to ensure an effective utilization of foreign exchange, strict foreign exchange controls (on imports, payments for services, and capital outflows) were instituted. These were the basic *tactics* designed to achieve the desired allocation of resources for improving national welfare. The export- and investment-led rapid economic growth, a rising income level, a reduction in hidden unemployment, and a narrowing of the dual wage structure, comprised the *strategy* for increasing the national welfare.

Underlying the tactics and strategy were the above-mentioned goals of monetary policy (1)–(3), which produced the following specific problems. When the business cycle became overheated, plant and equipment investment was overdone, and the level of effective demand (3) exceeded the supply capacity of existing plant and equipment, the balance of payments (2) would turn to deficit, and wholesale prices would start to rise (1). Also, in periods of business slowdown, available plant and equipment supply capacity exceeded the level of effective demand (3), the balance of payments (2) would switch to surplus, and wholesale prices (1) would drop sharply. In these cases the policy objectives were not contradictory. Domestic price stabilization (1) and an appropriate effective demand level for the available capital stock (3) were necessary conditions for equilibrium in the balance of payments (2). The tight-money policies of 1957 and 1961 are classic examples of the pursuit of these three policy objectives.

If one examines the record of changes in policy objectives as a guide to the ranking of objectives in these two periods, both for the timing of the start of tight money and the lifting of the policy, and judges by the rate of rise of wholesale prices, the balance of payments position, and the rate of increase in GNP, it is clear that among the three objectives the balance of payments (2) had priority. The reason is that in both cases, while wholesale prices fell after the start of the tight-money policy and while economic growth slowed down, the tight-money policy itself was not relaxed until after the balance of payments had returned to surplus. Of the two major resource constraints at this time—foreign exchange and capital equipment—

it is inconsistent with (*a*) reward corresponding to effort, (*b*) equality of opportunity, and (*c*) protection of the right to life.

For these reasons modern economics has come to the belief that maximum national welfare cannot be attained without policies which correct for market failure or assist in the redistribution of income.

the more serious was foreign exchange. Therefore, there was a tendency to judge whether prices or the level of effective demand by the foreign exchange position were rising too much, since both were liable to cause a deficit. In this sense also the constraint on capital plant and equipment was ultimately foreign exchange, because imports could not be brought in to augment supply capacity without confronting the foreign exchange constraint.

Within the Bank of Japan the three objectives (1)–(3) were never regarded as entirely independent of each other, since (1) domestic prices and (2) the international balance of payments were in essence two aspects of currency values, domestic and foreign, while (3) the appropriate level of effective demand tended to be regarded as one and the same instrument for achieving stable currency values. Thus, even if domestic prices were stable or declining, so long as this price movement was attained at the cost of a balance of payments deficit, then the tight-money policy must continue. From this standpoint, the policy objective of the Bank of Japan was stable money values, and because at this stage in its development Japan's key resource was foreign exchange, a decline in domestic money values would sometimes show up as a deficit in the balance of payments. Therefore, the effective level of demand was judged, not only in terms of capital plant and equipment, but also in relation to contraints on the supply capacity of foreign exchange. A simultaneous balance was the basic condition for price stability. And since foreign exchange was the more critical of the two, when adjustments were made to the level of effective demand, the achievement of external equilibrium appeared outwardly to be the chief objective.

The single exception during this period was the tight- or neutral-money policy from December 1959 through August 1960. Throughout the period the balance of payments remained in surplus, but the policy was maintained in order to arrest the rise in domestic wholesale prices and to restrain excess demand (i.e. objectives 1 and 3). The background to this preventive tight-money policy was that, following the so-called Jimmu Boom of 1955–57, a very severe tight-money policy had been imposed to meet a critical foreign exchange situation, and the economy had plunged into a deep recession. Judging from the fact that achievement of external equilibrium had caused such a large disruption, it was considered desirable in 1959 to impose a mild tightening of policy at an early stage to ensure a sustained cyclical upswing. Also, in this particular case the reason for restraining wholesale prices and the level of effective demand at such an early stage was in order to avoid a deterioration in the balance of payments at a later date. To this extent, the real, underlying motive or policy objective was equilibrium in the balance of payments (or the stability of money values in Japan relative to those abroad).

The separation of domestic price stability from balance of payments equilibrium as a policy objective was first deliberately enunciated in the early 1960s, when consumer prices started to rise rapidly. Stable wholesale prices were considered necessary to maintain international competitiveness abroad and to prevent the erosion of consumers' welfare at home. However, during this period the rise in consumer prices and the wide discrepancy between consumer and wholesale prices occurred against the background of an attempt to solve the problem of latent unemployment and the dual wage structure, and thus to produce a change in the distribution of income that would contribute to an improvement in national welfare. Hence any restriction of aggregate demand, which would have reduced the level of wholesale prices and produced a slowdown in economic growth (thus preserving the latent unemployment and the dual wage structure) in an attempt to stabilize consumer prices, was not part of the policy consensus. Thus, for example, neither of the tight-money policies of 1964 or 1967 were aimed primarily at holding down the rate of rise of domestic prices: both were initiated due to a deterioration in the balance of payments with the objective of restoring external equilibrium.

Internal price stability only became the primary objective of policy in name and in reality during the tight-money policy of September 1969–October 1970. Although the balance of payments was in surplus throughout the period, a sharp cyclical expansion of private investment against a background of rising effective demand had led to a sharp upturn in wholesale prices, and this induced the authorities to impose a tight-money policy. Similar to the precautionary tight-money policy of December 1959, this policy was adopted before the expansion of the business cycle had been allowed to develop too far, and with the deliberate intention of maintaining steady growth in the economy. On this occasion, however, the curbing of wholesale prices in order to forestall the possibility of loss of international competitiveness in the future was not an important consideration. Contrary to the situation in 1959, it was feared that the balance of payments surplus would increase rather than decrease under the tight-money policy. The reasons given for not wishing to allow wholesale prices to rise were: (a) that this would invite an even steeper rise in consumer prices, thus damaging welfare and distorting the distribution of income; and (b) such an upsurge in wholesale prices would instill inflationary fears in the corporate sector, thus undermining worthwhile investment activity and distorting the allocation of resources.

The difference between 1959 and 1969 reflects the fact that the economy had in the interim entered a new stage of development. From 1955 until around 1967 the economy was short of resources, mainly capital plant and equipment, and foreign exchange—particularly the latter—but from about 1968 the constraint imposed by the international balance of payments was notably less onerous, and as a result of the intensification of the problem of pollution, other problems such as constraints on the labor supply, social infrastructure capital, the availability of land, the natural environment, and imported natural resources came to the fore. Emphasis in policy therefore began to shift from concern about the efficient allocation of resources, priority for private investment in productive facilities, and the accumulation of foreign exchange, to concern about the provision of social capital related to national needs, the preservation of the environment through antipollution measures, and the elimination of the balance of payments surplus. These changes were evident in the plans for improving the level of social capital spelled out in the New National Overall Development Plan (1969), the New Economic and Social Development Plan (1970) and the hosting of the International Pollution Symposium (1970); but even more decisive changes were to follow the upward revaluation of the yen in 1971.

On the question of a fair distribution of income, the period 1955–65 saw the end of latent unemployment, and the late 1960s witnessed a trend toward greater equality of wage payments, so that the focus of debate shifted to the discriminatory effects of the rise in consumer prices on different income groups, such as the redistribution of income between land-owning and nonland-owning households, and the hardships faced by pensioners, the old, the physically disabled, and fatherless families.

These trends led to a simultaneous reappraisal of the competing requirements of efficient resource allocation and fair income distribution necessary to improve national welfare, and the emergence of a trade-off between the three objectives of monetary policy. (1) Internal price stability was necessary to avoid the unfair distribution of income that resulted from domestic inflation, but it could adversely affect corporate investment activity and hence the efficient allocation of resources; however, under a fixed exchange rate domestic price stability (1) was not necessarily consistent with the efficient allocation of resources in the sense of achieving equilibrium in (2) the international balance of payments (eliminating the surplus). Moreover, as the resource constraint moved from foreign exchange and capital plant and equipment to such factors as labor, the environment, and energy, (3) the level of effective demand could no longer be judged on the basis of the relation between overall supply capacity, available foreign exchange, and capital equipment, but had to be decided in the light of its relation with the scarcer resources of labor, a healthy environment, and oil supplies. Estimating the appropriate level of final demand (3) on the basis of these criteria was no guarantee that the result would be consistent with the other two objectives of (1) internal price stability and (2) equilibrium in the balance of payments.

This change can also be studied in terms of the conflict between domestic money values and foreign money values. During the period when foreign exchange was the main resource constraint confronting the Japanese economy, a decline in money values—that is, a decline relative to external values—normally appeared in the shape of a shortage of foreign exchange. The lack of foreign exchange led to supply shortages in the domestic commodity markets, and this produced a rise in prices in Japan in such a way that the internal decline in money values paralleled the external fall.

However, when the resource constraint moved from foreign exchange to manpower and the environment, the resources in short supply were labor, congenial cities, suitable sites for factories, antipollution technology, and oil reserves, so that the decline in domestic money values appeared in the form of rapid wage increases, spiraling rents, increasing costs of production and distribution, and more generally in domestic price inflation. Moreover, as long as the exchange rate was pegged, foreign exchange reserves continued to grow, causing an increase of values in Japan relative to those abroad, and aggravating the discrepancy between the movement of internal and external money values. The appropriate level of effective demand could not therefore be easily decided on the basis of either stability in internal money values (i.e. those based on the most efficient usage of labor, natural resources, the environment, and importable oil reserves) or stability of external money values (i.e. those based on the efficient utilization of foreign financial assets given surplus foreign exchange reserves).

From the perspective of a trade-off between the three objectives of monetary policy, the proper choice can only be between either: (*a*) the selection and pursuit of the optimum combination of the objectives (1) ∼ (3) capable of independent accomplishment by monetary policy, based on an efficient allocation of resources and a more equal distribution of income appropriate to the maximization of national welfare; or (*b*) the selection and pursuit of one of the policy objectives, leaving the other two policy objectives to an allocative mechanism outside the range of monetary policy.

The tight-money policy imposed between September 1969 and October 1970 was certainly not fully cognizant of these changed circumstances and, without resort to any other policy instrument to achieve equilibrium in the balance of payments, monetary policy set out solely to achieve domestic price stability. Herein lay a fundmental flaw. Conversely, because the contradiction in objectives (1) ∼ (3) was disregarded in allowing a complete relaxation of monetary policy, as evidenced by the successive reductions in the official discount rate in January, May, July, and December 1971 and June 1972, all three objectives were simultaneously pursued. However, the conflict between the three objectives even during a recession period became very apparent in the steep rise in wholesale prices after August 1972. Given the trade-off that exists between its three objectives, monetary policy is necessarily confronted with the choice between the two options (*a*) and (*b*) above.

1.3 *Objective Assessment of Monetary Policy Targets*

In the preceding section the ultimate objectives of monetary policy as pursued by the Bank of Japan were examined from a subjective standpoint. Here they will be examined objectively to determine the extent to which they were pursued by the authorities. For an empirical analysis of the relation between the objectively viewed behavior of central banks and their subjective policy targets, Dewald and Johnson [8] and Reuber [34] developed and computed central bank reaction functions. These functions took a monetary variable which was a direct operating target of the central bank in the United States or Canada (e.g. policy variables over which the monetary authorities had some discretionary control, such as the discount rate, a short-term money-market rate, or money supply) as the unexplained variable, and regressed them against a set of ultimate policy targets in the real economy (e.g. prices, the balance of payments, the unemployment rate, the economic growth rate, etc.) as explanatory variables. This technique enables the reaction of central banks to changes in ultimate policy objectives to be observed in terms of the policy instruments activated in response to those changes.

Kaizuka [16] has conducted empirical research on Japanese monetary policy for the decade 1955–65, and his analysis yields the following conclusions. The Bank of Japan did not pursue an optimum combination of multiple policy objectives between which there was a trade-off, but pursued one single policy objective. That policy was the maintenance of equilibrium in the current account of the balance of payments, stable wholesale prices, or the desired level of effective demand; but since these three objectives were not mutually inconsistent, it is difficult by econometric methods to determine which objective was dominant at any time. However, given the juxtaposition of all three objectives, the reaction function with the current account of the balance of payments is significant as an explanatory variable, whereas the significance of the other two explanatory variables is low, so it could be argued that equilibrium of the current balance was the direct objective, while the other two objectives were simultaneously accomplished as a result of the primary objective.

Kaizuka's conclusion (that equilibrium in the current account of the balance of payments was the primary objective among the three during the period 1955–65, while there was no trade-off between the three objectives) remains, in statistical terms, in the realm of hypothesis. Insofar as these results provide rough confirmation of the subjective analysis of the Bank of Japan's policy objectives, the hypothesis that, in an objective sense, the Bank of Japan's monetary policy between 1955 and 1965 was directed at achieving equilibrium in the international balance of payments is therefore persuasive.

2. Intermediate Monetary Policy Objectives

2.1 Credit Rationing among Japanese City Banks

The monetary mechanism of stabilization in Japan differs markedly from that in the United States or Britain. The main differences, examined in parts I–III, relate to the fact that high-powered money is supplied not solely by open-market operations, but by credit rationing operating through the system of overloan. Therefore, in the Japanese case, high-powered money is not supplied to any bank that is willing to acquire it through market transactions at the interest rate offered by the central bank, but it is allocated in a specific amount to a specific bank chosen by the central bank from among those wishing to obtain high-powered money. In other words, for a given level of the official discount rate there is excess demand from the commercial banks for scarce reserves, and these are controlled at the Bank of Japan's "loan window."

Such a policy is distinct from choosing a particular level of interest rate or a specific value for a monetary aggregate as an operating target for any given money demand function in order to select from a limitless number of possible combinations of interest rate and money supply. This policy implies the deliberate choice of a combination of a particular volume of money and a specific level of interest rate that is not located on the demand for money function. As a consequence, the demand for money at the chosen level of interest rate exceeds the volume of money supplied. The reasons for the adoption of this type of stabilization policy are set out in chapters 3 and 4.

Bank of Japan credit allocations $\bar{C}$ influence the cost and availability $[a : \bar{r}]$ of Bank of Japan credit as experienced by the city banks, and thereby affect (1) the loan volume L_1 of the city banks themselves, and (2) the banks' attitude toward borrowing call money and hence the call rate r_c. The intermediate or operating targets which the Bank of Japan has tried to control are therefore (1) the increase in loan volume of the city banks and (2) the call rate. The organizations within the Bank of Japan responsible for control over these targets are the Fund Section and General Administration Section of the Business Department. To strengthen its power in controlling the increase in city bank loan volume, the Bank of Japan has experimented with moral suasion in the form of loan supervision, ceilings on loan increases, and position guidance—together popularly known as "window controls" or "window guidance." In connection with the call rate, the bank maintains contact with the Sanmeikai,[4] a regular meeting of call market brokers

---

4. The Sanmeikai initially took its name from the fact that it met on the third Monday of the month (*San* = third; *mei* is a more euphonic but similar ideographic substitute for

(representing the lenders) and the heads of city bank fund departments (who are the borrowers). However, the real basis of the effectiveness of (1) and (2) is the credit allocation $\bar{C}$ made at the lending window. If unreasonably low loan limits were enforced, always in the past the incidence of "hidden" or "unreported" loans increased. Similarly, if an unrealistic call rate was imposed relative to the trend of supply and demand in the market, transactions at black market rates invariably increased.

The operating targets pursued subjectively by the Bank of Japan were (1) the increase in city bank lending and (2) the call rate; but the question one must ask is whether these two targets were successfully controlled in an objective sense. Again, Kaizuka's results with the Bank of Japan's reaction function provide interesting information.[5] His tests took total money supply, cash currency plus demand deposits at all banks, city bank loan volume, and the call rate, in turn, as four unexplained variables for the Bank of Japan's operating targets and computed the reaction function using the current account of the balance of payments, wholesale prices, and the index of mining and manufacturing production as explanatory variables corresponding to ultimate policy objectives. Satisfactory results were obtained only with the call rate as the unexplained variable. In an objective analytic sense therefore, the conclusion was that the best-controlled intermediate target of the Bank of Japan was the call rate.

At this time the Bank of Japan did not deliberately pursue money supply as an operating target, partly because for technical reasons the money supply statistics were announced with a lag of more than one month, and partly because the trend of money supply was set by the increase in bank lending, at least until the late 1960s. Hence, if the increase in city bank lending was controlled and the call rate was controlled (its impact being on the loan increases of noncity banks), then the money supply was in effect also being controlled.

The significance of fluctuations in money supply requires analysis of the economic units that hold money and why they hold it. In the investment-led Japanese economy, what mattered were variations in the money balances of the corporate sector and the motives behind those changes. It was for this reason that the Bank of Japan generally paid attention to changes in cash and deposits held by the corporate sector and the lending attitude of banks as perceived by firms (i.e. the availability of bank credit), as revealed by the "Short-Term Economic Forecast of Leading Enterprises," rather than to changes in the money supply itself.

---

getsu = Monday; *kai* = meeting). At first, the meeting was between heads of city bank finance departments, but now there is also a meeting of section chiefs of city bank finance departments, and this means there are now two meetings: the Bucho Sanmeikai and the Kacho Sanmeikai.

5. See Kaizuka [16].

14 The Effectiveness of Monetary Policy

The previous chapter was concerned with the ultimate objectives of monetary policy and with the operating or intermediate targets. In this chapter I shall be concerned with the transmission mechanism which links the two sets of objectives and targets, and this will lead to a discussion of the effectiveness of monetary policy in Japan.

1. *The Transmission Mechanism*

1.1 *The Impact on Bank Loans*
As we have seen from our study in parts I–III, since the mid-1950s overloan has existed as a structural feature of the economy in Japan, and therefore monetary policy has as its starting point the rationing of Bank of Japan loans to the city banks. Although the Bank of Japan's operations in bonds and commercial bills have been to a greater or lesser extent market transactions (i.e. nondiscriminatory purchases or sales through a broker at the going market rate), so long as the bank's discount window is open for low price, nonequilibrium credit allocations, one may say that in effect all Bank of Japan credit is supplied through a rationing mechanism. We now seek to confirm this point.

In its day-to-day regulation of the market the Bank of Japan has, as we saw in chapter 9, two major considerations to take into account: (1) the surplus or shortage of funds in the market resulting from the interaction of the demand for cash currency from the nonbank public, the net balance of the Treasury's account (including government bond issues), and the net balance of the Foreign Exchange Special Account with the private sector; and (2) the demand for cash currency and reserves to meet reserve requirements by the banks. In order to offset (1) and (2), the Bank of Japan may (3) carry out operations in securities and commercial bills at market interest

217

rates in order to balance the supply and demand for funds. Operations in (3) can either be conducted in order to balance the total of (1) and (2) exactly, or the bank has the option to leave a slight surplus or shortage of funds. If a slight shortage is engineered, either banks will be unable to accumulate reserves at the rate they intended (2) or they will become dependent upon borrowings at the Bank of Japan's loan window (4). Even in the former case (2), when the banks find they are short of reserves they will in the end be driven to depend upon Bank of Japan loans (4) to make up the shortfall of reserves. These loans are the ones available at the official discount rate—i.e. below prevailing market interest rates. Thus, both (3) bond or bill operations, and (2) reserve deposits are an instrument for forcing banks on to (4), the rationed Bank of Japan loans, and when the bank makes these allocations it is the bank's lending attitude which is the starting point for the effectiveness of policy.

This does not mean that either market operations or reserve requirement operations have no effect, but it does mean that the effects of Bank of Japan credit rationing are by far the most important. Here we may consider the effects simply in terms of a cost effect and a liquidity effect. Bond or bill market operations (3) are intended to prevent disruptive fluctuations in underlying market interest rates, and therefore—depending on one's definition—have no cost effect. In other words, the function of (3) is to ensure that seasonal fluctuations, irregular variations, and cyclical fluctuations have no cost effect on market interest rates. On the other hand, reserve requirement changes (2) definitely do have a cost effect insofar as they increase or decrease the "rate of the cash drain" due to loans, and therefore have the same effect as a change in the effective lending rate (= nominal lending rate ÷ rate of cash drain). Hence a rise in the reserve requirement rate is equivalent to a fall in the banks' lending rates. In practice, changes in Japan's reserve requirement rates are very small in magnitude, so their impact is negligibly small by comparison with the marginal return on bank lending, and we may therefore ignore the cost effects of reserve requirement changes.

Next, since the liquidity effects of (2) and (3) do not exist for banks that have no "sense of position" (i.e. banks which do not operate close to a corner maximum and whose fund position is not a fundamental determinant of their behavior), and we know that city banks do not operate in this manner, it is almost impossible to exert any liquidity effect on city banks through changes in reserve requirements or through operations in securities and commercial bills.

From the above discussion and the results of our study in part III, we may state that the starting point for the effects of policy in Japan's monetary policy is the Bank of Japan's loan rationing $\bar{C}$, as used in the theoretical model of part II.

In the transmission mechanism, Bank of Japan loan rationing to the city banks has two important effects. First, it affects the variable $[a : \bar{r}]$ in city banks' demand for call loans function, and hence determines L_1, and second, it induces changes in the call rate r_c through the same channel. Thus the availability of Bank of Japan's loans affects both the volume of city bank lending and the amount of money they borrow in the call market These two effects impinge directly on the Bank of Japan's operating targets. To reinforce the first effect, the Bank of Japan uses its Loan Assessments or Loan Limit System and Position Guidance, all of which are basically techniques of moral suasion. The second effect (on the call rate) is important not only for the city banks, but also for the other banks' lending function, because for them the call rate r_c is a key variable affecting their loan behavior. Given the imbalance of bank liquidity over the past fifteen years, the latter effect has been essential in controlling the aggregate of bank loans, since only 30–40 percent of all bank loans are made by city banks and thus subject to control through Bank of Japan credit allocations. By restricting its loans, the Bank of Japan causes the call rate to rise; this encourages the other banks who are not lenders in the call market to increase their loans to the call market and reduce their regular loans; and the city banks are guided by the Bank of Japan to use these funds from the call market to repay their loans from the Bank of Japan. Correspondingly, a relaxation in Bank of Japan credit produces a decline in the call rate that encourages other banks to reduce their loans to the call market and enables them to increase their regular loans.

Of course, if there were no effect through the call rate, variations in the loans of other banks would necessarily depend on either (*a*) changes in available funds resulting from changes in the loan position of city banks, or (*b*) changes in lending opportunities reflecting fluctuations in the business cycle also resulting from variations in city bank loans. If this were the case, changes in other banks' loans would lag behind changes in city bank loans, but the fact is that they do not. The evidence is presented in chart 14.1, which shows that there has been no change in this relationship even up to 1974, thus attesting to the continued importance of the call rate.

There is no major difference in opinion among specialists in monetary theory concerning the two propositions that the basis of the effectiveness of monetary policy is in bank lending policy, and that at the heart of loan policy is the effect of the Bank of Japan's credit rationing. As to the main route by which commercial banks' loan behavior is governed through Bank of Japan credit rationing, there is a difference of opinion. R. Tachi [52] and H. T. Patrick [33] appear to emphasize the direct effect of Bank of Japan credit on bank loans ($\bar{C} \to [a : \bar{r}] \to L_1$).[1] I emphasize the route whereby

1. Prof. Ryūichiro Tachi [52] expresses the view that the crux of the effectiveness of policy is the Bank of Japan's direct controls on bank credit, or "window controls." Since he is referring to controls on loans of city banks to their customers, he implies the following chain: $\bar{C} \to [a : \bar{r}] \to L_1$, plus moral suasion to supplement this mechanism. However, since Tachi

Chart 14.1   Fluctuations in City Bank and Other Bank Lending

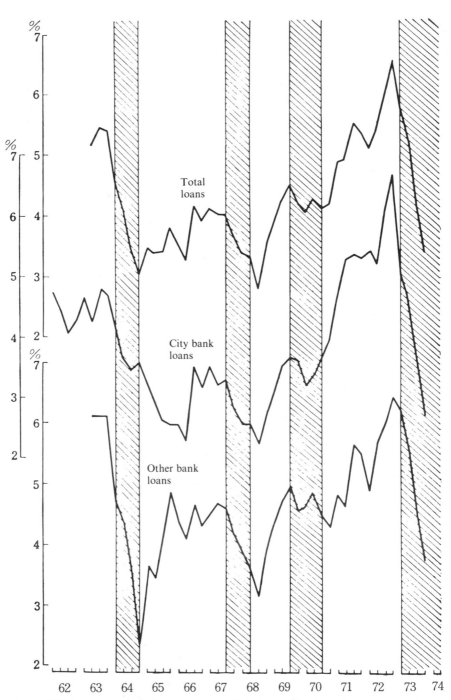

Total
loans

City bank
loans

Other bank
loans

Note: SAQ data, percentage change over preceding quarter. Average of month-end statistics, unadjusted for under-reporting after 1965.

Bank of Japan credit affects the call rate, and this affects not only city banks but also other banks ($C \rightarrow [a : \bar{r}] \rightarrow r_c \rightarrow L_1, L_2$).[2] If one tries to use econometric methods to verify which of these two routes is more realistic, one encounters some difficulties. The problem is that statistical identification of all banks' loan function (which includes the city banks) to separate the direct effects on bank loans of the cost and availability of Bank of Japan credit $[a : \bar{r}]$, and the indirect effects on bank loans of the same variable through the call rate r_c, is complicated by multicollinearity (see chap. 7, sec. 1.2). However, I believe that there are reasonable grounds for rejecting the hypothesis that only the first route is valid, since it is a statistical fact that, not only do city banks not lead, but also other banks either lead or are simultaneously affected, and therefore the second route is to be emphasized. Moreover, in chapter 7, section 1.2 it was shown that the call rate was statistically significant in the other banks' loan function. This is another reason for stressing the role of the second transmission route. (In the city bank loan function the call rate r_c is also statistically significant, but the effects of r_c and the effects of $[a : \bar{r}]$ again remain statistically indistinguishable.)

1.2 *Characteristics of the Transmission Mechanism and Its Effects on Real Economic Activity*

Given the predominance of indirect financing and the inflexibility of bank lending rates, city bank and other bank loans must be "allocated" to or "rationed" among corporate enterprises. In the presence of overborrowing, the determination of the corporate enterprise asset selection budget is crucially affected by bank credit allocations. Hence the availability of city bank credit (variable b) as subjectively felt by the corporate sector generally determines corporate expenditure levels, and particularly corporate investment decisions.

Variations in corporate investment in an investment-led economy greatly influence the level of effective demand, which in turn affects the supply and demand for commodities, the supply and demand for labor, and the balance of payments (current account). Thus the ultimate objectives of monetary policy—domestic prices and external equilibrium, etc.—are clearly affected, and in the longer term there is a broader impact on economic

---

uses the same expression in other contexts to refer specifically to Bank of Japan credit, if this is what is intended then there is no full explanation of the rest of the transmission process.

H. T. Patrick [33] clearly emphasizes the transmission effect $\bar{C} \rightarrow [a : \bar{r}] \rightarrow L_1$. His analysis is that bank behavior in Japan is not necessarily governed by profit-maximization motives, suggesting that the central control of the banking system is significantly influenced by the importance of human relations and by sanctions based on shame.

2. For the difference between these two views, see M. Rōyama [35], [36], and [37] and Kaizuka [16], [17].

growth. This is the basic transmission mechanism of monetary policy in Japan, but it is worth pointing out at least three special characteristics that can be identified.

First, the operating target is the short-term money-market interest rate (the call rate, and since 1972 also the bills discount rate). This rate plays a major role as a key variable in the transmission mechanism between the authorities and the other banks that do not receive Bank of Japan loans, and crucially affects their general behavior. Second, separate from the fact that the change in the call rate is a key variable affecting bank behavior, credit rationing is a determining factor in the transmission mechanism either between the Bank of Japan and the banking system or between the banks and business firms, but fluctuations in interest rates as a whole are not important.

Third, the transmission is a straight-line mechanism: Bank of Japan → banking system → business firms. With the exception of the announcement effect of changes in the official discount rate or in the reserve requirement rate, there is no feedback effect on monetary policy as a result of its direct impact on firms and households. (As shown in chapter 5, strictly speaking there is such a feedback mechanism in the general equilibrium structure, and it is not a perfect straight-line relation; but the feedback is very small, and insufficient to eclipse the main effect.) The reason for this is that, in Japan, business and households are cut off from the short-term money market (they cannot purchase short-term government bonds, bankers' acceptances, and certificates of deposit), and therefore actions of the Bank of Japan in the short-term money market do not directly affect firms or households. The separation of the nonbank private sector from the short-term money market is a necessary condition for the dual structure of interest rates described in chapter 3. In this sense, the direct-route transmission mechanism was a natural concomitant of the dual interest rate structure that evolved under the policy of maintaining artificially low interest rates.

2. *Contributory Conditions for the Effectiveness of Monetary Policy*

Based on our study of the transmission mechanism, we are now in a position to examine other conditions which have contributed to the effectiveness of monetary policy.

The first condition is the persistent dependence of city banks on Bank of Japan loans, namely, overloan. Because of the existence of overloan, the Bank of Japan's credit rationing has had a powerful effect on the asset selection behavior of city banks.

The second condition is the flexibility of the call rate and bills discount rate. When the Bank of Japan rations credit to its main clientele, the city banks, it has been able effectively to control the credit creation of other banks because the resulting variations in the call rate have had an impact on the overall behavior of these institutions. To put it another way, given the inflexibility of most interest rates, when the banks come to decide on the shape of their balance sheets, they will be significantly affected by variations in the one rate which does change to any degree. Bank behavior in Japan in this sense is rational, insofar as banks will seek to maximize profits when they make their asset portfolio selection. Other conditions being equal, any impediment to the flexibility of the call rate would result in a reduction in the effectiveness of monetary policy in Japan.

The third condition is that the banks whose credit-creating activities have been controlled in this way are by far the most important component of the totality of financial institutions. This is true both with respect to a comparison of the securities market and intermediary financial institutions (broadly defined to include banks), and to a comparison of banks in relation to nonbank institutions such as insurance companies, pension funds, and so on. Controls on bank behavior by the Bank of Japan imply an almost similar control on all credit-creating activities of the financial sector.

The fourth condition, not unrelated to the third, is that holdings of financial assets such as government bonds in the private sector are extremely small. The reasons for this are partly the almost total depreciation of privately held government bonds issued during the war, and partly the balanced-budget policy instituted in Japan from the time of the Dodge Line in 1949 until 1964. As a result, there was no mechanism by which the outstanding issues of government bonds could cushion the impact of money supplied by the banking sector on the real economy. Also, there was no undermining of monetary policy through pressure to support the price of government bonds in order to lessen the burden of interest debt for the government or to support the secondary market in government bonds.

The fifth condition for the effectiveness of monetary policy is the high degree of dependence of the corporate sector on bank credit, that is, overborrowing. Given overborrowing, bank credit supplied to the corporate sector profoundly affects the determination of corporate enterprises' capital expenditure budget, and therefore the availability of bank credit as subjectively experienced by business enterprises has had a powerful impact on fluctuations in investment.

A sixth condition for effective monetary policy was corporations' high expected rates of return. It is sometimes said that the effects of monetary policy have generally been asymmetrical: the effects of restrictive policy on the business cycle were larger than those of stimulatory policy. However, in the ten years preceding the revaluation of the yen, business confidence in the future of the economy produced a high expected rate of return among corporate enterprises. This in turn encouraged a prompt recovery in business investment based on the expansionary effect of bank credit and its availability as experienced by business enterprises. In this sense, the stimulatory effects of monetary policy were as powerful as the restrictive effects.[3]

The seventh condition was that corporate investment activity, itself intensely subject to monetary policy, was a leading force in the Japanese economy along with exports. Because the economy was investment-led, the control of corporate investment had a powerful impact on effective demand, and hence on prices and the balance of payments.

Finally, we cannot overlook the fact that the Japanese economy was insulated from foreign money markets by a strict system of foreign exchange controls. The distortions produced by having a single flexible rate—the call rate—in the interest-rate structure, the allocation of credit to the city banks by the Bank of Japan, and to business firms by the banking system— all these would have been difficult unless Japan had been isolated from the movement of funds in international markets. Conversely, by being able to neglect the effects of inflows and outflows of funds to and from international capital markets, the authorities were able to concentrate on maintaining effective instruments for the regulation of domestic demand without having to be concerned with the effect on inflows and outflows abroad. This was a necessary condition for an effective monetary policy in Japan.

3. The Limitations of Monetary Policy

The above-listed conditions for effective monetary policy also provide a clue to its limitations. The business cycle in Japan from the mid-1950s has been discussed from many angles, but the limitations relating to the effectiveness of monetary policy over this period may be classified under five headings.

First, recognizing that the contractionary and expansionary effects of monetary policy are large, the criticism is made that those effects ought to have been utlized preventively and flexibly to soften the business cycle, and that in this respect monetary policy was not necessarily effective. This criticism of the limitations of policy was first made at the time when the "Jimmu Boom" of 1955–57 gave way to the sharp recession of 1958.[4] It was

3. There was a tendency to suggest that monetary policy lacked stimulative power in each of the recessions of 1958, 1963, 1965, and 1971, but in each case after a slight time-lag monetary policy did exert a powerful expansionary force on the business cycle. Even after the revaluation of the yen in 1972, nonmanufacturing investment among medium and small enterprises and housing construction were encouraged to a major extent by the easy-money policy, and contributed importantly to the upswing in general business conditions. The basic reason was that firms involved in public-sector investment, housing, construction, and consumer spending—and these included many medium and small enterprises in the nonmanufacturing sector—were motivated by high expected profit rates.

4. See Motohiko Nishikawa [31].

also made in each of the recessions following the "Iwato Boom" of 1959–61 and the 1963–64 boom. In the five years after 1965 there was continuous economic expansion, but from 1970 there was an unexpectedly sharp reaction culminating in the revaluation of the yen. Again on this occasion, and when the very strong economic expansion of 1972–73 got under way, people were surprised by the size of the fluctuation. The only exception throughout the period was the preventive raising of the official discount rate in December 1959, which produced only an inventory recession and thereby enabled the upswing to continue somewhat longer.

If we examine the standard deviation of the average amplitude of fluctuation and the real economic growth rates of Japan and other leading countries for the period 1956–71, we may observe (see table 14.1) that the standard deviation for Japan is 3.5 percent, which is the largest among those countries listed. However, considering that Japan's growth rate was also the highest, it is only natural that its standard deviation should be the largest. If the deviations are divided by the growth rates to give a coefficient of variation, it turns out that although Japan's coefficient is larger than that of France, it is lower than that of the United States, Britain, and West Germany. It cannot be said, therefore, given its average profile, that Japan's business-cycle fluctuations are any larger, relatively speaking, than those of other countries.

The impression of severe fluctuation in the business cycle in Japan is due not so much to the average amplitude of fluctuation as to the sharp drop in business activity within half a year following any prolonged period of rapid growth. The rapidity of the slowdown is illustrated by the slowdown in real GNP from over 20 percent per annum (annualized) in the three quarters 1956 IV–1957 II to a complete standstill in the three quarters 1957 III–1958 I. Although not so dramatic, the slowdowns of 1961–62, 1964–65, and 1970–71 all represent reductions from about 15–20 percent p.a.

Table 14.1 International Comparison of Real Economic Growth Rates (1956–1971)

	Japan		United States	United Kingdom	West Germany	France
	56–62	63–71				
Standard deviation (%)	3.5	3.9	3.3	2.5	1.3	2.3	1.2
Average growth rate (%)	10.2	9.5	10.6	3.4	2.7	5.2	5.6
Coefficient of variation	0.343	0.405	0.311	0.736	0.508	0.452	0.208

Note: 1. Compiled from "International Comparative Statistics," Bank of Japan, Department of Statistics.

2. Coefficient of Variation $= \dfrac{\text{Standard Deviation}}{\text{Average Growth Rate}}$

(annualized) to below 5 percent. The criticism is therefore made that, in this respect, Japan's stabilization policy or countercyclical policy was not very effective and failed in its task of smoothing out the business cycle.

There are, perhaps, two main reasons why monetary policy is of limited effectiveness in preventing severe fluctuations. First, the intention to impose a mild sequeeze on business before the level of activity became overheated was hampered by the policy of low interest rates, and it was only when an increase in the balance of payments deficit threatened to put pressure on foreign exchange reserves that a tight-money policy was enforced. A classic case was in 1961. In January of that year there were already signs of business overheating in private corporate investment and other areas of the economy, but despite this the Ikeda Cabinet arranged to reduce the official discount rate, government bond yields, deposit interest rates, and long-term interest rates because they wanted artificially low interest rates. Finally, in July 1961, the official discount rate was raised by 0.1 sen per diem (0.365 percent p.a.), and the tight-money policy started in earnest in September, with the discount rate being raised by a larger amount; but it was already too late. The reduction of the discount rate in January 1961 and the tardiness of the timing of the tight-money policy in 1964 undoubtedly produced damaging effects from the point of view of stabilization policy.[5]

In addition to the problems caused by artificially low interest rates,[6] a second problem lies in the transmission mechanism of Japanese monetary policy. As indicated in the theoretical model of chapter 6 and empirically illustrated in chapter 7, section 1, table 7.2, the persistent overloaned position of the city banks and their ability to borrow from the Bank of Japan means that they are insensitive to their own fund position. They tend to be encouraged by the eager demand for credit when the business cycle heats up, and continue to expand their loans. Also, it is difficult for the Bank of Japan drastically to cut back its loans to city banks because the impact at every stage of the relation among the Bank of Japan, city banks, and business enterprises would mean either an inability of banks to meet demands for

5. Keimei Kaizuka [17] reaches a similar judgment to mine on the hampering effect of the discount-rate cut in January 1971 on stabilization, and on the dubious effectiveness of artificial low interest-rate policy in stimulating exports and investment. On the other hand, a representative justification of the artificial low interest-rate policy can be found in Osamu Shimomura [38].

6. Until February 1973, demands of a political nature were also imposed upon monetary policy, which limited its effectiveness in stabilization policy. First, there was a government decision to maintain the fixed exchange rate of the yen initially at ¥360, and from December 1971 at ¥308 per US$1.00. Second, the passage through the Diet of a supplementary budget designed to underwrite the "Plan to Remodel the Japanese Archipelago" and to stimulate the economy resulted in constraints on the timing and choice of monetary policy instruments, and was thus a factor contributing to the intensification of the inflation of 1973.

payment, or that commercial bills and exchange bills could not be settled and companies would be bankrupted. For this reason the Bank of Japan tends to be very accommodating to its client city banks, and the city banks in turn are very accommodating to their corporate clients. As long as this remains so, the brake will continue to be applied too late, and the business cycle will be amplified. One could even say that this is the fatal limitation of a monetary policy which depends for its basic effects on credit rationing. If, on the other hand, a self-regulating interest-rate mechanism were operating, the effects would be milder and emerge earlier than the effects of credit rationing.

It is clear from the above that credit rationing by the Bank of Japan under the overloan system, and credit rationing by the city banks under the overborrowing system, are two important conditions underlying the effectiveness of monetary policy in Japan. At the same time, the lag in the effect of policy, which itself reduces the stabilizing capability of monetary policy, was also caused by these two conditions. Whereas the effects of credit rationing and its accompanying lag amplify the cycle, a flexible interest rate mechanism would modify the cycle and make policy more rapidly effective.

Awareness of this limitation and determination to overcome the problem of stabilization was at the center of the discussion after 1955 of the question of "monetary normalization." This awareness also expressed in the return of free market interest rates, and in the more flexible operation of new instruments: the start of the Reserve Requirement System (September 1959), the preventive raising of the official discount rate (December and the linking of bank lending rates to the discount rate by the establishment of the Standard Rate System in March 1959.[7] In retrospect, no examination was made at the time of the basic elements of the rationing system by which the low interest-rate policy fed into the transmission mechanism of monetary policy, the drastic braking of activity continued to be a feature of Japanese cycles after 1960.

The second limitation of Japan's monetary policy, it is held, is to produce an efficient distribution of funds. The cause of this failure to be found in the credit rationing carried out between the Bank and the banking system and between the banking system and enterprises. This has been pointed out by numerous observers also one of the purposes of the monetary normalization debate above.

7. See Motohiko Nishikawa [31].
8. The earliest expositions of this view are to be found in Tachi and K [51] [52], Komiya [23], Nishikawa [31], Kaizuka [17], and Suzuki [40].

development in which public-sector investment, housing construction, and consumption are the leading sectors, and which is characterized by the growth of resource-saving and pollution-preventing industries.

Looked at in this light, the view that the profit rate of industry has taken an irreversible plunge, or that monetary policy will no longer be able to stimulate industry, is seen to be mistaken because it is too much obsessed with the historical pattern. The Japanese economy will not stiffen with age so rapidly. New incentives for private investment necessary to a new form of development will be born, which will be quite enough to guarantee the expansionary effect of monetary policy for a while yet. The sharp upswing of the economy after 1972, with its huge fiscal stimulus, can hardly be said to have been independent of the effects of the policy of monetary ease that preceded it.

In relation to the second fear that the internationalization of the money markets will undermine the effectiveness of monetary policy, while it is true, as we saw in chapter 3, section 1, that the lag in credit rationing amplifies the cycle, contrary evidence can be produced that a policy based on market interest rates would act sooner and yield a milder cycle. It would not, therefore, be true that the abandonment of credit rationing and a restoration of free market interest rates would necessarily be disadvantageous from the standpoint of regulating effective demand. The important thing is to have forward-looking, constructive, and flexible attitudes in the operation of policy. Further, with the diversification of monetary policy instruments such as the start of the system of reserve requirements and the creation of reserves against loans, the feared loss of freedom in domestic demand adjustment can be avoided to a large extent. But more important, with a flexible exchange rate policy, domestic policy can be made more effective by reducing the delay in the responsiveness of monetary policy to events outside.

Finally, concerning the fear that large-scale issues of government bonds will weaken the effectiveness of domestic monetary policy, it is certainly true that as the volume of bonds outstanding held by the private sector increases, a trade-off develops between the three objectives of government bond management—business stabilization, minimization of the interest cost burden, and maintenance of an orderly market in government bonds—so that harmonization of the three becomes a difficult task. However, as the experiences of the United States after the "Accord" of 1951 and Britain after 1968 show, if business stabilization is given priority and the principle is established that the reduction of the interest burden and maintenance of an orderly market must be achieved within that framework, the cramping effect on monetary policy is eliminated. From the standpoint of maximizing national welfare, which is the ultimate goal of economic policy, this is most desirable.

Above we have considered the implications of three possible shortcomings relating to the effectiveness of monetary policy. It is important to point out, however, that a more serious problem than all of these exists—namely inflation. With the severe inflation that started in the fall of 1972, a serious maldistribution of income occurred which monetary policy was by no means equipped to handle. This problem is touched on in the concluding chapter.

PART V

Prospects for the Future

In parts I–IV I have successively examined the Japanese financial structure, the monetary mechanism, policy instruments, and the effectiveness of monetary policy during the period from 1955 to the early 1970s.

In the late 1960s, with the emergency of continuous balance of payments surpluses and the subsequent upward revaluations of the yen in 1971 and 1973, coupled with the Supplementary Budget of 1972 (which resulted in a large expansion in government fiscal expenditures), and the constraint put on the world's natural resources following the oil crisis of late 1973, the Japanese economy again stood at the threshold of a new era. It is likely that in the aftermath of these events, the financial structure of part I and the monetary mechanism of part II will gradually change, and therefore the monetary policy instruments of part III and their effectiveness as described in part IV will enter a new phase.

In part V, as a concluding chapter for this book, I examine the implications of these new changes in direction.

15 The Japanese Economy at a Turning Point and Prospects for Finance in the Future

1. *A Historical Turning Point for the Japanese Economy*

The era of investment-led rapid economic growth that began around 1955 in Japan and had been based on a textbook-style application of the industrialization of Western society was the ultimate fruit of a hundred years of modernization since the Meiji Restoration, which had put Japan on the path to catch up with and overtake the West. As a result, from around 1970, Japan's total GNP moved up to become second in the free world, and as per capita GNP exceeded those of England and Italy, she attained a level of equality with the leading industrial nations of Europe and North America. If this process were to continue, many Japanese would not be at all surprised if the twenty-first century turned out to be, in Herman Kahn's phrase, "The Japanese Century."

However, the course of history is not so straightforward. At the start of the 1970s, having modernized and industrialized her economy on Western lines and pursued an investment-led rapid-growth economy, Japan was compelled to acknowledge that it stood at the start of a new and unknown age. The significant events which announced to the Japanese the advent of this historical turning point were the "Nixon Shock" and the "Oil Shock."

The announcement of the inconvertibility of the US dollar into gold on August 15, 1971 (anniversary of Japan's surrender in World War II), the subsequent Smithsonian Conference, the collapse of the Smithsonian exchange-rate parities in February 1973, and the shift to a floating exchange rate spelled the end for Japan's program of Western-style industrialization and modernization. Together these events marked the cool recognition by America that Japan was now a fully modernized and industrialized coequal partner. From the Japanese side, the very textbook Japan had been following—the Bretton Woods system—as the model for leading Western nations appeared to have been scrapped, and the Achilles heel of Western-style industrialization was revealed: the industrialized Western societies suffered from inflation, environmental pollution, and social instability. They were no longer her seniors to be followed, but her equal partners because Japan shared many of their problems. This was confirmed by the fact that Japan was invited to the November 1975 Summit Conference of Western Nations at Rambouillet to discuss the current economic difficulties facing leading Western nations.

But by far the most important event which impressed the Japanese people that the postwar era of investment-led growth had come to an end was the "Oil Shock" of November 1973. In fiscal year 1973, Japan's energy consumption was 77.4 percent dependent on oil, and 99.7 percent of that oil was imported. Even if other sources of energy are included, imported energy still accounted for 89.9 percent of Japan's consumption. Consequently, the restrictions on the quantity of oil exported by Middle Eastern countries and the rise in the price of oil starkly revealed Japan's poverty in energy and disastrously worsened her terms of trade so that from both angles a reduction in Japan's economic growth rate was inevitable. Moreover, as may be seen in the worldwide trends—not only in oil but in all mineral industrial materials—toward increasing shortages, Japan's exceptionally high dependence on imported food and industrial materials means the high growth she has so far achieved will become more difficult. Also, domestically within Japan the popular demand for pollution prevention and environmental protection is gathering momentum and restrictions on factory-building are imposing an obstacle to rapid economic growth. The Japanese economy today is confronted with two major problems. First, having achieved a hundred years of modernization since the Meiji Restoration, Japan requires a blueprint of objectives for its unique economy and society, not based on any Western European or North American model, but based on an economic policy which is adjusted to Japan's medium- and long-term aims. The aims of society in the age of postindustrialization would be an affluent society with a uniquely Japanese brand of welfare.

Second, having lost the necessary preconditions for rapid economic growth, growth should be slowed down to limit frictions to the minimum possible, and to adjust our industrial organization to that lower growth rate. In the past, when the first priority in economic policy was corporate investment, the level of incomes rose sharply, so that the hidden unemployment level and dual wage structure were eliminated, thereby promoting a more even income distribution and raising the level of economic welfare. But since these problems have largely disappeared, it will be important in future to ensure that, in considering the economic welfare of the nation, income redistribution receives more attention than in the past.

However, these two goals should be so harmonized that they never contradict each other; both are so inextricably interrelated that they must be harmonized. With slower economic growth, an affluent but more egalitarian welfare society must be built based on a high level of industrialization. The central problem of such a society is how to devise social security systems and old-age pension schemes which incorporate a national minimum together with more efficient house-building methods and more satisfying employment and education systems.

2. Financial Aspects of the Turning Point

It is natural that such a historical turning point in the Japanese economy should have an effect on the financial system. Signs of these effects were already evident in Japan after 1970, and will be discussed in the following order:

1. Change in the financial structure;
2. Problems with the artificial interest-rate policy;
3. Reappraisal of the institutional structure of the financial system;
4. A new monetary policy.

2.1 Change in the Financial Structure

As described in chapter 2, section 2, since investment as a proportion of GNE was extremely high under an investment-led rapid-growth economy, the corporate sector deficit was large and "overborrowing" was a standard characteristic of the Japanese financial structure. However, from 1970, as the growth of the economy slowed down, the proportion of GNE accounted for by private investment declined while government fiscal expenditures rose (see table 15.1). As a result, the rate of growth of the corporate-sector

Table 15.1 Slowdown in Economic Growth and Change in the Flow of Funds

		1956–60	*1961–65*	*1966–70*	*1971–75*
Real economic growth (annualized)		8.7	9.7	11.6	4.9
Share of GNE	Personal sector	65.3	63.0	62.0	63.6
	Corporate sector	18.1	19.1	19.7	16.7
	Public sector	16.5	18.1	17.3	19.3
	Foreign sector	0.1	−0.2	1.0	0.4
Shares of Financial Surplus/Deficit	Personal sector	100.0	100.0	100.0	100.0
	Corporate sector	−104.1	−84.7	−67.9	−54.4
	Public sector	4.9	−18.4	−22.0	−42.5
	Foreign sector	−0.8	3.1	−10.1	−3.1

Notes: 1. All data refer to fiscal years. FY 1975 statistics are estimated.
2. Shares of GNE are based on total GNE = 100.
3. Shares of Financial Surplus/Deficit are based on personal-sector surplus = 100.

deficit declined steeply, while the public-sector deficit began to accelerate sharply. This kind of trend is likely to be maintained in future when Japan switches to a less rapid economic growth rate and government expenditures grow with the building of a welfare society. In 1975 the public-sector deficit was already 2.5 times the size of corporate-sector deficit, and according to estimates in the Government's Medium-Term Plan 1976–80, the difference is likely to continue. In fiscal year 1975 this trend was accentuated by the cyclical decline in tax revenues produced by the recession, and the public-sector deficit is estimated to approach 8 percent of GNP for the year, or about twice the corporate-sector deficit. The public-sector deficit will continue into fiscal year 1976, and after that, with the cyclical influence of the rise in corporate tax payments, it may again decline, but not below the level of the corporate deficit until about 1978.

Thus there can be no doubt that in the future financial structure, corporate overborrowing will diminish while debt-issues by the public sector will grow to large dimensions. During fiscal year 1975 ¥5,480 billion of long-term government bonds were issued, and in fiscal year 1976 about ¥7,000 billion was scheduled. Similarly, the size of local government authority issues is also ballooning. Inevitably the increase in the size of these issues will have a considerable impact on the future of regulations governing interest rates, on the institutional structure of the financial system, and on monetary policy.

2.2 *Problems with the Artificial Low Interest-Rate Policy*

With the advent of the 1970s it was widely acknowledged that the policy of maintaining subequilibrium interest rates designed to promote exports and corporate investment had fulfilled its purpose and was no longer necessary. This was prompted by the depreciation in real terms of household savings, by the internationalization of the Japanese money markets, and by the expansion in size of government debt issues.

During the severe inflation of 1973–75, because real interest rates became negative, the household sector (which was in financial surplus) was a creditor yet lost money, while the corporate sector (which was in deficit) was a debtor yet profited, and this aroused popular feelings. Some representative consumers even started a constitutional suit against the Japanese government because of the unjust depreciation of household savings caused by the regulations on interest rates.

Now that the compensating mechanism whereby an increase in corporate investment or profit led to a rise in personal income and thus to a more favorable income redistribution was no longer functioning, criticism was voiced to the effect that the policy of fixing interest rates at an artificially low level was causing an unfair transfer of income from households to the corporate sector and a reduction in the people's welfare. Wherever inflation rates are high, real interest rates dip temporarily below zero, but because in Japan deposit interest rates and the yield on new bond issues have been artificially regulated, criticism of negative real interest rates was particularly harsh and provided one of the driving forces for liberalization of interest rates. The proposal to leave interest rates in Japan to market forces had been encouraged by the progress of the internationalization of Japan's capital markets after 1970. From 1971, a variety of controls were relaxed so that both investment in Japanese securities by foreigners and investment by Japanese in foreign securities increased. At the same time, Japanese brokerage houses were established abroad at a rapid rate, as were foreign brokerage houses in Japan, and yen-denominated foreign bonds and Eurobonds were sold within Japan.

With the movement toward internationalization, the principle whereby Japanese financial institutions may not engage in both banking business and bond underwriting began to run into difficulties. For example, Japanese banks operating overseas were doing underwriting business while Japanese brokerage houses abroad were engaging in banking business, and equally, when foreign financial institutions were admitted to Japan, various inconsistencies occurred. Further, the process of controlling interest rates on bond issues at an artificially low rate became increasingly troublesome because, with yields being decided by market conditions while domestic rates were decided by controls, international transactions were hampered. Hence the anomaly arose that the yield on a yen-denominated bond issued by Japanese was controlled, while yields on foreign yen-denominated issues were liberalized. Since Japan's international financial transactions tended to increase sharply, as long as the yield structure of Japanese interest rates was not fluctuating in accordance with market conditions there were certain to be distortions somewhere in the system. The policy of artificially low interest rates thus became an obstacle to the development of efficient money markets in Japan.

The third force acting in favor of the liberalization of interest rates is the reduction in corporate overborrowing and the large-scale issue of public-sector debt. On banks' balance sheets it is probable that the proportion occupied by loans to companies will decline, while the proportion occupied by holdings of public-sector debt will increase. Under the policy of artificially low interest rates, the rate of interest charged on loans and the yield on bonds (at time of issue) were forced down to subequilibrium levels, but by demanding compensating balances against loans the banks were customarily able to raise their effective lending rates. In the case of public-sector bonds, since banks hardly handled public-sector deposits (especially since all central government deposits are concentrated at the Bank of Japan), as long as nominal interest rates were at nonequilibrium levels, their profits were immediately squeezed. Consequently, when government bonds were issued in large quantities in 1975, both the banks and securities houses vigorously demanded that they be issued at market rates. Therefore, when long-term interest rates were revised in November 1975, just after the official discount rate was lowered for the fourth time and deposit interest rates and private-sector bond issue rates were lowered by 0.5–1.0 percent, the long-term government bond rates were only reduced by 0.1 percent. The trend toward the correction of the artificially low rate on government bonds will surely continue in 1976 and beyond.

These three forces have gradually been reinforced during the 1970s, bringing controlled interest rates back toward equilibrium levels, so that, in comparison with previous conditions, changes in interest rates have been much more frequent. Comparing the fifteen years 1956–70 and the five years 1971–75, the standard lending rates were altered eight and ten times, top-grade corporate bond-issuing rates were altered nine and fourteen times, and one-year fixed deposits rates were altered two and eight times, Thus, compared with the fifteen-year era of investment-led rapid growth, the five years after 1970 witnessed far more changes in long-term rates, though they were still far from being market-determined.

2.3 *Reappraisal of the Institutional Structure of the Financial System*
The attempt to restore interest rates to an equilibrium level at which supply and demand are equalized has involved, as we saw above, relatively frequent changes in regulated interest rates; but that process was not full liberalization—it merely implied slightly more flexibility. It did not imply the abolition of the policy of fixing interest rates at artificially low levels, only a retreat from that policy. The following factors still prevent the abolition of regulated lending rates, deposit rates, and bond-issuing conditions and hinder the adoption of a completely free market mechanism.

First, there are those who believe that the cheap money (= low interest-rate) policy should be continued in order to reduce the government's burden of interest payments. In order to move from investment-led growth to a less rapid growth path led by government expenditures, the public sector must become the chief borrower, and since private companies have lost the justification for low interest rates, the policy should now be pursued, it is argued, for the sake of the public sector—in other words, on behalf of the taxpayers. However, the counterargument is that low yields on government bonds tend to produce an artificially low general level of interest rates, so that for the net surplus household sector the effect is an unfair redistribution of income.

Second, since interest-rate liberalization implies the introduction of competitive interest rates, there is a strong possibility that some financial institutions conducting a steady business within the framework of regulated rates will find their base being undermined, and consequently they oppose interest-rate liberalization. Institutions affected would be the long-term credit banks, the trust banks, mutual banks, credit corporations, and agricultural cooperatives.

The long-term credit banks issue two-year and five-year debentures, and the trust banks receive deposits in trust of two years and five years and also money in trust in order to raise long-term funds for term loans to companies for plant and equipment investment purposes. However, with the end of the rapid growth era and the reduction in corporate overborrowing, these financial institutions will be faced with severe problems in making loans, and interest-rate liberalization can be expected to add to their difficulties in raising funds. Given the continuation of interest-rate controls, government bonds would normally carry a lower yield than debentures or deposits in trust, so that interest-rate liberalization would compel them to raise funds on competitive terms, and in times of financial stringency these types of instruments or borrowers might be crowded out. Also, both on the lending side and on the fund-raising side, the long-term credit banks and the trust banks would be compelled to cut back their business. Since these institutions played an instrumental role during the rapid growth era, their political power is quite significant, and together they form a political pressure group in opposition to free market interest rates.

The mutual banks, credit associations, and agricultural cooperative associations are smaller in scale than city banks or local banks, and there are several among them that are relatively inefficient in management by comparison. If interest rates were liberalized so that competition for deposits were to drive up deposit rates and force down loan rates, it would be reasonable to suppose that some of these institutions would come under pressure. As a result they also oppose interest-rate liberalization in cooperation with political powers who represent the interests of the medium- and small-sized enterprises and agricultural groups, who are clients of these institutions.

These factors suggest that progress toward a free market interest-rate structure will be impeded, but on the other hand, the three problems associated with artificially low interest rates are beginning to come into prominence. Considering the reform of the system, it is fair to say that the general proposition that nothing can be achieved without some conflict of interest applies to the problem of liberalizing Japanese interest rates.

From the fall of 1975 the government's Monetary System Research Council will be investigating the reform of the Banking Law over a two-year period; at present this study is still in progress. Although the topic for investigation is the city bank and local bank sector—namely, pure deposit-taking institutions—it is probable that the council will also pursue some topics relating to similar financial institutions, such as their position in relation to the long-term credit banks, trust banks, and mutual banks, and the question of interest-rate controls.

If at some stage in the future regulated interest rates are permitted to fluctuate freely at levels that accord with market equilibrium, and if in addition the yields on new bond issues and the rates payable on large deposits are also liberalized, the special characteristics of Japan's financial structure will change radically. With the development of the corporate bond market, the predominance of indirect finance and overborrowing would diminish. With the enhancement of the city banks' power to raise money, the imbalance of bank liquidity and the overloan situation would move toward a solution. In the process, a variety of other changes would also occur in the structure of financial institutions. The move by large brokerage houses into the banking business—at present only permitted outside Japan—and the move by some of the banks into underwriting, might be permitted to occur domestically. Simultaneously, the issue of negotiable CD's—again, at present only permitted outside Japan—might become common practice inside Japan, thus providing a new source of funds. However, since all of these questions pose radical problems for the Japanese financial system, progress will certainly not be straightforward. Nevertheless, it is certain that at its present historical turning point, the Japanese economy is groping for financial reforms.

2.4 *A New Monetary Policy*

The experience of 25–30 percent annual rates of expansion in the money stock from the early 1970s and the subsequent inflation in Japan brought about a major change in the operation of Japanese monetary policy. That change consisted of the three elements: (1) given the trade-off between the three policy objectives of price stability, equilibrium in the international balance of payments, and full employment (or economic growth), it was appreciated that monetary policy alone was not sufficient to achieve these objectives; (2) the money stock should be adopted as the operating target of monetary policy; and (3) in order to implement more effectively the role of interest rates in the transmission mechanism, interest rates must be allowed to move more flexibly, or be completely freed. These three points have received growing acknowledgment at the Bank of Japan and growing support from the academic community.

As explained in chapters 13 and 14, under the policy of investment-led growth there was no trade-off among the three policy objectives of prices, balance of payments, and the level of employment. In the tight-money policy of 1969–70, while domestic price stability was achieved, the balance of payments remained in massive surplus and the level of domestic economic activity slumped, thus dramatizing the trade-off among the three objectives. Subsequently, in 1971–73, with the 25–30 percent annual growth in the money stock, the level of economic activity and the domestic price level was raised, but the balance of payments remained in surplus: the trade-off relationship remained in effect. It was not until after the yen had been revalued by 16.88 percent (taking the yen exchange rate from ¥360 to ¥308 per US$1.00) in December 1971 at the Smithsonian Conference, and the floating of the yen exchange rate in February 1973 (so that at one time the rate moved to a level only slightly above ¥250 per US$1.00) that the balance of payments surplus was eliminated. Because the "Oil Shock" of October 1973 caused a serious deterioration in Japan's terms of trade, the yen later floated back down to around ¥300 per US$1.00.

These events showed that if the yen was floated so that the balance of payments was no longer a constraint upon policy objectives, monetary policy could be released from the balance of payments constraint to concentrate on the two domestic objectives of price stability and full employment. The Japanese authorities are now content to conduct a managed float, so that the balance of payments adjusts through the exchange rate responding to the forces of supply and demand in the longer run, though they will intervene in the short run to prevent sharp upward or downward fluctuations in the foreign exchange market.

Monetary policy today is thus designed to pursue a dual set of policy objectives: the minimum permissable rate of inflation coupled with a desirable rate of economic growth (or employment). It is considered important that fiscal policy should be implemented to achieve a suitable policy mix. In order to execute this kind of policy, the Bank of Japan has begun to pay attention to the money supply M_2 (cash currency and all deposits of the private nonbank sector) as an operating target. The "Monthly Review" of the Bank of Japan for July 1975 contains a paper on this topic, which begins with the following paragraphs:

> Close statistical correlation exists between the money supply and real economic activity in Japan. This is particularly true of the co-variation between the stock of M_2 and prices after a time-lag of 2 to 4 quarters— observable through the two decades of 1955–64 and 1965–74. The close relation between the two is seen in the influence on prices— through multifarious channels—caused by changes in liquidity of the private sector (excluding banks) represented by the stock of M_2.
>
> To explain further, changes in the M_2 stock affect investments in plant and equipment, in inventories, and in housing, and through these processes, invite changes in gross national expenditure. Not only will changes in GNE affect the demand and supply balance of the total economy thereby influencing prices but they also influence prices from the cost factor through the impact, more or less, on wages, and prices of imported raw materials. Besides, changes in the M_2 stock influence prices through channels not directly related to GNP, such as speculative transactions in commodities by traders and also trading in existing

assets as land and equities. Moreover, changes in the stock of M_2 affect the demand and supply attitudes on a wide variety of commodities via stimulation of inflationary psychology. It should be noted, however, that in the complex transmission mechanism are numerous factors unrelated to movements in the M_2 stock, and therefore, the quantitative relation between the rate of change of the M_2 stock and the rate of change of prices, as well as the time-lag of the transmission effect, is subject to change according to the economic situation.

In the process of realizing optimum economic development while maintaining stable prices, sufficient attention should be paid to the money supply in the operating of monetary policy in order to prevent excesses. However, in view of the fact that the quantitative relation between the money supply and prices is subject to change depending on the economic situation, it is not desirable or appropriate to set a specific target of growth of the stock of M_2 and attempt to realize the target mechanically. In the actual operation of policy, a realistic policy attitude will be to maintain or revise the growth of the M_2 stock by keeping in mind a desirable economic pattern as the objective while carefully and constantly analyzing the relation between the prevailing M_2 growth and economic conditions.

Looking to the future, the money supply will expand through channels that will vary with the structural changes in the flow of funds as the supply of bank credit to the public sector grows. The most important objective of monetary policy is therefore to control the total credit supply from the banking sector to the public sector and to the private nonbank sector within an appropriate amount of money supply. If this distribution of funds is attempted through credit rationing, there is the danger that the banks will be forcibly compelled to purchase government bonds. To avoid such a deliberate method of fund distribution, the policy of artificially low interest rates must be revised, the interest-rate mechanism brought into action, and public and private nonbank credit demands reconciled while at the same time monetary growth is controlled. In other words, it is a necessary condition for the achievement of an appropriate M_2 growth under the new flow-of-funds structure that free market interest rates be utilized as a primary instrument for the transmission mechanism of monetary policy. At this point in Japanese economic history there is a historic need for interest-rate liberalization.

References

[1] Bank of Japan Economic Research Department. *The Japanese Financial System*. Tokyo, 1978.

[2] Bank of Japan Research Department. *Nihon Ginkō—sono Kinō to Soshiki*. April 1967, rev. ed.

[3] Bank of Japan Research Department. "Money Supply no Zōka ni tsuite." *Chōsa Geppō*, February 1973.

[4] Bank of Japan Research Department. "Waga Kuni no Kinri Hendō ni tsuite." *Chōsa Geppō*, May 1973.

[5] Bank of Japan Research Department. "Waga Kuni Kinyu Kikan no Shōhisha Kinyū ni tsuite." *Chōsa Geppō*, August 1973.

[6] Bank of Japan Statistics Department. "Nihon Ginkō Keiryo Keizai Model—sono Shiten to Kōsei." *Chōsa Geppō*, September 1972.

[7] Brainard, W. C. "Financial Intermediaries and a Theory of Monetary Control." Yale Economic Essays 4 (Fall 1964).

[8] Dewald, W. G., and Johnson, H. G. "An Objective Analysis of the Objectives of American Monetary Policy, 1952–61." In Carson, D., *Banking and Monetary Studies*, 1963.

[9] Eguchi, Hidekazu. "Ginkō Kōdō no Riron to Kinyū Model no Kōsei." In *Keizai Seichō to Sangyō Kōzō*, edited by Yamada, Shionoya, and Imai. Shunjyū-sha, 1965.

[10] Fujino, Shozaburō. *Nihon no Keiki Jyunkan* 1965. Keiso-shobō.

[11] Iida, Tsuneo; Taishitsu, Kaizen; and Kinyū, Seijyoka. *Keizai Seichō to Nijyū Kōzō*. Tokyo: Keizai Shimpō-sha, 1962. Chapter 2.

[12] Ikura, Kazuya. "Madoguchi Shidō no Mechanism." *Kinyū Journal*, July 1961.

[13] Ishida, Sadao. *Money. Flow Bunseki*. Rev. ed., Tokyo: Nihon Keizai Shimbun-sha, 1966.

[14] Ishii, Yasunori. Ginkō Kōdō no Riron. *Kikan Riron Keizai Gaku*, August 1971.

[15] Ishikawa, Michitatsu. *Yasashii Nihon Kinyū-Shi.* Tokyo: Bungado Kenkyū-sha, 1965.

[16] Kaizuka, Keimei. Antei Seisaku no Mokuhyō to Kinyū Seisaku. In Kazuo Kinoshita, ed., *Keizai Antei to Zaisei Kinyū Seisaku.* Nihon Keizai Shinbun-sha, 1967.

[17] Kaizuka, Keimei. Showa 30 Nendai no Kinyū Seisaku. *Bankingu,* vol. 226 (January 1967).

[18] Katō, Kazumasa. Kojin Kinyū Shisan no Hendō. In Shōzaburō Fujino, ed., *Tomi no Kōzō.* Nihon Keizai Shimbun-sha, 1969.

[19] Kawaguchi, Hiroshi. *Kahei to Keizai.* Kobundō, 1958.

[20] Keizai Kikaku-chō, Keizai Kenkyūsho. *Waga Kuni Toshi Ginkō no Kōdō Bunseki.* Kenkyū Series, vol. 13, 1963.

[21] Kinyū Seido Chōsakai [Monetary System Research Council]. *Overloan no Zesei.* Kinyū Seido Chōsakai-Tōshin, May 1963.

[22] Klein, L. R. *The Keynesian Revolution.* New York: Macmillan, 1947.

[23] Komiya, Ryūtarō. Nihon ni okeru Kinyū Seisaku no Yūkōsei. Tokyo University, *Keizaigaku Ronshū,* July 1964.

[24] Kure, Bunji. *Kinyū Seisaku.* Tokyo: Tōyō Keizai Shimpō-sha, 1973.

[25] Miyazaki, Giichi. Katōkyōsō no Ronri to Genjitsu. *Syūkan Economist,* Supplement, 1962.

[26] Moriguchi, Shinji. Call Loan Jyūyō Kansū to Kyōshiteki Kinyū Model no Seigosei. *Kikan Riron Keizaigaku,* August 1970.

[27] Mundell, R. A. "The Appropriate Use of Monetary and Fiscal Policy under Fixed Exchange Rates." IMF Staff Papers, March 1962.

[28] Nishikawa, Motohiko. Kinyū Chōsei no Hōhō. *Kinyū Gakkai Hōkoku.* Tōyō Keizai Shimpō-sha, June 1955.

[29] Nishikawa, Motohiko. Waga Kuni ni okeru Tsūka no Kyōkyū Keitai. *Miyata Kiyōzō Hakase Kanreki Kinen Ronbunshū.* Dobunkan, 1958.

[30] Nishikawa, Motohiko, and Tsūka, Seisaku. *Gendai Kinyū Jiten Dai 5-kan.* Shunjyū-sha, 1960.

[31] Nishikawa, Motohiko. Nihon ni okeru Kinyū Seisaku no Hōkō. *Keizai Hyōron,* July 1960.

[32] Nishikawa, Shunsaku. Futsū Ginkō ni okeru Kibo no Keizaisei. *Kinyū Gakkai Hōkoku 32.* Tokyo: Tōyō Keizai Shimpō-sha, 1970.

[33] Patrick, H. T. *Monetary Policy and Central Banking in Contemporary Japan.* Bombay: University of Bombay Press, 1962.

[34] Reuber, G. L. "The Objectives of Canadian Monetary Policy, 1949–1961: Empirical 'Trade-offs' and the Reaction Function of the Authorities." *Journal of Political Economy,* April 1964.

[35] Rōyama, Masakazu. Critique of Yoshio Suzuki's *Kinyu Seisaku no Kōka.* In Tokyo University, *Keizai Gaku Ronshū,* April 1967.

[36] Rōyama, Masakazu. Waga Kuni no Tsūka Kyōkyū to Kinyū Seisaku. Hitotsubashi University, *Keizai Kenkyū,* July 1969.

[37] Rōyama, Masakazu. Waga Kuni no Kinyū Mechanism, edited by Takuji Shimano and Koichi Hamada. *Nihon no Kinyū*. Tokyo: Iwanami Shoten, 1971.

[38] Shimomura, Osamu. Kinyū Seijyōka to Teikinri Kakumei, *Nihon Keizai wa Seichō suru*. Tokyo: Kōbundo, 1963. Chapter 2.

[39] Suzuki, Kinzō. *Ginkō Kōdō no Riron*. Tokyo: Tōyō Keizai Shimpō-sha, 1968.

[40] Suzuki, Yoshio. *Nihon no Tsūka to Bukka*. Tokyo: Tōyō Keizai Shimpō-sha, 1964.

[41] Suzuki, Yoshio. *Kinyū Seisaku no Kōka—Ginkō Kōdō no Riron to Keisoku*. Tokyo: Tōyō Keizai Shimpō-sha, 1966.

[42] Suzuki, Yoshio. Kokusai Hakkō to Kinyū Seisaku no Kōka. In Ryuichirō Tachi, Ryūtaro Komiya, and Yoshio Suzuki, *Kokusai Kanri to Kinyū Seisaku*. Nihon Keizai Shimbun-sha, 1968.

[43] Suzuki, Yoshio. Nihon no Kinri Hendō to Kashidashi Tōshi. *Kikan Ronri Keizaigaku*, March 1968.

[44] Suzuki, Yoshio. Kawaru Nihon no Kinyū Kōzō. In *Gendai no Keizai-gaku*, edited by Masahirō Tatemoto and Tsunehiko Watanabe. Nihon Keizai Shimbun-sha, 1972.

[45] Suzuki, Yoshio. Kokusai Kanri Seisaku no Kakuritsu o. In *Kōkyo Keizaigaku no Tenkai*, edited by Yasukichi Anjyō and Keimei Kaizuka. Nihon Keizai Shimbun-sha, 1973.

[46] Suzuki, Yoshio. Toshi Kōzō no Henka to Kinyū Seisaku no Sentaku. *Shūkan Tōyō Keizai*. Kindai Keizaigaku Series. Special issue, March 1973.

[47] Suzuki, Yoshio. Saikin ni okeru atarashii Bukka Mondai no Tōjyō. In *Keizai Seichō to Bukka Mondai*, edited by Masahiko Yoshino. Shunjyū-sha, 1973.

[48] Suzuki, Yoshio. Kinyūmen kara mita Bukka Jyōshō Mechanism. *Kikan Gendai Keizai*, summer 1973.

[49] Suzuki, Yoshio. Bukka Mondai wa Fukushi no Kanten de. *Debates on Inflation*, Nihon Keizai Shimbun edition. Nihon Keizai Shimbun-sha, 1973.

[50] Suzuki, Yoshio. *Inflation to Tsūka Kiki*. Nihon Kokusai Mondai Kenkyūsho, 1971.

[51] Tachi, Ryuichiro. "Kinyū Seido Chōsakai Tōshin 'Overloan no Zesei' o Meguru Shomondai." *Keizaigaku Ronshū*. Tokyo: Tokyo University, July 1963.

[52] Tachi, Ryūichiro. "Kinyū Seisaku no Yūkōsei." *Keizaigaku Ronshū*. Tokyo: Tokyo University, July 1965.

[53] Tachi, Ryūichirō. Jyunbi Yokin Seido no Kakujyu ni tsuite. *Kinyū*, April 1972.

[54] Tachi, Ryūichirō, and Komiya, Ryūtarō. Nihon no Kinyū Seisaku wa ikani arubekika. *Keizai Hyōron*, April 1960.

[55] Tachi, Ryūichirō, Komiya, and (Ryūtarō.) "Under-liquidity and Monetary Policy in Japan." In Hitotsubashi University edition of *Keizai Kenkyū*, July 1960.

[56] Tachi, Ryūichirō, and Hamada, Kōichi, *Kinyū*. Iwanami Shoten, 1972.

[57] Tinbergen, J. *The Appropriate Use of Economic Policy*. Rev. ed. North Holland, 1955.

[58] Tobin, J. "A General Equilibrium Approach to Monetary Theory." *Journal of Money, Credit and Banking*, February 1969.

[59] Tobin, J. Manuscript, chapter 8 (incomplete), "The Theory of Commercial Banking."

[60] Tobin J., and Brainard, W. C. "Financial Intermediaries and the Effectiveness of Monetary Controls." *American Economic Review*, May 1963.

[61] Yoshino, Toshihiko. Wagakuni Shichu Ginkō no Overloan ni tsuite. In Bank of Japan Research Department, *Chōsa Geppō*, February 1947.

[62] Yoshino, Toshihiko. *Wagakuni no Kinyū Seido to Kinyū Seisaku*. Shisei-dō, 1954.

Index

DATE DUE

MAR 28 '84			
JAN 23 '85			
NOV 9 '87			
OCT 28 '88			
DEC 01 '88			
AUG 9 '89			
DEC 10 '89			
NOV 1 2 1990			
DEC 27 '90			